Object-Oriented Test & Measurement Software Development in C++

Hewlett-Packard Professional Books

Atchison	Object-Oriented Test & Measurement Software Development in C++
Blinn	Portable Shell Programming: An Extensive Collection of Bourne Shell Examples
Blommers	Practical Planning for Network Growth
Costa	Planning and Designing High Speed Networks Using 100VG-AnyLAN, Second Edition
Crane	A Simplified Approach to Image Processing: Classical and Modern Techniques
Fernandez	Configuring the Common Desktop Environment
Fristrup	The Essential Web Surfer Survival Guide
Fristrup	USENET: Netnews for Everyone
Grady	Practical Software Metrics for Project Management and Process Improvement
Grosvenor, Ichiro, O'Brien	Mainframe Downsizing to Upsize Your Business: IT-Preneuring
Gunn	A Guide to NetWare® for UNIX®
Helsel	Graphical Programming: A Tutorial for HP VEE
Helsel	Visual Programming with HP-VEE
Kane	PA-RISC 2.0 Architecture
Knouse	Practical DCE Programming
Lewis	The Art & Science of Smalltalk
Madell, Parsons, Abegg	Developing and Localizing International Software
Malan, Letsinger, Coleman	Object-Oriented Development at Work: Fusion in the Real World
McFarland	X Windows on the World: Developing Internationalized Software with X, Motif®, and CDE
McMinds/Whitty	Writing Your Own OSF/Motif Widgets
Phaal	LAN Traffic Management
Poniatowski	The HP-UX System Administrator's "How To" Book
Poniatowski	HP-UX 10.x System Administration "How To" Book
Poniatowski	Learning the HP-UX Operating System
Thomas	Cable Television Proof-of-Performance: A Practical Guide to Cable TV Compliance Measurements Using a Spectrum Analyzer
Weygant	Clusters for High Availability: A Primer of HP-UX Solutions
Witte	Electronic Test Instruments

Object-Oriented Test & Measurement Software Development in C++

Bridging the Gap Between Object-Oriented Programming and Test & Measurement

Lee Atchison

Hewlett-Packard Company

Prentice Hall PTR
Upper Saddle River, New Jersey 07458

Acquisitions editor: *Karen Gettman*
Editorial assistant: *Barbara Alfieri*
Production supervision: *Mary Sudul*
Copyeditor: *Tracy Wanamaker*
Cover design: *Wanda Ispania*
Cover design director: *Jerry Votta*
Manufacturing manager: *Alexis R. Heydt*
Manager, Hewlett-Packard Press: *Patricia Pekary*

Published by Prentice Hall PTR
Prentice-Hall, Inc.
A Simon & Schuster Company
Upper Saddle River, New Jersey 07458

The publisher offers discounts on this book when ordered in bulk quantities.
For more information, contact Corporate Sales Department,
Prentice Hall PTR, One Lake Street, Upper Saddle River, NJ 07458.
Phone: 800-382-3419; Fax: 201-236-7141; E-mail: corpsales@prenhall.com

Printed in the United States of America

10 9 8 7 6 5 4 3 2 1

ISBN 0-13-227950-9

Prentice-Hall International (UK) Limited, *London*
Prentice-Hall of Australia Pty. Limited, *Sydney*
Prentice-Hall Canada Inc., *Toronto*
Prentice-Hall Hispanoamericana, S.A., *Mexico*
Prentice-Hall of India Private Limited, *New Delhi*
Prentice-Hall of Japan, Inc., *Tokyo*
Simon & Schuster Asia Pte. Ltd., *Singapore*
Editora Prentice-Hall do Brasil, Ltda., *Rio de Janeiro*

Acknowledgments

This book would not be possible without the help and support of many individuals. In particular, I'd like to thank Bob Helsel for the encouragement to get started, Pete Stone for his word processing help and letting me bounce ideas off of him, and Joe Mueller for his help on SCPI and object oriented instrumentation brainstorming. Also, I'd like to thank my OO coworkers, Pete Stone, Nate Berg, and Jon Eisele. In addition, I could not have written this book without the help of many in HP management, namely Brian Sippy, Larry DesJardin, Steve Schink, Dave Palermo, and Dave Kepler.

I'd like to give a special thanks to George Sparks, MXD's division manager, who has given me support, encouragement, and the opportunities to succeed. I can honestly say, I would not be where I am professionally if it were not for him.

Of course, I couldn't have written this book without the support of my wife, Beth, who is always there for me. But I also got support from our purring six: Boo, Baby, Rusty, Lucy, Gus, and Nellie. Plus the one that keeps them all in line, Kiita our Husky-Malamute.

To Beth
My Buddy

Table of Contents

PART 4 - ADVANCED TOPICS

APPENDICES

Preface

History of Test Development

The need to control test instrumentation has been around as long as instrumentation itself. Historically, test control applications have started with simple BASIC programs to control simple functionality of an instrument remotely. Over time, those simple BASIC programs grew into complex, almost unwieldy applications. Many of these applications written 10 or more years ago are still in use today, but many are difficult to maintain.

Since these test applications have become so complex, the cost of creating and supporting them have grown dramatically. Companies have put substantial amounts of resources into building applications. Now, many companies are recognizing the cost of these applications and have been working on ways to reduce the cost of test development. One way is to contract out the work to develop the applications, rather than developing the expertise in house. Another is to develop dedicated in-house groups that develop and maintain these test applications.

In either case, the responsibility for developing these test applications has increasingly become the responsibility of software engineers, engineers whose whole job it is to develop and maintain complex software systems. These software engineers work not only for end-user companies, but for custom system integrators, instrument and component manufacturers, and third party application companies as well. These engineers have had a variety of ideas designed to make building and supporting test systems easier.

Several companies have developed applications specifically designed to make test development easier. Some have been quite successful, others less successful. There is a current trend toward high-level iconic programming languages such as HP VEE. These languages remove much of the complexity of programming languages and allow test engineers to develop simple to medium size test systems themselves, without the help of specialized test software engineers. While these languages and others like them have a fair amount of success, most test engineers still concentrate on text-based programming languages because of their versatility and cost.

Why Object Oriented Test Development?

While these changes have been going on in the test and measurement community, the software engineering community has undergone their own revamping. Standardized software packages, portable applications, and standardized languages have become more prevalent. Many years ago there were a variety of languages used for programming (BASIC, FORTRAN, Pascal, C, etc.). Now, however, the industry has almost unanimously standardized on C as the programming language of choice because of its wide availability, portability, and adaptability.

At the same time, the software engineering community has embraced the concept of object oriented (OO) programming. Object oriented programming is a programming methodology that encourages re-use of code, abstraction, and design-for-support. It encourages early design of applications, modularizing large applications, and documenting during development. Using OO concepts can dramatically ease the task of developing and supporting large applications. The OO language of choice for software engineers is C++.

As the test and measurement community has moved more and more toward hiring software engineers to develop their test applications, the software engineers have been bringing their "tools-of-choice" into the realm of test and measurement. As a result, fewer test applications are written in BASIC, and more are being written in C. As OO concepts continue to grow popular, object oriented programming will become much more pervasive in the test and measurement community.

What's the Difference?

Programming a test in a traditional non-OO way is very different from programming a test using OO methods. Figure 1 shows an admittedly simple example of a test using traditional programming techniques. Figure 2 shows a similar example of a test using some OO principles. The tests basically do the same thing: They perform two measurements on a device after correctly setting a switch matrix for the test. The resulting measurements, when compared against success values, indicate whether the device "passed" or "failed" the test. The test is repeated for many devices.

```
dotests(){
    INST dmm,switch;
    double result;
    int tmp,i;

    dmm=iopen("vxi,24");
    switch=iopen("vxi,48");

    for(i=0;i<MAX_TESTS;++i){
        /* Set switch card to right settings */
        iprintf(switch,"R3D0C2P2\n");
        iprintf(switch,"WAIT\n");
        iscanf(switch,"&d\n",&tmp);

        /* Send Measure command to voltmeter */
        iprintf(dmm,"MEAS:VOLT:DC?\n");
        /* Get Result */
        iscanf(dmm,"%f\n",&result);

        /* See if result is in range */
        if((result<3.2e3)||(result>3.5e3)){
            log("FAILURE");
            fail(i);
            continue;
        }

        /* Set switch card to new settings */
        iprintf(switch,"R0D3C2P2\n");
        iprintf(switch,"WAIT\n");
        iscanf(switch,"&d\n",&tmp);

        /* Get next measurement */
        iprintf(dmm,"MEAS:VOLT:DC?\n");
        /* Get Result */
        iscanf(dmm,"%f\n",&result);

        /* See if result is in range */
        if((result<12.5)||(result>45.2)){
            log("FAILURE");
            fail(i);
            continue;
        }

        /* Success */
        log("SUCCESS");
        pass(i);
    }
}
```

Figure 1: Non-Object Oriented Test Program

```
dotests(testvec& tv){
    dmmswitch dmm;
    double result;
    hpx1234_state sA,sB;
    test tt;
    sA=...;
    sB=...;

    for(tt=tv.first();!tv.done();tt=tv.next()){
        // Get first reading
        result=dmm.measstate(sA);
        if(!tt.goodvoltA(result)){
            tt.fail();
            log(tt,"FAILURE");
            continue;
        }

        // Get second reading
        result=dmm.measstate(sB);
        if(!tt.goodvoltB(result)){
            tt.fail();
            log(tt,"FAILURE");
            continue;
        }

        tt.pass();
        log(tt,"SUCCESS");
    }
}
```

Figure 2: Object Oriented Test Program

As can be seen in Figures 1 and 2, there are many differences between the two tests. For example:

- The first test requires intimate knowledge of the instrument and its language, as well as its location and interface type. The second stores this instrument knowledge within an object that is specific to this instrument. In object-oriented programming terms, this is called *information hiding*. While non-object-oriented techniques can be used to implement information hiding, object-oriented techniques are very well suited to providing this capability.

- The first test requires knowledge of an I/O library syntax, and forces a "SEND, then RECEIVE" metaphor for communicating with the instrument. The second makes no such assumptions. If a new instrument comes along that does not require the communication metaphor (such as a LAN RPC-based instrument), it can be substituted in the system without restructuring the test. In object-oriented terms, this is called *polymorphism*.

- The first test uses simple C data types for information exchange. The second makes use of a "test" variable type, which can contain all the information necessary to perform a test (more than just demonstrated here). In object-oriented terms, these new data *types* are simply objects that act as new data types added to the language.

Most of these things can be accomplished in a non-OO programming language. However, OO programming makes these things easy, straightforward, and natural, and therefore encourages the use of these mechanisms. This is just some of the benefits that OO programming can afford the programmer. They provide a powerful motivation to explore this new, ever-growing, programming paradigm.

The Purpose of This Book

This book brings the test and measurement community and the OO programming community together. By combining these two communities, test and measurement application developers can learn from and take advantage of the wealth of programming experience available in the OO world.

Who Should Read This Book?

This book is written for the software engineer who is learning how to develop object oriented test applications. As such, the reader should:

1. Be familiar with test and measurement instrumentation and have a need to develop T&M applications.

2. Understand the basic *concepts* of OO programming, but may never have designed or written any OO programs.

3. Have programming experience in some programming language, such as C.

The Structure of this Book

This book is divided into four sections. Section 1, "*Programming Test Systems,*" describes what a test system is, the types of test systems, what composes a test system, and how to program a test system. This is a discussion of the *classical* approach to test application development. For test engineers, much of this material may be review.

Section 2, *"Object Oriented Programming and Design"*, describes object-oriented concepts. It first describes object oriented programming in general terms, then it discusses how object-oriented concepts map into C++ programming concepts. Finally, the object-oriented design process is discussed. For existing test engineers, this material should be new and is important core information.

Section 3, "*Object Oriented Test & Measurement Systems,*" describes applying object-oriented concepts to T&M system development. It starts with a high-level object-oriented design of a sample test system. The section then provides details on constructing I/O control classes, instrument classes, and measurement and test classes. Finally, a complete working example of an object-oriented test system is presented. For test engineers, this material should be new and is the heart of this book.

Section 4, "*Advanced Topics,*" describes in more depth several object oriented topics and how they relate to instrumentation. Topics include creating new data types, advanced error handling, and advanced instrument classes.

In addition to the four sections listed, a series of appendices are provided at the end of this book. Appendix A describes a proposal for creating a *standard* object oriented interface to instrument drivers in C++. Appendix B discusses the contents of the enclosed disk, and Appendix C contains answers to exercises at the end of each chapter.

It is hoped that this book can help bridge the gap between the two very different worlds of test and measurement and object-oriented programming. At the same time, this book can provide the test and measurement world more tools that will help bring the cost of test development down.

Lee Atchison
Scientist/Engineer
Hewlett-Packard
Measurement Systems Division

Part I

Programming Test Systems

1. Test Systems

All test systems are different. Each is used to satisfy a very specific need. However, all test systems generally fall into one or more of several different categories. Each of these test systems serve a very different purpose, contain different components, and satisfy different user needs. The following categories will be used throughout this book when describing different aspects of test systems.

Topics Covered:

- Test System Categories
- Characteristics of Test Systems
- Data Acquisition Systems
- Production Test Systems
- R&D Bench Test Systems
- Monitor and Control Test Systems
- Mixed Test Systems

- **Data Acquisition Systems.** Sometimes known as "Data Acq" systems, these are test systems whose primary purpose is to collect data, usually from some physical process. After the data is acquired, it can be correlated with other data, filtered, adjusted, reduced, and so forth to extract the information desired. This data can be further analyzed, plotted, or graphed as needed.

  An example of a data acquisition system is a device monitoring the temperature of a test tube during a chemical reaction. The device can monitor temperatures at a periodic interval and store the results in a log file. Later, the log file can be examined to determine characteristics of the chemical reaction.

  Typically, a data acquisition system must collect a large amount of data rapidly, but analysis of the data can occur later at a much slower rate.

- **Production Test Systems.** A production test system typically provides a pass/fail status for each device that is tested in the production line. Based on the outcome of the test, appropriate actions can be taken. If the test passes, the device can continue on in the production process. If the test fails, the device can either be scrapped, or returned for repair.

Typically, a production test system must collect data, calculate results, perform analysis on those results, and come to a decision before the device can go on to the next stage of testing.

The results of a test, other than pass/fail, may or may not be important. If the device fails, it may be scrapped with no further action required. However, the results of why the device failed could be passed along with the device to a repair station where the device's failures can be fixed.

Some production test systems also log the results of the test for later analysis to determine failure rates, conditions, and so forth. Such data can be used to determine production efficiency, parts reliability, and so forth. This data, analyzed later, can provide positive input into correcting or improving the production process.

- **R&D Lab Bench Systems.** An R&D Lab Bench System is a set of test instrumentation used by an R&D engineer in the design and evaluation of prototype devices. An R&D engineer will have a series of either disconnected test instruments or loosely connected instruments. The engineer will typically develop several quick-and-dirty test applications. Some of these test applications may only be used once, while others may be transferred eventually to a production test system when the prototype device goes into production.

- **Monitor and Control Test Systems.** These test systems are used for controlling processes of various kinds, especially industrial and environmental systems. An example is an oil refinery, where a test system makes sure that various systems are operating correctly and within specified parameters. If some system deviates from specified parameters, the test system can apply corrective actions to bring the system back into specifications. This is a classic closed-loop feedback system.

  Another example is the computer controlling the engine in an automobile. It makes sure the engine operates at the correct temperature, fuel and air consumption, and other parameters. The computer control makes corrections as necessary.

  Typically, a monitor and control test system must collect a large amount of data, like the data acquisition system, but must also calculate results, perform analysis on those results, and make decisions based on the analysis much like a production test system. However, unlike any of the other systems mentioned here, the monitor and control test system must apply corrective actions to bring the system back into proper running order when problems are detected.

Common Test System Characteristics

As can be seen, each of these test systems are used in very different ways. Yet, they all have many of the same basic characteristics. Table 1-1, "Test System Characteristics", is a summary of each of the various basic characteristics of test systems and how they apply to each of the basic test system types.

Referring to Table 1-1, the types of test systems discussed as "categories," above, are listed across the table. The common characteristics of each are listed in the left-most column. Each interior square represents the given characteristic in the given system category. An "X" means that test system type generally contains that characteristic. An "S" means that test system type occasionally contains that characteristic.

The following list summarizes the different characteristics discussed in Table 1-1:

- **Device Monitoring.** This characteristic describes the ability to monitor a device under test. Essentially, this is the "measurement" part of test and measurement. The device is measured using some number of instruments and data is collected from those measurements.

- **Device Stimulation.** This characteristic describes the ability to provide stimulus to a device. The device is stimulated using some means, such as applying a pulse, ramp, or more complex signal, to an input pin. This stimulation is typically used to generate some response from the device that is monitored and examined.

- **Device Control.** This characteristic describes the ability to control a device under test. The device is controlled by some means, such as closing a relay, or supplying a voltage to some control device. This control is typically used to modify the actions of the device or system in monitor and control systems.

- **Real-Time Data Analysis.** This characteristic describes the ability to take data acquired from the "Device Monitor" characteristic, and process the data real-time. This means the data is analyzed during the measurement and monitoring process.

- **Real-Time Analysis Decision.** This characteristic describes the ability to take data analyzed real-time and make decisions based on this data real-time. This means the decisions must be made automatically during the measurement and monitoring process. This decision could be a simple pass/fail decision, or a more involved decision such as "turn up temperature by 10° Celsius."

- **Real-Time Data Logging.** This characteristic describes the ability to take data acquired from the "Device Monitor" characteristic, possibly analyzed and reduced further, and log it to some logging system (such as database, hard disk, or tape drive) for later analysis.

- **Post-Process Data Analysis.** This characteristic describes the ability to take data logged from the "Real-Time Data Logging" characteristic and perform analysis on the data later, after the measurement and monitor process is complete. This analysis may be more involved than is possible real-time, or the analysis is not determined until after the data is collected (such as deciding to perform a specialized test with satellite high-energy data that has been collected for a previous test).

Table 1-1: Test System Characteristics

Test System Characteristics	*Data Acq*	*Production Test*	*R&D Lab Bench*	*Monitor & Control*
Device Monitoring	*X*	*X*	*X*	*X*
Device Stimulation	*S*	*X*	*X*	
Device Control				*X*
Real-Time Data Analysis		*X*		*X*
Real-Time Analysis Decision		*X*		*X*
Real-Time Data Logging	*X*	*S*		*S*
Post-Process Data Analysis	*X*	*S*		*S*

Legend: *X - Test System contains that characteristic.*
S - Test System sometimes contains that characteristic.

Data Acquisition Systems

Data Acquisition and Logging systems are T&M test systems designed to collect large amounts of data for later analysis. This data can be of almost any type: electrical (voltage, current, frequency, complex signal), mechanical (vibration, stress, etc.), chemical (pH, etc.), physical (temperature, pressure), and so forth.

The purpose of a data acquisition system is to collect data from a system in a real-time manner and store the data until it can be analyzed later. The key is that data must be captured in a real-time manner, typically faster than the data can be analyzed. Sometimes, data collected over a few milliseconds may take weeks or months to analyze completely. In addition, data collected from a data acquisition system may be needed for future, yet unknown, analysis.

Data acquisition systems are used in a variety of places. Some examples include:

- Analyzing a chemical reaction in a test tube.
- Analyzing the stress on the structural supports to a bridge.
- Analyzing the data from a rocket engine firing test.

Components of a Data Acq System

A data acquisition system is broken into two sections. The first is the real-time section. The second is the post-processing, or data-analysis section, which is not time-critical.

The real-time section is composed of these parts:

- **Measurement Probes.** This is the device or devices that convert the electrical, mechanical, chemical, or physical data to be measured into some form of electrical signal.
- **Instrumentation.** This is the device or devices that convert the electrical signal from the measurement probes to digital data that can be analyzed by a computer.
- **Data Logger.** This is a software application that takes the data from the instrument and stores it in a database, hard disk, or tape drive for later analysis. This application may do a limited amount of data reduction, which is essentially a limited amount of data analysis in order to reduce the amount of data that must be stored to a more manageable level.
- **Data Store.** This is the database, hard disk, or tape drive that is used to store the data being collected.

The data-analysis section is composed of these parts:

- **Original Data Store.** This is the database, hard disk, or tape drive that contains the original data from the real-time section of the test. This is the data to be analyzed.

- **Data Analysis.** This is the processing used to analyze the data. This analysis can be used to filter unnecessary or irrelevant data. The analysis can reduce the data by combining pieces of the data, change the data into a more useable form (such as doing FFT analysis, etc.), and correlate the data with other data to find patterns.

- **Data Store.** This is a data store, like the original data stored, used to log data for later analysis. This is used to store post-processed data for further analysis and later display.

- **Display.** This displays the data or the results of the analysis. It can be in the form of a number, a chart, a graph, a plot, or other means of presenting the results of the analysis.

Example Data Acq System

An example of a data acquisition system is a device monitoring the temperature of a test tube during a chemical reaction. The device can monitor temperatures at a periodic interval, and store the results in a log file. Later, the log file can be examined to determine characteristics of the chemical reaction.

Figure 1-1, shows graphically this example data acq system. In this figure, the measurement probe is a thermister and the instrumentation is an Ohm meter.

Figure 1-2, shows graphically the processing that may go on after the data acquisition has occurred. For this example, the analysis involves correlating the temperature readings with the chemical reaction, and the display is a temperature vs. time plot.

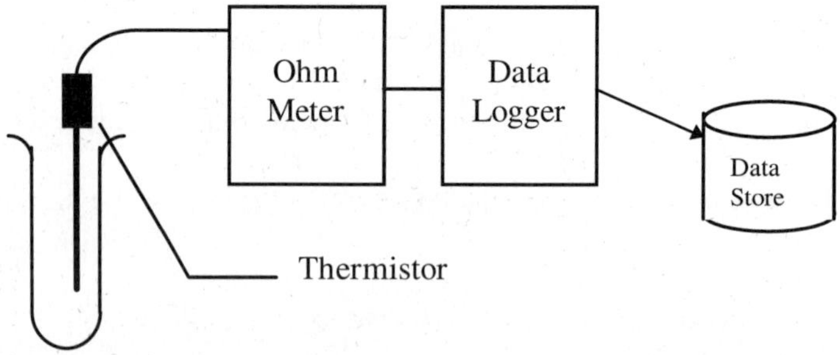

Figure 1-1: Example Real-Time Data Acq System

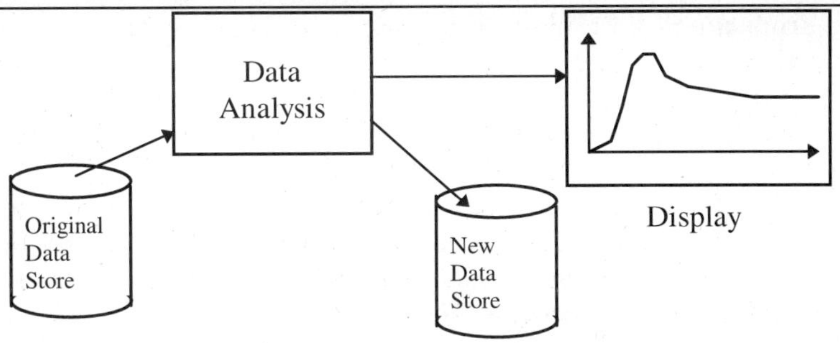

Figure 1-2: Data Acq Post Analysis

Production Test Systems

Production Test Systems are test systems designed to analyze devices and decide whether the given device meets specified criteria or not. The device is typically a PC board or other electronic box, but it could be a device requiring mechanical or chemical testing.

The purpose of a production test system is to collect data from a device, possibly stimulate the device in some way and monitor how it reacts, then take the data collected and compare it against norms. Finally, the test must decide if the device is operating within acceptable limits from the norms. If it is not, the device is tagged for repairing, recycling, or destruction. If it is within limits, it is allowed to go on to the next step in the manufacturing process.

The production test system provides:

- Immediate feedback on the quality of manufacturing devices.
- Mechanisms to weed out borderline or failed devices.
- Data that can be used to repair a problem device.
- Data that can be used to track the sources of problems (e.g., 25% of the devices failed for this reason...).
- Data that can be used to improve the overall reliability of the manufacturing facility.

Components of a Production Test System

A production test system consists of:

- **Production Line.** This is the manufacturing production line. While not technically part of the test system, it is the mechanism that brings the devices to the device fixturing for testing. It also passes the device on or sends it to the repair station as necessary.

- **Device Fixturing.** This is the mechanism by which the device is connected to the test system. It usually consists of connections and contacts that can withstand a large number of insertions and removals, along with the mechanics to move and hold the device during the testing.

- **Switches.** These connect the various instruments, sources, and other instrumentation to the various test points on the device. Since a device may typically have a large number of test points to be tested, it is impractical to have a test instrument for each test point. A switch matrix makes it possible for a single test instrument to share multiple test points, as well as to have a single test point connected to a number of test instruments during the course of the test.

- **Instruments, sources, power supplies.** These are the actual measuring devices used to perform the test, along with the sources that provide input stimulus to the device. Also, various power supplies may be provided to power the device during the testing process.

- **Test Software.** This is the software that controls the fixturing, switches, instruments, sources, and power supplies in order to perform the actual testing needed. Typically, several different tests will be run with each requiring several set ups. The test software provides all of this control, along with actually performing the test and determining if the device passed or failed the test.

- **Pass/Fail Indicator.** This is typically a mechanical device that the test software tells whether the device passed or failed. Based on this decision, this mechanism diverts the device on the assembly line to either continue down the correct path, or send it to the repair or recycle station.

Example Production Test System

An example production test system is shown in Figure 1-3, where a PC board is being tested. The PC board is passed up the assembly line from the bottom of the figure. When the board reaches the test fixture, the fixture attaches itself to the device and the test begins. The test could take anywhere from milliseconds to tens of minutes. In fact, the test software may regularly apply a short test (milliseconds or seconds), and occasionally spot check devices by applying a more rigorous test (tens of seconds or minutes).

After the test is complete, the pass/fail indicator is set correctly. If the test passed, the PC board continues along the assembly line by going off the top of the figure. If the test failed, the board is diverted to the left to the "Device Failed" bucket, where the device may be repaired or scrapped. If it is to be repaired, the test results are passed along with the device.

The results of the test and any supporting data is also passed to the data store. Here, all the data is collected so post-processing data analysis can occur. The post-processing data analysis in this case would probably try to correlate problems with individual components, assembly lines, or suppliers

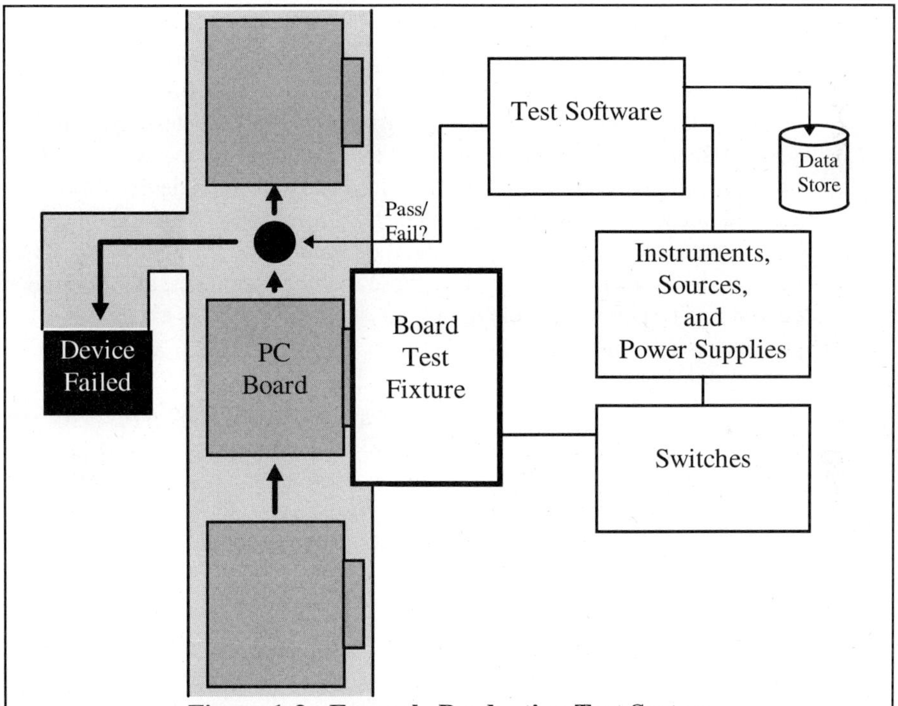

Figure 1-3: Example Production Test System

R&D Lab Bench Systems

R&D Lab bench systems are test systems used by R&D engineers during the prototyping phase of development. They typically consist of a wide variety of test instrumentation, sources, and power supplies. All of these components are loosely coupled or completely uncoupled.

An engineer will typically do one of two things with this setup:

- **Construct a simple test application.** Using a few instruments, the engineer will temporarily connect the instruments to the device using clips. The engineer will then write a simple program (or use an existing application) to run a simple test and collect some data. The data is typically examined on the computer, not the instrument displays. The engineer may use some simple switches to avoid having to move the probe clips. Typically very little to a moderate amount of programming is required.

- **Build a production test application.** Using some number of instruments, sources, and power supplies, and making extensive use of switching and fixturing, the R&D engineer will construct a test stand to test a prototype device. Once the test stand is built and the prototype device is installed, the engineer will write a series of test applications to test the device. Some of these applications will be quick and dirty "throw away" applications. Others will be more involved and will make their way to the manufacturing floor. A single test stand may be used by more than one engineer, all of whom are developing tests for the same or similar device. Typically, extensive programming is needed in these systems.

The last category of R&D Lab test systems is the category that will benefit most from the concepts in this book.

Components of an R&D Lab Bench System

An R&D Lab Bench test system is composed of these components:

- **Prototype device.** The prototype device being tested.

- **Probes.** Temporary connections between the test instrumentation and the prototype device. Probes can be easily moved from one test point on the prototype device to another.

- **Fixturing.** More permanent component providing the connection between the test instrumentation and the prototype device. It is typically a custom built interface that holds the device and all the test connections together so that testing can be performed without touching or modifying the prototype device or its connections.

- **Switches.** Used with a fixture to connect the prototype device in the fixture to the test instruments in a way such that the instrumentation can test multiple test points on the device, and a test point can be connected to multiple instruments.

- **Instrumentation.** The devices that measure data from the prototype device, as well as provide input stimulus to the device.

- **Test Software.** The software that controls the instrumentation.

Example R&D Lab Bench System

An example R&D test system is shown in Figure 1-4. It shows two different setups. The first setup is a fixturing to the prototype device. The fixturing is connected to a switch matrix and test instrumentation. The instrumentation is under the control of test software that displays results on the display.

The second setup uses probes to the prototype device from a single instrument (in this case, an oscilloscope). These probes are manually moved from point to point on the prototype device. The results can either be read directly from the oscilloscope screen, or can be downloaded to the test system for later analysis.

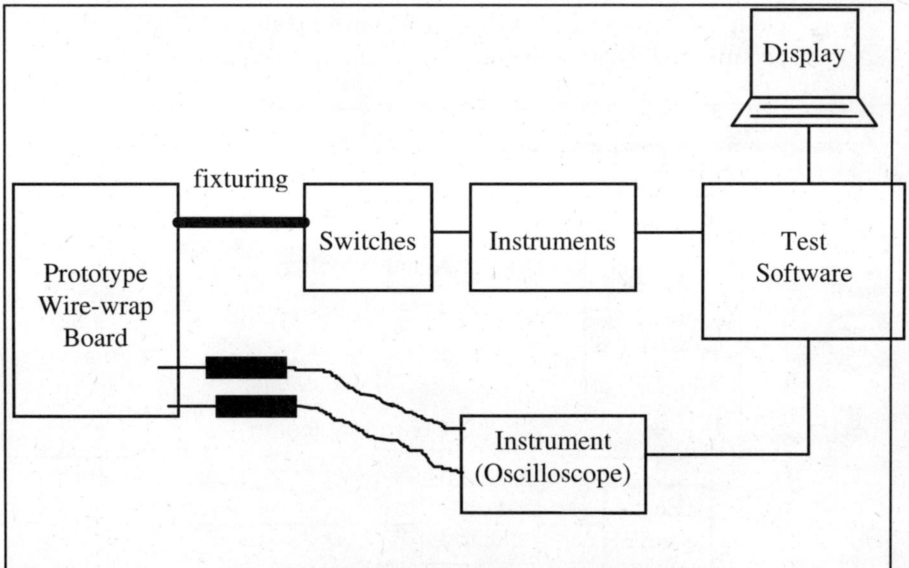

Figure 1-4: Example R&D Test System

Monitor and Control Test Systems

A Monitor and Control test system is designed to provide stability and control to a system or process. It monitors the system and when the system begins to move away from its stability position, the test system sends control pulses to the system or process to adjust its actions, bringing it back into a stable position. A monitor and control test system provides closed-loop feedback control to a system or process.

Typically, a monitor and control test system must collect a large amount of data, like the data acquisition system, but must also calculate results, perform analysis on those results, and make decisions based on the analysis much like a production test system. However, unlike any of the above, the monitor and control test system must apply actions to the system to bring the system back into proper running order when problems are detected.

Components of a Monitor and Control System

- **Instrumentation.** Devices that measure how the controlled system or process is doing.
- **Monitor and Control Software.** The software that monitors the data collected from the instrumentation and makes decisions about corrective actions needed.
- **Control Mechanisms.** Devices that convert requests from the monitor and control software into stimulus to the controlled system or process.

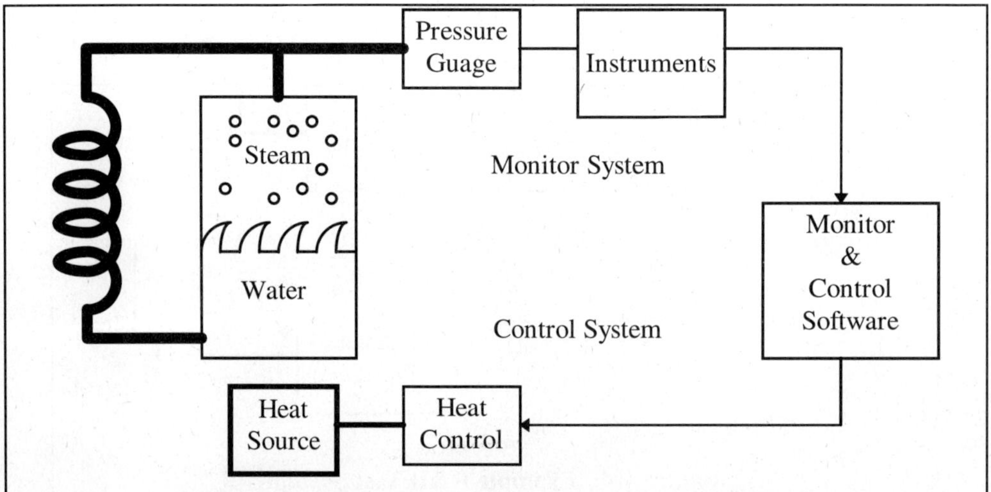

Figure 1-5: Example Monitor and Control Test System

Example Monitor and Control System

Figure 1-5 shows an example monitor and control system. It shows a greatly simplified steam and water system. In this case, the monitor and control system monitors the pressure of the steam. When the pressure is too great, the system turns down the heat. When the pressure is too low, the system turns up the heat.

A more realistic example of a monitor and control test system is an oil refinery, where a test system makes sure that various systems are operating correctly and within specified parameters. If some system deviates from specified parameters, the test system can apply corrective actions to bring the system back into spec. This is a classic closed-loop feedback system.

Another example is a computer controlling the engine in an automobile. It makes sure the engine operates at the correct temperature, uses the correct fuel and air consumption ratios, and other parameters.

Mixed Test Systems

Sometimes a test system does not fit into a single category, but more appropriately fits into more than one category. This is called a mixed test system. Table 1-2, show some example test systems of mixed types. Some of these examples have been presented in previous sections, but are discussed here to show how they can be considered in multiple categories.

There are, obviously, many other types of mixed test systems. In some ways, most test systems contain components of more than one of the generic categories presented in this chapter.

Table 1-2: Mixed Test Systems Usage

Mixed Systems	Uses
Production Test with **Data Acq**	Production test data acquired for post-process system analysis to determine % failure rate, etc.
Monitor and Control with **Data Acq**	Monitor and control data acquired for performance checking, check for limits violation, environmental verification, etc.
R&D Lab Bench with **Production Test**	R&D tests created in a way such that they can be passed easily to production
R&D Lab Bench with **Data Acq**	R&D test data acquired during prototype system run for analysis

Summary

This chapter described the different types of T&M test systems and categorized them into the following categories:

- **Data Acquisition Systems.** A system that collects data and stores it for later analysis.

- **Production Test System.** A system that tests a device, decides if it passes or not, and sends it on its way down a production assembly line.

- **R&D Lab Bench System.** A system that is a "roll your own" system where the test system is setup, usually temporarily, to meet the needs of a R&D engineer during the prototyping stage of development.

- **Monitor and Control System.** A system that provides a closed-loop feedback control to a system or process.

This chapter then described common characteristics of each. Examples of different types of test systems were given. Finally, examples of mixed test systems were discussed.

The exercises that follow continue building on the sample test systems presented here.

Exercises

Exercise 1-1. Think of four different uses for a data acquisition system. Describe the components needed to perform the test.

Exercise 1-2. What data would each data acq system in Exercise 1-1 collect?

Exercise 1-3. What analysis might be done on data in Exercise 1-2? What graphing and plotting would be performed?

Exercise 1-4. Think of a simple electrical device. Imagine you are building a production test system to test this device. What types of tests would you perform on the device? How would you determine if the device passed the tests or not?

Exercise 1-5. Describe the instrumentation and fixturing needed to test the device used in Exercise 1-4. Try and reuse test instrumentation by using switches, when possible, to reduce the cost of the test system.

Exercise 1-6. Think of a specific process that can be monitored using a setup that is similar to Figure 1-5.

Exercise 1-7. Describe the components needed to implement a complete monitor and control system for the process described in Exercise 1-6.

Exercise 1-8. Describe algorithmically the steps involved in the monitor and control software used to control the system described in Exercise 1-7. Make and document any reasonable assumptions you make.

2. Components of a Test System

While each test system is different, many follow similar patterns and work in similar ways. In particular, each test system contains many of the same components connected in the same manner.

Figure 2-1 shows a model test system and the standard components that comprise it.

The following components are contained in this diagram:

- **DUT.** "Device Under Test" is the device or component that the test system is evaluating.
- **Fixture.** The mechanical and electrical connection between the DUT and the test instrumentation.
- **Switching.** Electrical switches that connect the test instrumentation to a variety of test points on the DUT, or connect a test point on the DUT to a variety of test instrumentation.
- **Instrumentation.** The actual test & measurement devices that perform the measurements requested in the system.
- **Measurement Library.** The software that reads the digital data from the instrumentation and converts it into a form usable by the test library.
- **Test Library.** The software that takes the measurement data from the instrumentation and performs the appropriate analysis on the data.
- **Sequencer.** The software that controls which tests are executed, and the order the tests are executed in.
- **Data Logger.** The software that stores the data and results of a test execution for later analysis.

- **Analysis.** The software that performs post-processing analysis of the data logged from the test system.

In Figure 2-1, the sequencer is in control of the entire test process. It decides what steps to be made and when for a given DUT. The sequencer executes specific tests in the test library.

The test library contains one or more specific tests to perform. When the sequencer decides to execute a given test, the test library performs the necessary measurements using the measurement library to determine the status of the DUT.

The measurement library contains several routines for performing various measurements with the instrumentation available. The measurement library communicates directly with the instrumentation to perform the required measurements.

The measurement library also controls the switching to connect the various instruments to the required test points in the DUT. Once the correct switch connections are made, the measurement library can have the instrumentation perform the required measurements.

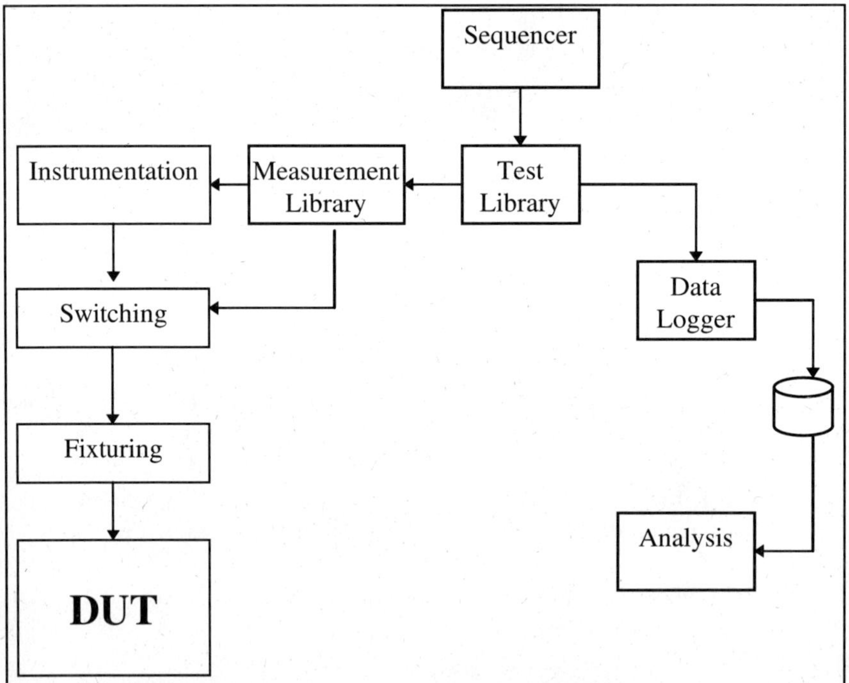

Figure 2-1: Test System Components

Once the test library has determined the outcome of the specified test, it must perform the actions necessary based on that outcome. The test may determine a success/failure status of the DUT and perform physical actions based on that status (such as routing the DUT to a failure station), and/or it may take the results of the test (and, possibly, the raw or processed data) and pass it on to the data logger for storage.

The data logger will store the data, along with other relevant information such as time stamps, DUT identification, and so forth, in the database.

Later, the data stored in the database is analyzed and is used, condensed, and processed. The exact use of the stored data is process specific.

Hardware Components

This section discusses the individual components of the basic model that comprise the test hardware used to perform the DUT testing.

There are four parts to this subsystem. The DUT is the device being tested. The instrumentation is what actually performs the physical measurement. The fixturing and switching connects the DUT to the instrumentation. Each of these components will be discussed in turn.

Device Under Test

The Device Under Test, or DUT, is the specific component being evaluated by the test system. It may be:

- A PC board or component on an assembly line to be tested.
- A prototype board or component on a lab bench.
- A probe or series of probes monitoring a physical process or system.
- A physical, chemical, biological, or electrical system whose characteristics are to be examined.

The exact nature of the DUT varies for each individual test system.

Fixturing

The fixturing is the mechanical and electrical connection between the DUT and the test instrumentation. It may consist of:

- Connections to instrumentation and switch matrixes.
- Patch panels connecting instrumentation modules together and connecting instrumentation modules to the DUT.
- Probes and terminals connected to the DUT.
- Circuits attached to the probes and terminals that must, for various reasons, be physically close to the DUT.
- Cables connecting all of the above.

There are two types of fixturing, permanently connected and automatically connected. The difference has to do only with how the DUT is connected to the fixturing.

In permanently connected fixturing, the DUT is mechanically connected to the probes and to the rest of the fixturing. This is used in cases where there is a single DUT that is to be tested over an extended period of time in the test system. An example is a data acquisition system used to measure the temperature of a test tube, or a monitor and control system controlling the chemical reaction in a factory.

Figure 2-2 is an example of a simple permanently connected fixture. It contains only probes connected to the device and cables to connect those probes to the instrumentation. Figure 2-3 is an example of a typical permanently connected fixture. It contains probes and cables, along with a patch panel to connect the instrumentation to the probes.

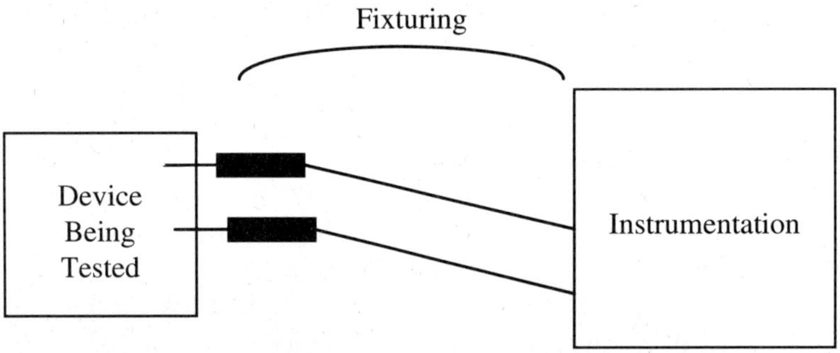

Figure 2-2: Simple Permanently Connected Fixturing

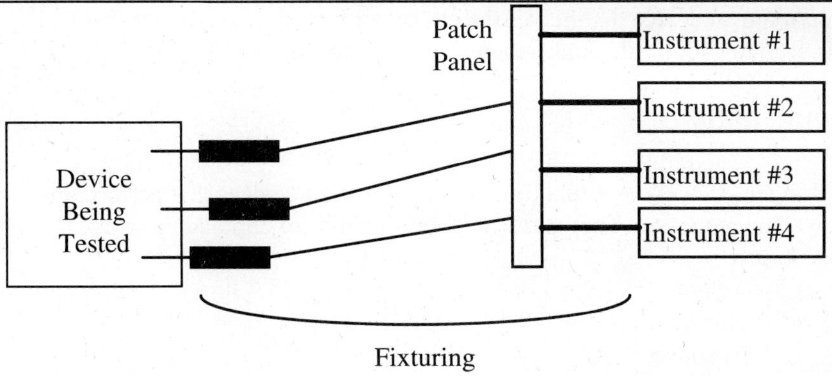

Figure 2-3: Typical Permanently Connected Fixturing

In automatically connected fixturing, the DUT is automatically connected to and disconnected from the probes and the rest of the fixturing. This is used in cases where there are multiple DUTs that are to be tested by the same test system. An example is a manufacturing test system where the devices are being manufactured on an assembly line and passed by the test system before being shipped. Since a large number of DUTs must be connected and disconnected from the test system over a period of time, the reliability of the connections is important.

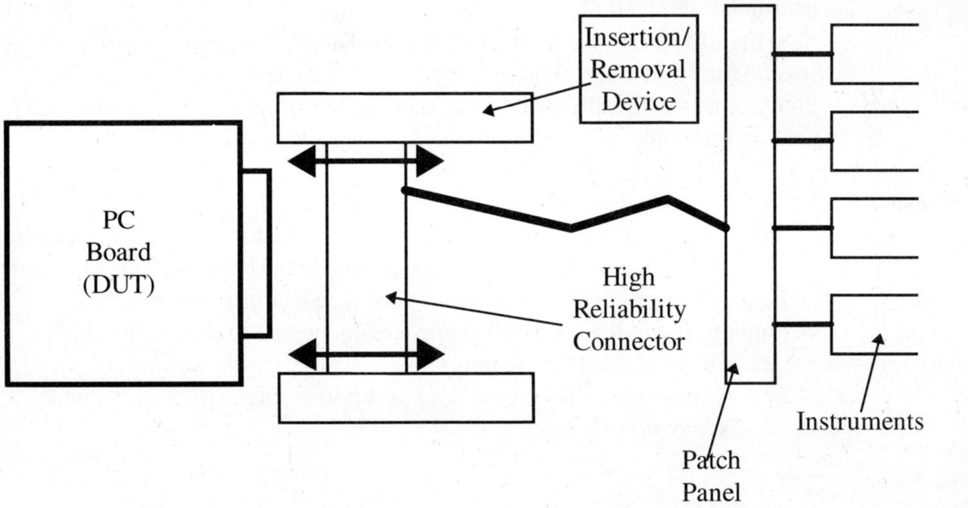

Figure 2-4: Typical Automatically Connected Fixturing

Figure 2-4 is an example of a typical automatically connected fixturing system. It consists of a high-reliability connector that connects the DUT to the cabling. It also consists of an insertion/removal device that moves the connector into place on the DUT. Finally, a patch panel is used to connect the high-reliability connector to the test instruments.

Instrumentation

The instrumentation is the actual test and measurement devices that perform the measurements requested. They turn electrical signals into digital data. Some examples of instruments are:

- Voltmeters
- Oscilloscopes
- Spectrum Analyzers
- Sources

Switching

The switching in a test system is used to connect the DUT test points to the test instrumentation. Switching allows:

- **Sharing of test instruments.** A single test instrument may have to be connected to several points on the DUT. Rather than having a separate instrument for each test point, switch cards can be used to connect the instrument sequentially to different test points.
- **Sharing of DUT test points.** A single DUT test point may have to have several different measurements made on it by different test instruments. Switch cards allow different test instruments to be sequentially connected to a given test point.

Switch cards are usually created in either multiplexer or matrix arrangements. A switch multiplexer is a series of switches that allow connecting one input pin to one of n output pins. A multiplexer cards would have m such pin arrangements. Therefore, a multiplexer switch card will have m input pins and $n*m$ output pins. The test instruments are connected to the input pins and the DUT test points are connected to the output pins. Changing the switch settings during the duration of a test suite allows various test instruments to be connected in turn to various DUT test points. Figure 2-5 shows an example of a multiplexer switch arrangement.

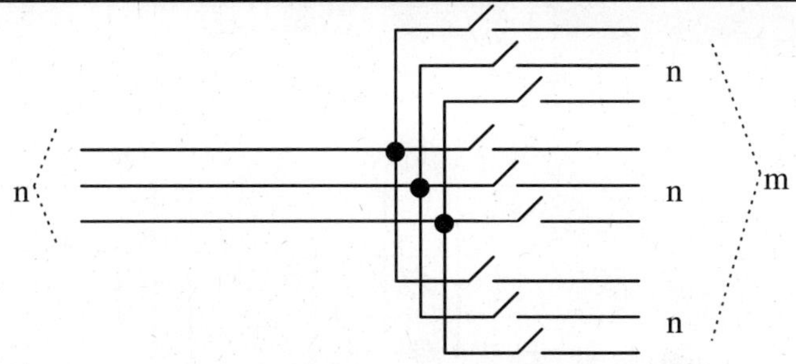

Figure 2-5: 3x3 Multiplexer Switch Card

A matrix switch is a two-dimensional matrix with *n* rows and *m* columns. Each intersection point contains a switch that can either be opened or closed. A closed switch shorts the row line to the column line at the intersection point. A *n* x *m* switch card has *n*m* intersection points, and therefore *n*m* switches. By creatively opening and closing the switches, one or more rows may be connected to one or more columns. When the test instruments are connected to the rows, and the DUT test points connected to the columns, one or more test instruments can be connected to one or more DUT test points.

Figure 2-6 shows a graphical view of a matrix switch card. The view shows the row and column lines intersecting, along with the switch that connects them at the intersection. This view shows four switches closed, and the remaining twenty switches open.

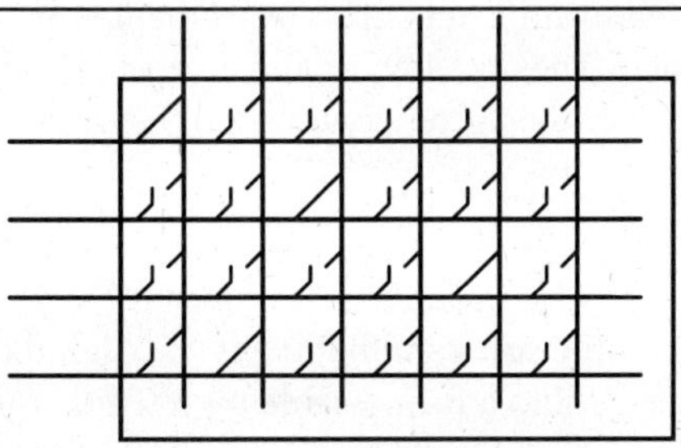

Figure 2-6: A 6x4 Matrix Switch Card

Figure 2-7 shows two switch cards connecting several test instruments to a DUT. In this case, one switch matrix is used to connect sources to DUT inputs, and one switch matrix is used to connect test instruments to DUT outputs.

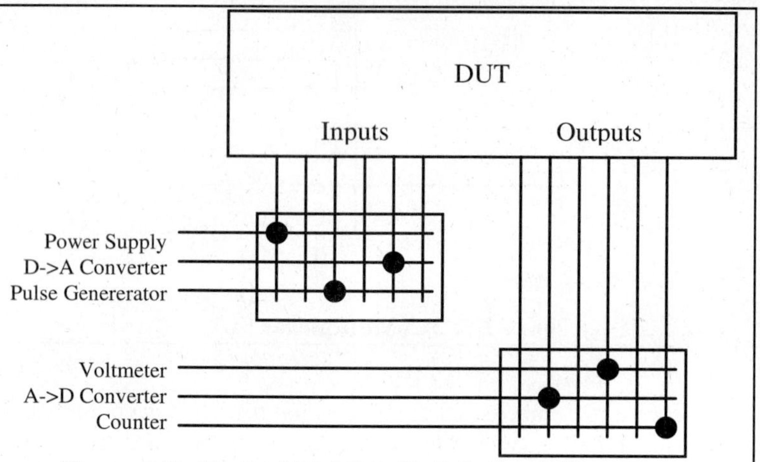

Figure 2-7: Typical Multiple Switch Cards Usage

Software Components

This section discusses the individual components of the basic model that comprise the test software used to perform the DUT testing.

There are five parts to this subsystem. The measurement library and the test library are the primary subsystems used to control the test instrumentation. The sequencer decides what tests are executed when. The data logger and data analysis are used to store and process the test results. Each of these components will be discussed in turn.

Measurement Software

The measurement software is the software that reads the digital data from the instrumentation and converts it into a form usable by test software. It consists of software that:

- Controls the I/O interface between the test controller and the instrumentation.
- Manages the instrument-specific data and command formats.
- Manages switch card activations.
- Changes the data acquired from the instrumentation into a form usable by the test software.

Figure 2-8 shows the software layers involved in taking measurements. The I/O hardware drivers are the low-level hardware control routines that manage communications to the hardware interface that connects the computer to the test instrumentation. The I/O library is the software interface to the low-level I/O hardware drivers. The instrument drivers are the instrument-specific software libraries that manages the control of a given instrument, and converts the data to the correct formats.

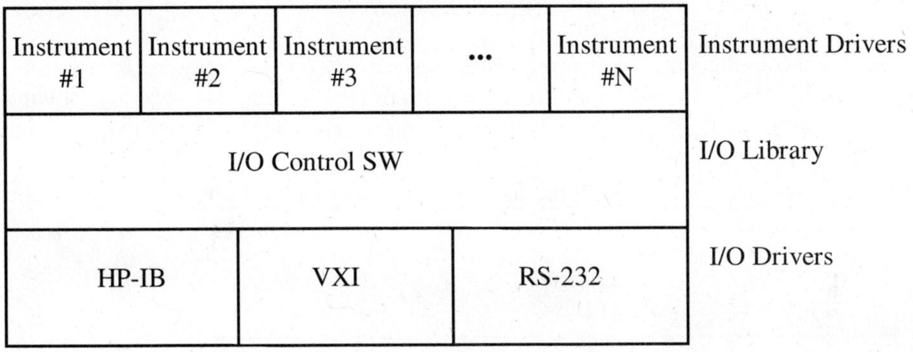

Figure 2-8: Instrument I/O Software Layers

Test Library

The test library is the software that takes the measurement data from the instrumentation and performs analyses to determine whether the DUT passed the various requirements imposed by the test. This includes:

- Verifying the DUT is acting correctly.
- Verifying the DUT results are accurate.
- Verifying the DUT results are within specified limits and bounds.
- Verifying other results of the DUT.

The test library may:

1. Give a pass/fail indication as to the status of the DUT. This is typically used in production test systems.

2. Indicate if a DUT is approaching its operational limits or specs. This is typically used in production test systems, and monitoring and control systems.

3. Trigger other actions based on the measurement data, such as perform feedback processing. This is typically used in monitoring and control systems.

4. Reduce the quantity of data to a more manageable level, such as removing redundant, repetitive, inaccurate, and unusable data. This is typically used in data acquisition systems.

Figure 2-9 shows the same software layer diagram as Figure 2-8, with the addition of the test library layer and the test sequencer layer. There are multiple test libraries shown in this example, all under the control of the one sequencer. Each test library has access to each of the instrument drivers. The sequencer may decide to execute the tests sequentially, or in parallel if multiple tests may be executed without affecting the others.

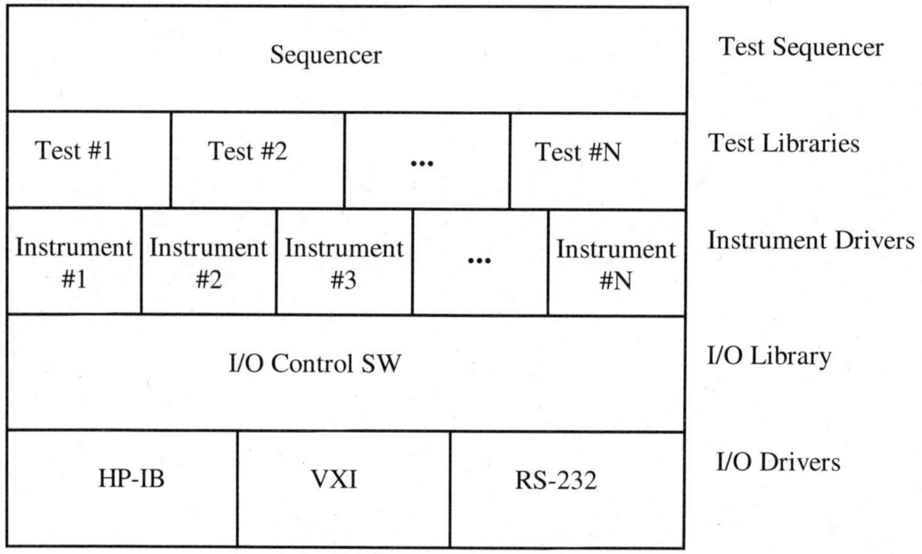

Figure 2-9: Software Layers Including Test Libraries

Sequencer

The sequencer is software that controls which tests are executed, and the order the tests are executed in, for a given system. The sequencer may take on many different roles.

In a production test system, it may read a serial number from a DUT to determine its characteristics. From that information it may pick and choose from a library of tests which tests make sense for the particular DUT. It then executes these tests and makes a conclusion as to the disposition of the DUT.

In a production test system, it may determine that a certain combination of tests may execute concurrently, while others must be serialized. The sequencer can attempt to optimize the order the tests are executed in to reduce the overall test time for the DUT.

In a process control system, the sequencer may decide to perform various checks and tests at various times during the process execution, such as once every hour verifying the emissions output from an exhaust system.

In a simple test system, there may be no sequencer, or only a basic sequencer.

Data Logger

The data logger is a software database that stores the data and results of a test execution. This data may be the raw instrument data, the reduced instrument data, or simply the results of pass/fail testing of various DUTs. This data is stored for later analysis.

Data Analysis

The analysis software may be used to determine:

- The percentage of DUTs that passed. This can be useful for determining the yield of particular manufacturing processes.
- The types of failures that DUTs contained. This can be useful feedback to R&D and manufacturing to improve designs and processes to try and increase manufacturing yields.
- The reliability of a process control system feedback loop. This can be used to determine if the control software should be updated to provide better control.
- The post analysis of data acquisition data for characterizing a particular DUT, looking for trends, and other such analyses. This can be used to, for example, determine the mean temperatures of a building and the reliability of heating/cooling systems.

Components for Different Test System Types

The basic model of a test system can be applied to each of the basic test system types described in Chapter 1.

Data Acquisition Systems

A basic data acquisition system has the structure as shown in Figure 2-10.

The basic data acquisition system typically has no switching to choose which DUT test points to use, as typically a data acquisition system will test all test points simultaneously, as time sequencing is important (this, of course, is not always the case).

The data acquisition system typically has fixturing which is static, that is, the fixturing "permanently" connects the instrumentation to the DUT.

The measurement library and instrumentation are the same as the model test system. The test library and sequencer becomes a "control library," which combines many of the functions of test library and sequencer. However, this "control library" typically does no data analysis, other than perhaps some reduction in the amount of data. The data analysis typically occurs after the test system has run.

The data logger and data store are of primary importance to a data acq system. Typically all data (or a reduced set of data) is stored and virtually all of the data analysis occurs later.

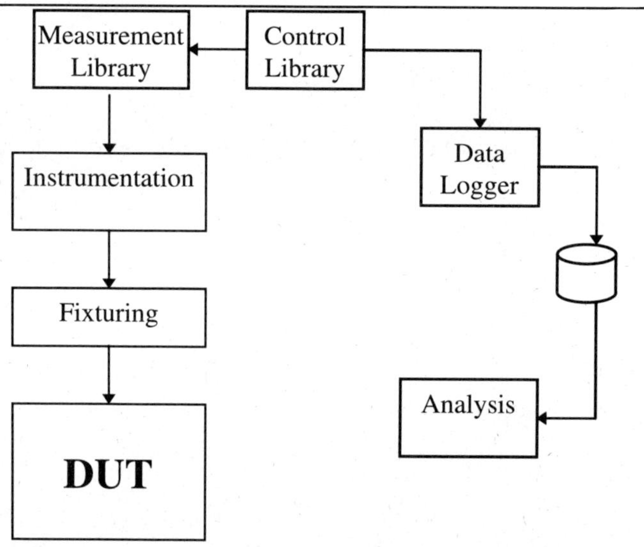

Figure 2-10: Components of a Data Acquisition System

Production Test Systems

A basic production test system has the structure as shown in Figure 2-11.

A production test system has all the basic components of the model test system, without the data acquisition components, namely the data logger, data store, and analysis.

However, many production test systems are actually mixed production and data acq systems, where the data being logged for later analysis is the outcome of the production test of the DUTs.

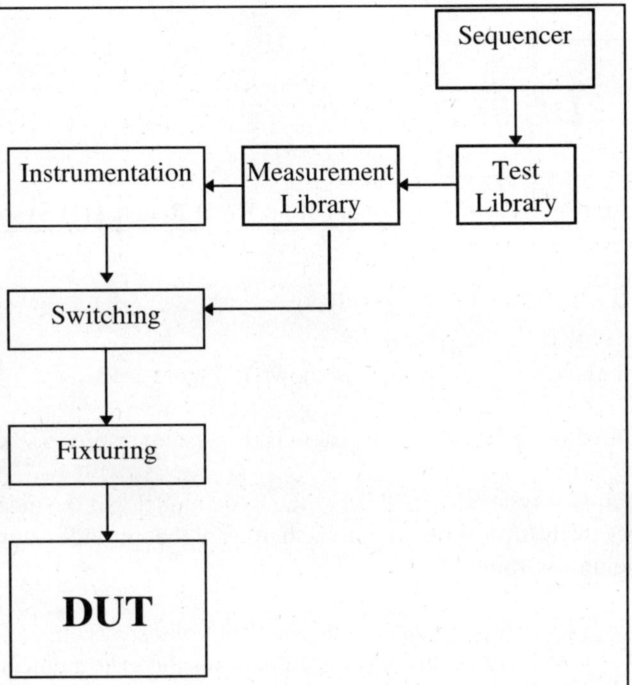

Figure 2-11: Components of a Production Test System

R&D Bench Test Systems

Since an R&D bench test system is a "roll-your-own" system, there is no basic model that applies for all systems. However, Figure 2-12 contains the components of an example bench test system. This example is fairly simple, as are most R&D bench test systems. It contains the DUT directly connected to the test instrumentation. The "measurement library" may simply be an I/O library, or more advanced instrument drivers. The "custom software" is nothing but home-brewed software for controlling the instrumentation. This software may be throw-away software, or may later become part of the "test library" of a full-fledged production test system.

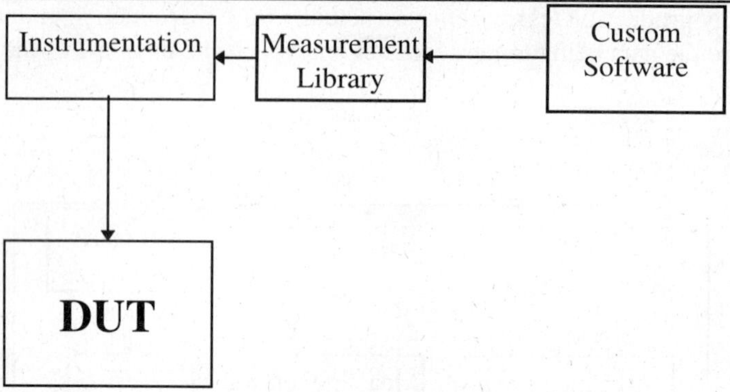

Figure 2-12: Components of an R&D Bench Test System

Monitor and Control Test Systems

A basic monitor and control test system is shown in Figure 2-13.

The DUT in a monitor and control test system is the system or process being controlled.

The instrumentation is typically the same as the basic model, but the measurement library controls not only the instrumentation, but the hardware that provides stimulus and control to the system being controlled.

Rather than having a test library, the monitor and control test system has a "control library," which provides the feedback control that takes the measurements, and provides the stimulus and control needed to keep the process/system operating correctly.

The sequencer decides what portions of the process/system should be monitored and when.

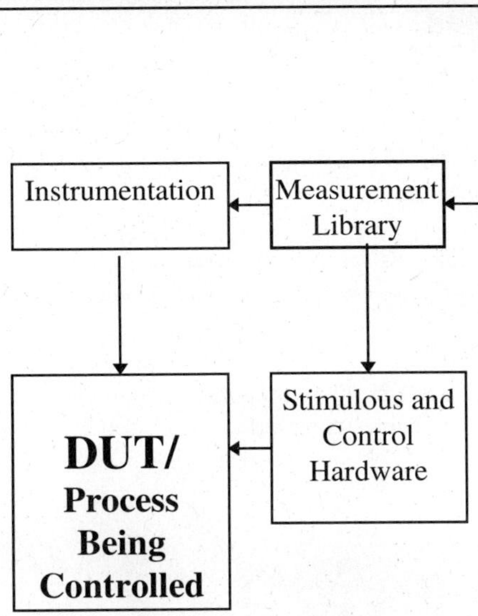

Figure 2-13: Components of a Monitor and Control Test System

Summary

This chapter described the basic components that all test systems contain, along with how these components fit into typical test systems.

The exercises continue from the exercises in Chapter 1. They set the stage for the construction of a demonstration of a non-object-oriented, "C"-based, instrument test system.

Exercises

Exercise 2-1. Using the electrical device and instrumentation used in the exercises in Chapter 1, create a specific schematic of the DUT, fixturing, switching, and instrumentation used to test the DUT. Be specific.

Exercise 2-2. For the system created in Exercise 2-1, describe specifically what instruments are needed, how they are connected to the switch matrix, and how the DUT is connected to the switch matrix.

Exercise 2-3. What size of switch matrix is needed for the system described in Exercise 2-2? Assuming you only have 2x3 switch matrixes available, how many switch matrixes are needed to implement the switch matrix needed? How are they connected?

Exercise 2-4. Think of the tests needed to test the DUT in Exercise 2-1. Break the tests needed into individual test routines and describe specifically what they will do.

Exercise 2-5. Describe a "C" style programming interface to each of the individual test routines described in Exercise 2-4. This is the interface described by the "test libraries" layer in Figure 2-9.

Exercise 2-6. Using the instruments described in Exercise 2-2, and the test routines created in Exercise 2-5, think of the measurements needed to implement these test routines.

Exercise 2-7. Describe a "C" style programming interface for each of the measurements described in Exercise 2-6. This is the interface described by the "instrument Drivers" in Figures 2-8 and 2-9.

3. Software for Test Systems

Many types of software are available for programming test systems. Engineers have available to them a variety of off-the-shelf software that provides support for a number of standard functions. In addition, engineers make use of semi-custom and custom software to link the off-the-shelf software pieces together.

In order to build a complete test application, typically a combination of off-the-shelf, semi-custom, and custom software is needed. Different tradeoffs must be made as to how much software to purchase, how much to build, and how much to have custom built.

This chapter discusses different types of off-the-shelf, custom, and semi-custom software that is available for test engineers to use.

Off-the-Shelf Software

There are three basic types of off-the-shelf test software discussed in this chapter:

- **Programming Languages**. All test systems make use of some type of programming language to write the custom pieces of the test system. This may be an iconic or visual programming language, such as HP VEE, or it may be text-based languages such as C, C++, or BASIC.

- **I/O Software**. I/O software is the software that allows a test application to communicate with the I/O hardware and the test instrumentation.

- **Misc. Software**. A variety of other software packages may be used, including database programs, spreadsheet programs, and data analysis programs.

Programming Languages

There are two types of programming languages. Visual, or Iconic programming languages provide a graphical view of a test application. Text-based programming languages provide a non-pictorial, text-instruction based view of a test application.

Visual/Iconic Languages

A visual programming language is a programming language that describes the program execution or data flow using pictures (or icons) to describe the actions of the application. This type of programming has many advantages and disadvantages.

Advantages of iconic programming:

- Programs are typically easier to read and understand.
- Programs can be created quickly and easily with a very small learning curve.
- Visual programming languages provide very good support for displaying and graphing data.
- Simple programs can be prototyped quickly and easily.

Disadvantages of iconic programming:

- Complex programs are often difficult or impossible to write.
- Complex programs are often more difficult to read and understand than text-based programs.
- Many functions are not possible or not easy to use.
- Each iconic programming language is different, so moving from one environment to another requires a new learning curve.

There are many examples of iconic programming languages. For test and measurement systems, one popular choice is Hewlett-Packard's VEE, or Visual Engineering Environment.

Hewlett-Packard's VEE provides a high-level interface to programming instruments. It provides an easy to use interface to perform many activities needed to program an instrument application, but it requires applications to fit within its environment. Not all applications fit easily into this model, but many applications, especially simpler applications, fit this programming model quite well.

The VEE model is a data-flow model. Each icon in a VEE program represents one of the following:

- A physical device, such as an instrument or source.
- A graph or plotting icon, representing a mechanism for displaying data.
- A calculation icon, which performs operations on data.
- A control icon, which controls the flow of data and control of the program.

These icons are connected by lines that represent either data flowing from one icon to another (connecting icons left to right), or flow-of-control flowing from one icon to another (connecting icons top to bottom).

A sample VEE application is given in Figure 3-1. This sample program calculates a simple Fibonacci sequence. Figure 3-2 shows a run of this application.

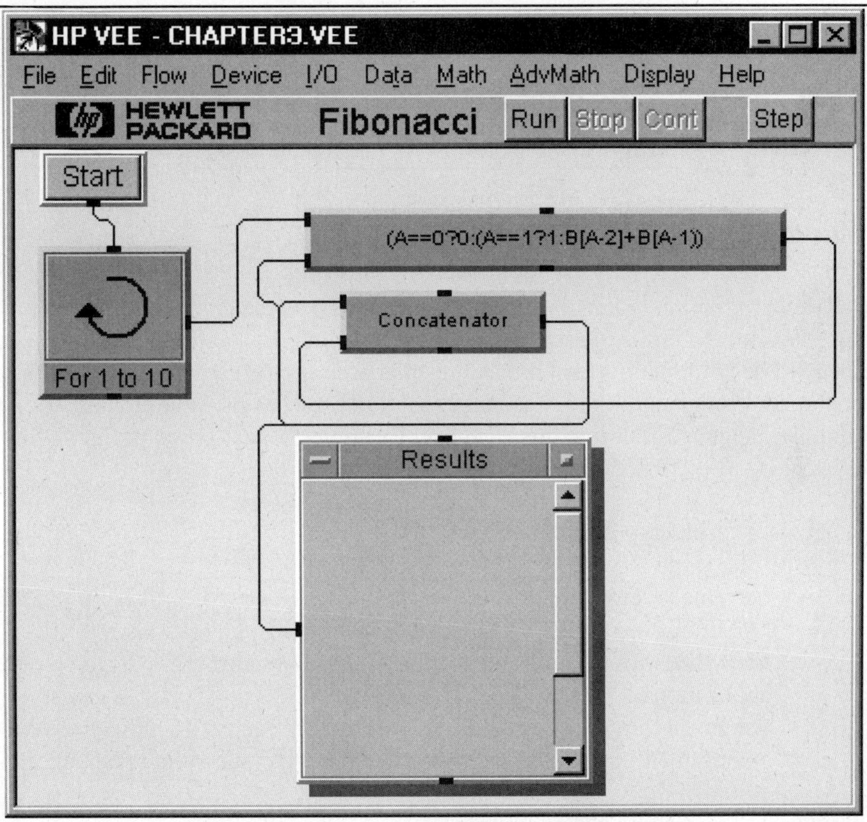

Figure 3-1: Fibonacci Sequence using HP VEE

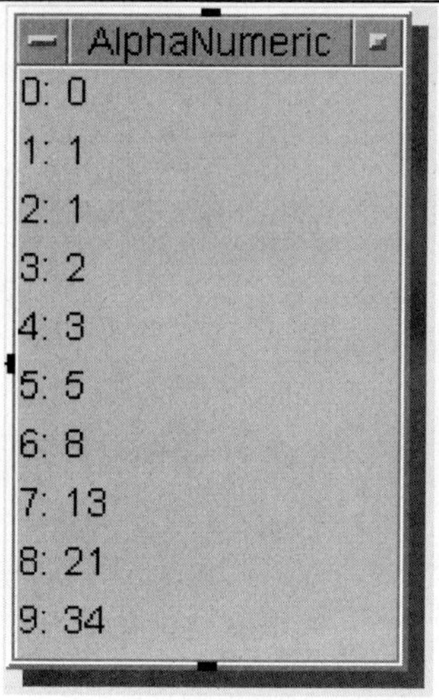

Figure 3-2: Run of HP Vee Application

Text-based Languages (Procedural and Object Oriented)

A text-based programming language is a programming language that describes the program execution in terms of sequential textual instructions. Typically, the language describes a series of functions and procedures that are executed sequentially, plus a set of textual commands that alter the sequential execution flow (loops, conditionals, etc.). Most programming languages fall into this category. Examples of text-based programming languages are C, C++, BASIC, Pascal, and Fortran.

Advantages of text-based programming:

- Extremely complex applications can be developed.
- Maximum versatility is available in developing applications.
- Many libraries of tools and utilities are available for use in developing applications.
- Languages are fairly standard, so a developer can easily move from one environment to another and still apply the principles of the language.

Disadvantages of text-based programming:

- A learning curve is necessary before even a basic application can be developed.
- Involves "real" programming, which typically requires more up-front thought in the creation of an application.

- Provides little or no built-in support for graphing and data display, all such functions are provided by external libraries.

For test and measurement purposes, the most popular text-based languages are BASIC and C, with C++ becoming more prevalent.

Historically, test control applications used BASIC for the test-development language. This was because most test applications were simple, and BASIC allowed quick development of simple programs and the ability to grow these programs over time.

However, as time went on, test applications became more complex. As such, software engineering principles became increasingly important. Application supportability, portability, reuse-ability, and so forth started becoming important. Test development became a full time software engineering job – a specialty rather than a side job for engineers. As such, languages such as C and C++ have begun to become much more prevalent.

Listing 3-1 contains a sample C program that performs the same actions as the VEE program shown in Figure 3-1. Listing 3-2 is the same program written in BASIC. Figure 3-3 shows the output of these two programs.

```
/*
 * Fibonacci:
*/
#include <stdio.h>

main(){
   int i;
   int fib[10];

   /* Generate the sequence */
   fib[0]=0;
   fib[1]=1;
   for(i=2;i<10;++i)
      fib[i]=fib[i-1]+fib[i-2];

   /* Print the sequence */
   printf("First Ten Fibonacci Numbers\n");
   for(i=0;i<10;++i)
      printf(" fib(%d) = %d\n",i,fib[i]);
}
```

Listing 3-1: Fibonacci Sequence Using C

```
100  REM
110  REM Fibonacci:
120  REM
130  DIM FIB[10]
140  REM Generate the Fibonacci Sequence
150  FIB[0]=0
160  FIB[1]=1
170  FOR I=2 TO 9
180     FIB[I]=FIB[I-1]+FIB[I-2]
190  NEXT I
200  REM
210  REM Print the Sequence
220  PRINT "First Ten Fibonacci Numbers"
220  FOR I=0 TO 9
230     PRINT "fig)";I;") = ";FIB[I]
240  NEXT I
250  END
```

Listing 3-2: Fibonacci Sequence Using BASIC

```
First Ten Fibonacci Numbers
 fib(0) = 0
 fib(1) = 1
 fib(2) = 1
 fib(3) = 2
 fib(4) = 3
 fib(5) = 5
 fib(6) = 8
 fib(7) = 13
 fib(8) = 21
 fib(9) = 34
```

Figure 3-3: Run of C and BASIC Program

I/O Software

I/O software is used to control interface hardware that connects the computer to the test instrumentation. There is a variety of I/O software available, for use with a variety of I/O control hardware.

While there are many examples of I/O software packages for use with I/O well beyond the scope of test instrumentation control, there are several designed specifically for T&M and test instrumentation. The two best examples of T&M specific I/O software are SICL and VISA.

SICL

SICL, or Standard Instrument Control Library, is a portable, interface independent I/O library that works on a variety of software and hardware platforms. It was developed in 1989 by Hewlett-Packard, and was the first T&M I/O software standard that was adopted and supported by most of the major I/O vendors. It is designed to provide an easy-to-use interface to control a variety of T&M I/O interfaces, including HP-IB, VXI, and RS-232. It is designed so that a well-written SICL application can be moved from one interface type to another and from one hardware platform to another with little or no changes to the application, thus making software portability easier. SICL added many concepts to I/O software that were not traditionally available in previous I/O software systems. In particular, it added the ability to trap and process errors independently of the main I/O program path. In addition, it added formatted I/O which allowed an application to process data to standard ASCII-based instrumentation, especially IEEE 488.2 style instruments.

Listing 3-3 contains a sample SICL application. It shows a simple application used to talk to a HP-IB based voltmeter to take a basic voltage measurement. This example shows a basic error-handler that simply causes the application to terminate if an error occurs. It also shows formatted I/O being used to talk to the instrument and process the result returned.

VISA

VISA, a subset of which is also known as VTL (the VISA Translation Library), is a much newer I/O software interface. It has many of the same concepts as SICL, and much of the same semantics, but does make some changes and has some additional functionality. VISA was developed by the *VXIplug&play Systems Alliance*[1] as a standard I/O interface library for VXI based systems. Although VISA was designed to control VXI-based systems, it does support HP-IB and RS-232 based systems as well.

Listing 3-4 contains a sample VISA application. It shows the same sample application as the SICL application in Listing 3-3, except it uses VISA to perform the I/O. Notice that many of the same sorts of commands are available, however not everything. First, VISA has no error handling, so each command must check its own error status. In addition, there is extra code to process something called a `defaultRM`, which is a logical

[1] The *VXIplug&play Systems Alliance* is a consortium of most of the major VXI systems manufacturers, including Hewlett-Packard. It has many of the same members as, but is a separate organization from, the *VXI Consortium*.

grouping of similar types of instruments into a structure called a *resource manager*[1]. Other than these changes, and some slight syntactical difference, SICL and VISA are much the same.

Comparing SICL and VISA

So, why are there two very similar I/O libraries in existence? The answer is simple: SICL was developed several years before VISA and serves some different needs than VISA. SICL was designed first and foremost to be easy-to-use and portable. These were the primary goals of SICL. It was because of these goals that it was accepted for many years as a defacto industry standard.

VISA, on the other hand, had the foremost goal of being industry standard. It was developed by a committee of engineers who had various needs and desires. Also, since it came later, it took many of the successes of SICL, and added more features that were missing from SICL.

As such, VISA has more growth potential than SICL, but at the cost of being harder to use than SICL. The tradeoff between portability/ease-of-use and functionality is a tough one, and each of the libraries chose a different balance. Neither is right or wrong, just different.

Ultimately, both SICL and VISA are important I/O libraries within the T&M community.

```
/*
 * Sample SICL Application
 */
#include <stdio.h>
#include <sicl.h>
main(){
   INST id;
   double volt;

   ionerror(I_ERROR_EXIT); /* Catch Errors */
   id=iopen("hpib,24");

   iprintf(id,"MEAS:VOLT:DC?\n");
   iscanf(id,"%lf\n",&volt);
   printf("Voltage Read = %g\n",volt);

   iclose(id);
}
```

Listing 3-3: Sample SICL Application

---

[1] The VISA/VTL resource manager should not be confused with a VXI resource manager.

```
/*
 * Sample VISA Application
 */

#include <stdio.h>
#include <visa.h>

void CheckError(vi,err){
    char buf[256];
    if(error==VI_SUCCESS)
        return;
    viStatusDesc(vi,err,buf);
   printf("Error: 0x%lx: %s\n",err,buf);
}

main(){
   ViStatus err;
   ViSession dRM,vi;
   double volt;


   err=viOpenDefaultRM(&dRM);
   CheckError(dRM,err);

   err=viOpen(dRM,"GPIB::24",0,0,&vi);
   CheckError(dRM,err);

   err=viPrintf(vi,"MEAS:VOLT:DC?\n");
   CheckError(vi,err);
   err=viScanf(vi,"%lf%*t",&volt);
   CheckError(vi,err);

   printf("Voltage Read = %g\n",volt);

   viClose(vi);
   viClose(dRM);
}
```

Listing 3-4: Sample VTL/VISA Application

Summary

This chapter discussed the following main points:

- Both off-the-shelf and custom/semi-custom software are needed for a complete test system.

They are very different concepts and have no connection to each other.

- HP VEE is one of the prevalent iconic-programming languages used extensively in T&M application development, especially where ease-of-use and "non-programming programming" is desired.

- BASIC and C are prevalent textual-programming languages commonly used for test systems were more extensive programming is needed.

- A Fibonacci sequence program written in VEE, BASIC, and C shows a simple comparison among the three languages.

- T&M applications need an I/O library to talk to test instrumentation. The two most prevalent examples are SICL and VISA. SICL was designed primarily for ease-of-use and portability, while VISA/VTL was designed primarily for multivendor standardized systems.

Exercises

Exercise 3-1. Write a simple SICL application in C or C++ that configures a source to generate a 10Khz sine wave signal with amplitude of 1V P-P. Then read from a voltmeter the voltage on a DUT output pin (expected voltage is between 3-5V). You may either use existing instrumentation that you are aware of, or you may create and describe fictional instruments that perform the commands desired. You may need to refer to a SICL manual in order to complete this exercise.

Exercise 3-2. Write the same application described in Exercise 3-1, but use VISA or VTL to write the application. You may need to refer to a VISA/VTL manual in order to complete this exercise.

Exercise 3-3. Write the same application described in Exercise 3-1, but use HP-VEE.

4. Programming a Test System

This chapter describes a simple DUT that must be tested, and a set of criteria for testing the DUT. From this information, a simple test system is constructed. The purpose of this test system is to perform a simple production test of the DUT to determine if it passes or fails the given test criteria.

Topics Covered:

Construction of an Example Test System

Software Components Needed for the Test System

Writing Test Software for Example Test System

Demonstration of a Complete Example Test Application

The test system that will be constructed in this chapter will use traditional programming techniques, that is, procedural-based programming, top-down modular design, and written in ANSI C (without using C++ extensions). The purpose of this application is to show how traditional programming techniques are typically applied to solving a T&M test problem. During the object oriented discussions in Part III of this book, this same problem description will be used to demonstrate object oriented techniques and C++ programming. At the end of Part III of this book, this same test application will be rewritten as an object oriented program.

The Problem

The problem that this application must solve is to test a simple band-pass filter to make sure it satisfies a specific set of conditions. This test application will be the basis for a production test system where a continuous supply of band-pass filters will be passed by the test station on the assembly line and tested. Filters that pass the tests will be sent on their way, while filters that do not pass the test will be discarded.

For the purposes of this book, the mechanics of the assembly line processing and the complexities of the fixturing will be ignored. Instead, the band-pass filter will simply be a black-box circuit board sitting on an R&D bench, and will be tested for conformance to the test criteria.

In review, a band-pass filter is a simple circuit that passes frequencies between two specified frequencies, and does not pass frequencies that are below or above the specified range. The range of frequencies where the signal is passed is called the *passband.* As a black box, the DUT can be modeled as shown in Figure 4-1.

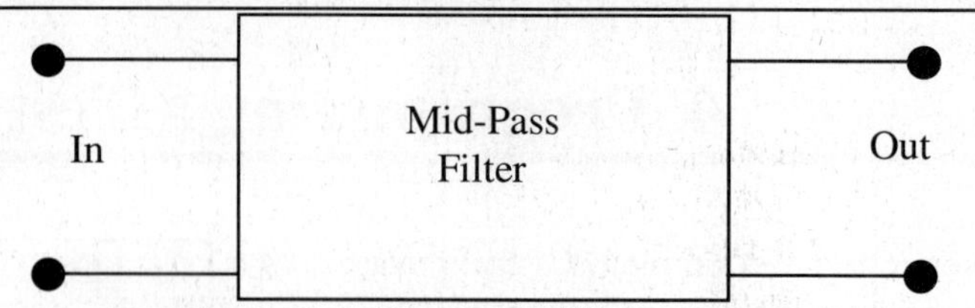

Figure 4-1: Black-Box View of DUT

The frequency response of a typical band-pass filter is shown in Figure 4-2. The frequency response has several aspects, in particular:

- ω_0 - **The center frequency**. This is the frequency at which the output voltage is maximized.
- ω_1 - **The low frequency**. This is the frequency where the output voltage is $1/\sqrt{2}$ of the voltage at ω_0. Lower frequencies have a lower voltage, higher frequencies have a higher voltage. This is the low-end of the passband.
- ω_2 - **The high frequency**. This is the frequency where the output voltage is $1/\sqrt{2}$ of the voltage at ω_0. Lower frequencies have a higher voltage, higher frequencies have a lower voltage. This is the high-end of the passband.
- β - **The Bandwidth**. This is the width of the frequency response between ω_1 and ω_2.

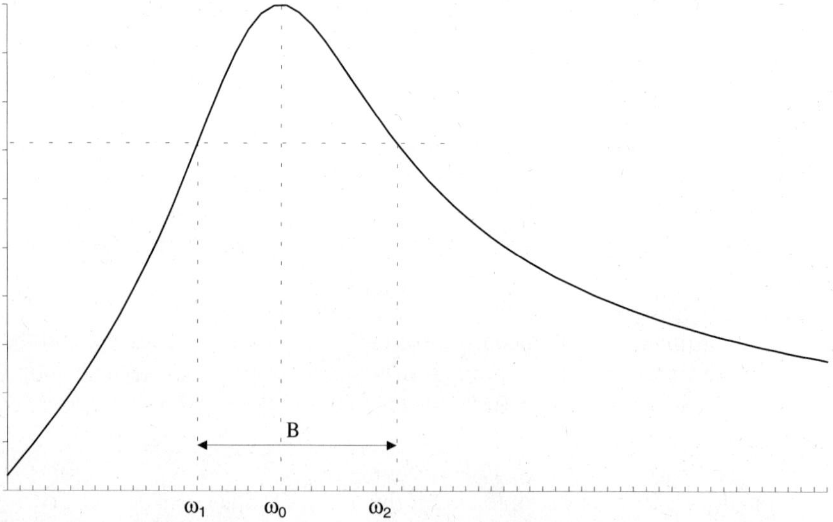

Figure 4-2: Typical Band-Pass Filter

For the band-pass filter that will be tested by this example test application, the following characteristics are desired:

$$\omega_0 = 2250Hz$$
$$\omega_1 = 1455Hz$$
$$\omega_2 = 3045Hz$$
$$\beta = 1590Hz$$
$$0.5V \le V_o \le 1.0V$$

This is for an ideal DUT. Obviously, no real device is ideal. The purpose of the test is to decide whether a given instance of a DUT does a satisfactory job of meeting these conditions. This will be discussed later.

DUT

Before we describe the test application, we will describe the DUT in more detail. In "The Problem", we described the DUT in black-box terms. In other words, we described it as a band-pass filter with a specific set of characteristics. In this section, we will describe the implementation of the DUT that meets the requirements. We will use a simple RLC circuit as our band-pass filter. The RLC circuit is shown schematically in Figure 4-3.

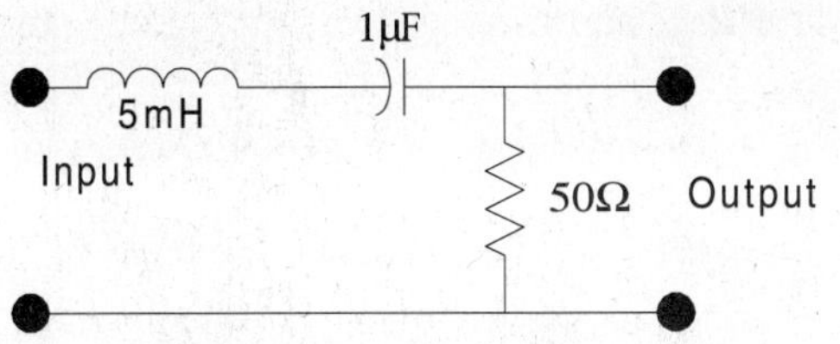

Figure 4-3: DUT - RLC Band-Pass Filter

We have chosen the following values for the various components in this circuit:

$$R = 50\Omega$$
$$L = 5mH$$
$$C = 1\mu F$$

So, the center frequency, ω_0, can be calculated:

$$\omega_0 = \frac{1}{\sqrt{LC}}$$

Plugging in our values for L and C:

$$\omega_0 = \frac{1}{\sqrt{5 \cdot 10^{-3} \cdot 1 \cdot 10^{-6}}} = 14142 \tfrac{rad}{\sec} = 2251Hz$$

The low and high end of the passband, ω_1 and ω_2 can be calculated:

$$\omega_1 = -\frac{R}{2L} + \sqrt{\left(\frac{R}{2L}\right)^2 + \frac{1}{LC}}$$

$$\omega_2 = +\frac{R}{2L} + \sqrt{\left(\frac{R}{2L}\right)^2 + \frac{1}{LC}}$$

The bandwidth can be calculated:

$$\beta = \omega_2 - \omega_1 = \frac{R}{L}$$

Plugging in our values for *R*, *L*, and *C*:

$$\omega_1 = 9142 \tfrac{rad}{\sec} = 1455Hz$$

$$\omega_2 = 19138 \tfrac{rad}{\sec} = 3046Hz$$

$$\beta = 9996 \tfrac{rad}{\sec} = 1591Hz$$

These values are within .1% of the desired values. Of course, real-world tolerances with the given parts will cause the variance to be greater. Therefore, several DUTs will be constructed and tested. Depending on the reliability of the parts, somewhat different results are expected. Thus the need for this test system.

Design Methodology

Since the purpose of this application is to show how traditional programming techniques are typically applied to solving a T&M test problem, we will be making several fundamental assumptions on how the application will be designed.

We will be using a typical top-down design. In this design, we will take the problem at a high level, and break it down into smaller problems that will be solved independently. This will create a layered design. You will see as we go through this process that the layers will match very closely to those discussed in Chapter 3. The application will be structured into modules that match these design layers.

No object oriented concepts will be used in this example. It will be a complete procedural-based application.

Designing the Test System

Now, we must design the test system itself. This involves creating the test criteria that we will use for testing the DUT, along with deciding what hardware components we will need to build the test system.

This section will not discuss the design of the test software. After we have finished the design of the test system, we will design the software that will be used in the test system.

Test Criteria

The first step, and probably the most important step, in designing the test system is to decide what criteria will be used for testing the DUT. This includes:

- determining the characteristics to be tested
- determining acceptable range of values
- determining input values to use
- creating list of specific tests needed

Determining Characteristics to be Tested

First, we need to decide what characteristics of the DUT we will test. We have chosen the following:

ω_0 - The center frequency.

ω_1 - The low-end of the passband. The frequency where the output voltage is $1/\sqrt{2}$ the input voltage.

ω_2 - The high-end of the passband. The frequency where the output voltage is $1/\sqrt{2}$ the input voltage.

β - The bandwidth.

V_{om}- The output voltage at its maximum, when the frequency is at ω_0.

I_{om} - The "output" current (current across *R*) at its maximum, when the frequency is at ω_0.

V_L - The output voltage at ω_0 – 2000Hz.

V_H - The output voltage at ω_0 + 2000Hz.

There are obviously many more characteristics that could be tested, but only these will be used in this example. The first five are specific design characteristics of the band-pass filter. The last two are simply check points for other frequencies. A less thorough test may not test these values, and a more thorough test may test V at other frequencies as well.

Determining Acceptable Range of Values to Test

Now that we know what characteristics to test, we must decide what are acceptable ranges for the specified values. These will normally be determined based on the needs of the DUT user.

First, let us discuss the acceptable ranges for the frequencies. For this example, we will arbitrarily choose an acceptable frequency tolerance of ±10%. Therefore, ω_0 must be

10% of 2250Hz is 225Hz
2025Hz ≤ ω0 ≤ 2475Hz,

while ω_1 must be

10% of 1455Hz is 145Hz
1310Hz ≤ ω1 ≤ 1600Hz,

and ω_2 must be

10% of 3045Hz is 304Hz
2741Hz ≤ ω2 ≤ 3349Hz.

Finally, β must be:

$$10\% \text{ of } 1590\text{Hz is } 159\text{Hz}$$
$$\mathbf{1431Hz \le \beta \le 1749Hz.}$$

Notice that it is possible for a device to pass the ω_0, ω_1, and ω_2 tests, but still fail the β test. This can happen when, for example:

$$\omega_0 = 2250\text{Hz}$$
$$\omega_1 = 1310\text{Hz}$$
$$\omega_2 = 3349\text{Hz}$$
$$\beta = \omega_2 - \omega_1 = 2039\text{Hz}$$

Even though all the values necessary to calculate β are within acceptable range (ω_1 and ω_2), the value of β may be out of range.

Next, we must decide on criteria for V_{om} and I_{om}, the output voltage and current at the center frequency ω_0. We will arbitrary choose an acceptable voltage attenuation of ±5%. Therefore, V_{om} must be:

$$V_i{*}95\% \le V_{om} \le V_i{*}105\%$$

where V_i is the input voltage and I_{om} must be:

$$I_{exp}{*}95\% \le I_{om} \le I_{exp}{*}105\%$$

where I_{exp} is the expected current (at load impedance R), which is:

$$I_{\exp} = \frac{V_i}{R}$$

Next, we must set criteria for V_L and V_H. Since the frequencies where these voltages are to be measured are outside the passband, we desire to make sure the voltages are less than a certain threshold. We choose to make sure that:

$$V_L \le V_i{*}20\%$$

and:

$$V_H \le V_i{*}50\%$$

In other words, make sure the voltage at ω_0-2000Hz is ≤ 20% of the input voltage, and the voltage at ω_0+2000Hz is ≤ 50% of the input voltage. These values are arbitrary. More specific tests could be made.

Determining Input Values

Now, we must decide the input values that will be used during the tests. Because of the values used in the RLC circuit, in particular, the low value of R, we must be careful when choosing an input voltage such that the current requirements on the various components, and the power requirements on R are not too great.

We choose to use three different input voltages: 0.5V, 1.0V, and 1.5V. This generates a maximum current draw in the circuit of:

$$I_{max} = \frac{V_i}{R}$$

$$I_{max}(0.5V) = 10mA$$

$$I_{max}(1.0V) = 20mA$$

$$I_{max}(1.5V) = 30mA$$

and maximum power requirement of R:

$$P_{max} = \frac{V^2}{R}$$

$$P_{max}(1.5V) = .045W$$

which is well within reasonable limits for this simple test.

Therefore, the test will be run for three different input voltages[1]:

1. $V_i = 0.5V$
2. $V_i = 1.0V$
3. $V_i = 1.5V$

---

[1] It is an arbitrary choice to perform the tests at three different voltages (instead of simply using one), given the characteristics of this particular DUT. However, for demonstration purposes, we will test at all three voltages.

Specific Tests to Perform

Now that we know all the characteristics we want to test, we can finally decide the specific list of tests tó perform. Based on the above information, the following tests will be performed.

Do the following for V_i=0.5V, V_i=1.0V or V_i=1.5V:

Verify ω_0 is within expected limits (2025Hz $\leq \omega_0 \leq$ 2475Hz).
Verify ω_1 is within expected limits (1310Hz $\leq \omega_1 \leq$ 1600Hz).
Verify ω_2 is within expected limits (2741Hz $\leq \omega_2 \leq$ 3349Hz).
Verify β is within expected limits (1431Hz $\leq \beta \leq$ 1749Hz).
Verify V_{om} is within expected limits (V_i*95% $\leq V_{om} \leq V_i$*105%).
Verify I_{om} is within expected limits (I_{exp} *95% $\leq I_{om} \leq I_{exp}$ *105%).
Verify V_L is within expected limits ($V_L \leq V_i$*20%).
Verify V_H is within expected limits ($V_H \leq V_i$*50%).

Test Components Needed

Now, we must decide on the hardware needs of this test system. This consists of instrumentation, controller hardware, and off-the-shelf software.

Instrumentation

In order to implement the above tests, the following types of instrumentation are needed:

Voltmeter. A device that measures AC voltage.

Ammeter. A device that measures AC current.

Source. A device that generates a sine wave at various amplitudes and frequencies.

Switch. A device that connects the instruments in various ways to the DUT.

Of course, the voltmeter and ammeter may (and probably will be) contained in a single digital multimeter (DMM) that performs both functions. Notice that in order to connect the ammeter, we need to insert it into the DUT inline with the resister, as shown in Figure 4-4.

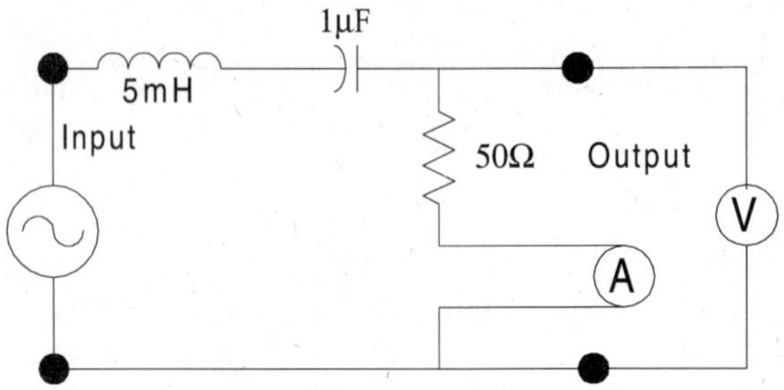

Figure 4-4: DUT - RLC Band-pass Filter

For these instruments, the following range of values must be supported:

Voltmeter. Measure AC voltage from 0-2V. We will assume we need a voltmeter with at least a .1% accuracy. This corresponds to at least a 3 1/2 digit voltmeter.

Ammeter. Measure AC current from 0-40mA. We will assume we need an ammeter with at least a .1% accuracy. This corresponds to at least a 3 1/2 digit ammeter.

Source. Must generate a sine wave with an amplitude from 0-2V and a frequency of 1000Hz to 4000Hz. There will be a maximum current draw of 40mA. We will assume we need a source with at least a .1% accuracy. This corresponds to a .02V and a 4Hz variation at various current draws.

The switch card must have the following characteristics:

Switch. A matrix switch that connects the voltmeter, ammeter, and source to the DUT. We will assume that we will connect each of the instruments to *row* lines, and each of the DUT pins to *column* lines. Given that we have three instruments with two terminals each, and the DUT has three terminals (one is common to input and output), we therefore need a 6x3 matrix switch. The switch must handle up to 2V at 40mA. We will assume that all switching will be done with the source disabled.

We will assume that the fixturing needs of these instruments is straight-forward enough that we can create the custom wiring necessary to connect the instruments together.

Designing the Test Software

We will now do the top-down design of our test software.

Sequencer

The top of our test hierarchy is the *sequencer*. This is the software component that schedules specific tests and returns a status of passed or failed. The top-level interface to the sequencer looks like this:

Module:	*Sequencer*
Inputs:	<none>
Outputs:	DUT Passed/Failed Module Success/Failure

This module needs no inputs, but returns an indication as to whether the DUT passed or failed the tests. It also returns an error status, which is an indication as to whether the test itself was successful in testing the DUT, not an indication of DUT success. Table 4-1 describes the meaning of different combinations of outputs from the sequencer.

Module Success/Failure	DUT Passed/Failed	Description
Failure	Unknown	The test failed. Status of DUT is unknown.
Success	Passed	The DUT passed the test.
Success	Failed	The DUT failed the test.

Table 4-1: Success/Failure Modes of Tests

The sequencer simply calls all the individual tests that perform the actual DUT testing. It records the results of each DUT test and returns error and status codes as appropriate. In more involved test systems, the sequencer also decides which tests to execute on a given DUT and when. But in our simple model, we will assume that all tests will always be run and will be run in a fixed order.

The sequencer will execute the tests specified in the "Specific Tests to Perform". In order to perform these tests, the following test routines are needed:

- **Test ω_0**. A test routine that verifies the value of ω_0.
- **Test ω_1**. A test routine that verifies the value of ω_1.
- **Test ω_2**. A test routine that verifies the value of ω_2.
- **Test voltage**. A test routine that verifies the output voltage is within a specific range given a specific frequency, ω.
- **Test current**. A test routine that verifies the output current is within a specific range given a specific frequency, ω.

The sequencer will use these routines to perform all the tests expected. These routines constitute the next level down in abstraction and will be discussed next.

Test Routines

The next level of our test hierarchy is the *test routines*. These are the software components that execute specific tests. The tests are called by the sequencer, which knows what needs to be tested and when. There are five modules that make up the test routines:

Test ω_0.
Test ω_1.
Test ω_2.
Test voltage.
Test current.

The top-level interface to these functions look like this:

Module:	*Test ω_0*
Inputs:	V_i - Input voltage to use.
Outputs:	ω_0 - Frequency where V_o is maximized.
	DUT Passed/Failed
	Module Success/Failure

This module takes as input a V_i (input voltage) to use. The output is ω_0, the frequency where V_o is maximized, an indication as to whether the ω_0 is acceptable (i.e., did the DUT pass?), and an indication as to whether the test routine was successful or failed. This routine returns ω_0 so that it can be used in other tests by the sequencer later.

Module:	*Test ω_1*
Inputs:	V_i - Input voltage to use.
Outputs:	ω_1 - Frequency where V_o is $1/\sqrt{2}$ of V_{om}, but greater than ω_0.
	DUT Passed/Failed
	Module Success/Failure

This module takes as input a V_i to use. The output is ω_1, an indication as to whether the ω_1 is acceptable, and an indication as to whether the test routine was successful or failed. This routine returns ω_1 so that the sequencer can calculate and verify β.

Module:	*Test ω_2*
Inputs:	V_i - Input voltage to use.
Outputs:	ω_2 - Frequency where V_o is $1/\sqrt{2}$ of
V_{om}, but	
	greater than ω_0.
	DUT Passed/Failed
	Module Success/Failure

This module takes as input a V_i to use. The output is ω_2, an indication as to whether the ω_2 is acceptable, along with an indication as to whether the test routine was successful or failed. This routine returns ω_2 so that the sequencer can calculate and verify β.

Module:	*Test voltage*
Inputs:	V_i - Input voltage to use.
	ω - Frequency to use.
	V_L - Minimum acceptable V_o.
	V_H - Maximum acceptable V_o.
Outputs:	DUT Passed/Failed
	Module Success/Failure

This module takes as input: V_i, the input voltage; ω, the frequency to use; V_L, the minimum acceptable output voltage;

and V_H, the maximum acceptable output voltage. This routine will make sure the output voltage at the given input voltage and frequency is between V_L and V_H.

Module:	*Test current*
Inputs:	V_i - Input voltage to use.
	ω - Frequency to use.
	I_L - Minimum acceptable I_o.
	I_H - Maximum acceptable I_o.
Outputs:	DUT Passed/Failed
	Module Success/Failure

This module takes as input: V_i, the input voltage; ω, the frequency to use; I_L, the minimum acceptable load current; and I_H, the maximum acceptable load current. This routine will make sure the current at the given input voltage and frequency is between I_L and I_H.

In order to perform these actions, these modules must take measurements. The following measurement routines must be provided:

- **Get frequency that maximizes voltage**. A measurement routine that calculates the frequency that generates the maximum output voltage (use to find ω_0).

- **Get frequency that matches specific voltage**. A measurement routine that calculates the frequency that generates a specific output voltage (used to find ω_1 and ω_2).

- **Get voltage**. A measurement routine that measures the output voltage using a given input voltage and frequency.

- **Get Current**. A measurement routine that measures the current using a given input voltage and frequency.

These routines constitute the next level down in abstraction and will be discussed next.

Measurement Routines

The next level of our test hierarchy is the *measurement routines*. This is the software component that takes various measurements needed by the test routines. There are four functions that constitute this level of abstraction:

Get frequency that maximizes voltage.
Get frequency that matches specific voltage.
Get voltage.
Get current.

The top-level interface to these functions look like this:

Module:	*Get frequency that maximizes voltage.*
Inputs:	V_i - Input voltage to use.
	ω_s - Start frequency.
	ω_e - End frequency.
Outputs:	ω_0 - Actual peak frequency.
	Module Success/Failure.

This routine takes an input voltage, a start frequency, and an end frequency. It scans frequencies between ω_s and ω_e until the actual peak frequency, ω_0, is calculated.

Module:	*Get frequency that matches specific voltage.*
Inputs:	V_i - Input voltage to use.
	V_e - Expected output voltage.
	ω_s - Start frequency.
	ω_e - End frequency.
Outputs:	ω - Frequency that generates V_e.
	Module Success/Failure.

This routine takes an input voltage, an expected output voltage, a start frequency, and an end frequency. It scans frequencies between ω_s and ω_e until a frequency that generates the expected output voltage, V_e, is achieved.

Module:	*Get Voltage*
Inputs:	V_i - Input voltage to use.
	ω - Input frequency to use.
Outputs:	V_o - Output voltage at given input
voltage and	
	frequency.
	Module Success/Failure.

This routine takes an input voltage and input frequency. It then measures and returns the output voltage.

Module:	*Get Current*
Inputs:	V_i - Input voltage to use. ω - Input frequency to use.
Outputs:	I_o - Current at given input voltage and frequency. Module Success/Failure.

This routine takes an input voltage and input frequency. It then measures and returns the current.

In order to perform these actions, these modules must talk to instrumentation. The following instrument routines must be provided:

- **Set Source Voltage**. Set the output voltage of the sine-wave source. This is the input signal to the DUT.

- **Set Source Frequency**. Set the output frequency of the sine-wave source. This is the input signal to the DUT.

- **Enable Source Output**. This turns on the sine-wave source at the previously set voltage and frequency.

- **Disable Source Output**. This turns off the sine-wave source. This is the default value. The source must be disabled during test set-up and while the switch card is switching.

- **Set DMM Range**. Set the range of the DMM to the given setting.

- **DMM Measure**. Measure the signal on the DMM input. This is typically the output of the DUT.

- **Set Switch**. Set the switch card to the given setting. This sets the switch to connect the correct DMM input pins to the DUT output, and the correct source output pins to the DUT input.

These routines constitute the next level down in abstraction and will be discussed next.

Instrument Drivers

The next level of our test hierarchy is the *instrument drivers*. This is the software component that communicates directly with the given instrumentation. The instrument drivers are called by the measurement routines to perform specific measurements with specific instrumentation. There are seven functions that make up the instrument drivers:

Set Source Voltage.
Set Source Frequency.
Enable Source Output.
Disable Source Output.
Set DMM Range.
DMM Measure.
Set Switch.

The top-level interface to these functions look like this:

Module:	*Set Source Voltage*
Inputs:	V - Source output voltage to use.
Outputs:	Module Success/Failure.

This function sets the sine-wave source output voltage to V.

Module:	*Set Source Frequency*
Inputs:	ω - Source output frequency to use.
Outputs:	Module Success/Failure.

This function sets the sine-wave source output frequency to ω.

Module:	*Enable Source Output*
Inputs:	<none>
Outputs:	Module Success/Failure.

This function enables the sine-wave source output.

Module:	*Disable Source Output*
Inputs:	<none>
Outputs:	Module Success/Failure.

This function disables the sine-wave source output.

Module:	*Set DMM Range*
Inputs:	range
Outputs:	Module Success/Failure.

This function sets the range of the DMM. The possible values are:

- Voltage: 0-2V
- Current: 0-50mA

Module:	*DMM Measure*
Inputs:	<none>
Outputs:	measured value Module Success/Failure.

This function causes the DMM to take the reading specified by a previous range setting, and returns the results.

Module:	*Set Switch*
Inputs:	setting
Outputs:	Module Success/Failure.

This function sets the switch to the specified setting. The possible values are:

- Voltage: Connect the voltmeter terminals of the DMM to the DUT output, and the source to DUT input.
- Current: Connect the ammeter terminals of the DMM across the DUT resister, and the source to DUT input.

In order to perform these actions, these modules must be able to send commands to and from the instrumentation. This is where the HP-IB I/O library comes into play. In this example, the I/O library used is Hewlett-Packard's VTL library.

Mapping Design to Test System Model

Figure 4-5 shows how the test system design looks. Compare this picture to the "Software Components" section of Chapter 2. This is a typical breakdown of a test system.

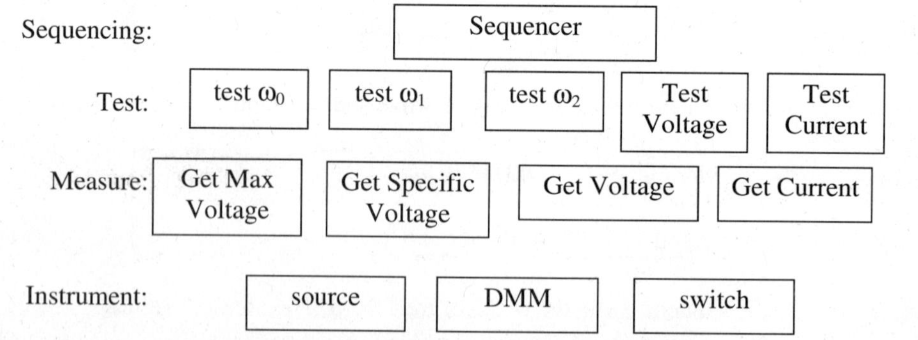

Figure 4-5: Example Test System Design

Constructing the Test Software

Next, we must construct the test system. We will only discuss the construction of a few of the modules. Many of the rest will be left as exercises. In addition, a complete working example of this application is contained on the disk included with this book.

Error and Status Reporting

All functions in our examples will return a result of type "error." This value will be 0 for success and a non-0 error code if a failure of some type occurs. A value of <0 means the test failed in some way. A value of >0 means the test was successful, but the DUT did not meet the specific criteria.

The instrument library and measurement routine layers will only return success and <0 test failures. The test library and sequencer will return success, <0 test failures, and >0 DUT failures. This is because layers below the test layer have no knowledge of the DUT itself. Only at the test layer and above does the application have any knowledge of the meaning of measurements taken and what that means to the DUT.

Instrument Drivers – Sine-Wave Source

The sine-wave source instrument driver will have five entry points, as follows:

```
error sourceInit(); /* Initializes the source */
error sourceSetVolt(double voltage); /*Sets voltage*/
error sourceSetFreq(double freq); /*Sets frequency*/
error sourceEnableOutput(); /*Enables output */
error sourceDisableOutput(); /* Disables output */
```

To set the output voltage, the following SCPI command must be sent to the source:

```
SOUR:VOLT voltage
```

To set the output frequency, the following SCPI command must be sent to the source:

```
SOUR:FREQ frequenecy
```

To enable the sine-wave output, the following commands must be sent:

```
SOUR:FUNC SINE
SOUR:ENABLE
```

To disable the sine-wave output, the following command must be sent:

```
SOUR:DISABLE
```

The `sourceInit` function simply opens an I/O session to the source:

```
#include <visa.h>
ViSession dmmVi;
error sourceInit(){
    ViStatus err;
    err=viOpen(
                    defaultRM,
                    "GPIB-VXI0::24::INSTR",
                    VI_NULL,
                    VI_NULL,
                    &dmmVi
                );
    if(err!=VI_SUCCESS)
        return ERROR_OPEN_FAILED;

    return SUCCESS;
}
```

The `sourceSetVolt` function sends the corresponding SCPI command to the source:

```
error sourceSetVolt(double voltage){
    ViStatus err;
    err=viPrintf(vi,"SOUR:VOLT %g\n",voltage);
    if(err!=VI_SUCCESS)
        return ERROR_INST_IO;

    return SUCCESS;
}
```

The other functions have similar implementations.

Measurement Library -- Measure Voltage and Current

One of the modules in the measurement library is the `getVoltage` function. The implementation of this function has the following prototype:

```
error getVoltage(
                    double inpVolt,
                    double inpFreq,
                    double *outVolt
                    );
```

The `inpVolt` is the voltage and `inpFreq` is the frequency of the sine-wave source during the measurement. The measured output voltage is returned in `*outVolt`.

This function makes use of the source and the DMM to make the measurements. The prototypes for the functions to control the source are shown above. The prototypes for the

DMM are given on the enclosed disk, and are also shown in a simplified form for reference here:

```
#define DMM_RANGE_20V 20 /* 0-2.0V range */
error dmmInit();
error dmmSetRange(int range);
error dmmMeasure(double *value);
```

The `range` is the range to set the DMM. The `DMM_RANGE_20V` is one of the specific values to use for `range`. The `*value` is the value measured.

So, given all of this, the following is a simplified implementation of `getVoltage`:

```
error getVoltage(
                double inV,
                double inF,
                double *outV
){
    /* Disable the source output */
    sourceDisableOutput();

    /* Set up the source */
    sourceSetVolt(inV);
    sourceSetFreq(inF);

    /* Set up the DMM and Switch */
    dmmSetRange(DMM_RANGE_20V);
    switchSet(SWITCH_VOLTAGE);

    /* Turn on the source */
    sourceEnableOutput();

    /* Measure the output voltage */
    dmmMeasure(outV);

    /* Disable the output */
    sourceDisableOutput();

    return SUCCESS;
}
```

This example does not show error handling, logging, and so forth.

Measurement Library -- Peak Voltage

One of the modules in the measurement library is the `getFreqMaxVoltage` function. The purpose of this function is to calculate the frequency (within a given range of frequencies) that maximizes the output voltage. The implementation of this function has the following prototype:

```
error getFreqMaxVoltage(
                                    double inV,
                                    double startFreq,
                                    double stopFreq,
                                    double *resFreq
                                );
```

The `inV` is the voltage to set the sine-wave source. The `startFreq` and `stopFreq` values are the range to test the output voltage. The `*resFreq` is the output of this function that is set to the frequency between `startFreq` and `stopFreq` where the output voltage is maximized.

This function is not as simple as the other functions, since there is no function within the instrument that directly corresponds to it. Therefore, this function must be implemented in software.

This function will be implemented by first approximating the maximum voltage by scanning frequencies between `startFreq` and `stopFreq` with a large step frequency (amount to increase the frequency each scan). Then, using a more restricted frequency range and a smaller step frequency, the maximum voltage is again calculated. This process is repeated until an accurate `*resFreq` can be determined.

So, to implement this function, we define a helper function:

```
error scanFreqMaxVoltage(
                                    double startF,
                                    double stopF,
                                    double stepF,
                                    double *resFreq
                                );
```

This function scans frequencies from `startF` to `stopF` with a step between scans of `stepF`. At each step, the output voltage is calculated. The frequency tested that returns the greatest output voltage during the one scan is returned in `*resFreq`. This function assumes the sine-wave source output is disabled, but the sine-wave output voltage has been set. This function also assumes that there is only one frequency peak in the range of `startF` to `stopF`, which is the case for the given DUT.

Here is a simplified implementation of `scanFreqMaxVoltage`:

```
error scanFreqMaxVoltage(
                            double startF,
                            double stopF,
                            double stepF,
                            double *resFreq
                           ){
    double currF;
    double lastVal;
    double val;

    /* Set original peak value to 0 (all peaks are >0)
*/
    lastVal=0.0;

    /* Scan thru frequency range */
    for(currF=startF;currF<stopF;currF+=stepF){
        /* Set source output frequency */
        sourceSetFreq(currFreq);

        /* Enable the source output */
        sourceEnableOutput();

        /* Measure the output voltage */
        dmmMeasure(&val);

        /* See if last time was a peak */
        /* This is true if this value is less than */
        /* the last value (we are over the peak) */
        if(val<lastVal){
            /* We have peaked, last value was peak */
            *resFreq=currF-stepF;

            return SUCCESS;
        }

        /* We have not yet peaked */
        lastVal=val;
    }

    /* No peak value was found */
    return ERROR_NO_W0_FREQ;
}
```

Listing 4-1: `scanFreqMaxVoltage` Implementation

This function is used by `getFreqMaxVoltage` during its progressive approximation. It makes several calls to `scanFreqMaxVoltage` using increasingly smaller frequency ranges and increasingly smaller step frequencies. Each approximation will get an increasingly more accurate estimate of the peak voltage frequency. The following is a simplified implementation of `getFreqMaxVoltage`:

```
error getFreqMaxVoltage(
                                double inV,
                                double startF,
                                double stopF,
                                double *resFreq
                              ){
    double tmpF;

    /* Disable the source output, and setup */
    sourceDisableOutput();
    sourceSetVolt(inV);
    switchSet(SWITCH_VOLTAGE);

    /* Try a step of 200Hz (entire range) */
    scanFreqMaxVoltage(startF,stopF,200,&tmpF);

    /* Use a step of 20Hz (range: tmpF+/-200Hz) */
    scanFreqmaxVoltage(tmpF-200,tmpF+200,20,&tmpF);

    /* Use a step of 1Hz (range: tmpF+/-20Hz) */
    scanFreqmaxVoltage(tmpF-20,tmpF+20,1,&tmpF);

    /* Return the last tmpF (it will be +/- 1Hz) */
    *resFreq=tmpF;

    return SUCCESS;
}
```

Listing 4-2: `getFreqMaxVoltage` Implementation

This example does not show error handling, logging, and so forth.

We wrote this routine because our DMM did not have a "find maximum voltage over frequencies" function. If it had, we would not have had to write this function. But, now that this function exists, from the perspective of the test routines (the layer above the measurement library), it does not matter if the DMM implemented this function or we wrote it. We essentially added a function to our DMM. This is a sample of a *virtual instrument* function. We created new instrument functionality from existing instruments. In this case, we used both a DMM and a sine-wave source to produce an instrument that calculates ω_0.

Object oriented programming is well suited for developing virtual instruments and virtual instrument functions. This will be discussed in detail in a later chapter.

Test Library -- Test Various Frequencies

One of the modules in the test library is the `testVoltage` function. The implementation of this function has the following prototype:

```
error testVoltage(
                double inpVolt,
                double inpFreq,
                double lowV,
                double hiV
                );
```

The `inpVolt` is the voltage and `inpFreq` is the frequency of the sine-wave source during the measurement. The output voltage is measured and compared to `lowV` and `hiV`. If it is within the given range, the test returns SUCCESS; else it returns an error.

The following is a simplified implementation of `testVoltage`:

```
error testVoltage(
                   double inV,
                   double inF,
                   double lowV,
                   double hiV
                ){
    double result;

    /*Use Measurement Library to get output voltage*/
    getVoltage(inV,inF,&result);

    if(result < lowV)
        return ERROR_V_TOO_LOW; /* Output too low */
    if(result > hiV)
        return ERROR_V_TOO_HIGH; /* Ouptut too high */

    /* Good result! */
    return SUCCESS;
}
```

This example does not show error handling, logging, and so forth.

Completed Example

A complete working example of this test application is contained on the disk included with this book. Also included is a makefile to build the system using Microsoft Visual C++ 2.0. This example includes all of the functions necessary to implement this test application. This includes functions that we have designed in this chapter and not implemented, as well as complete versions of functions we have implemented in this chapter. These complete versions also include logging and error handling.

There are two different instrument libraries included with the example. The first is the real instrument library that talks to the test hardware discussed in this chapter. The second uses *pseudo-instruments*. It emulates the behavior of test instruments connected to the given DUT without actually connecting to any hardware. This instrument library can be used to test the software or to run it when the test instrumentation needed is not available.

They are also useful for debugging the rest of the application without tying up test hardware. The existing makefile is set up to use the pseudo-instrument version of the instrument library.

The ability to substitute one instrument library for another in order to replace or eliminate test hardware, is a mechanism well suited for object oriented programming. This will be a topic of a later chapter.

Summary

In this chapter we started with a T&M testing problem. We then went through all the steps necessary to design and build a test application to solve the given problem. In this example, we used traditional, non-object oriented programming techniques. During the course of this chapter, however, we introduced concepts that object oriented programming may be able to help us implement. We will cover these concepts in later chapters.

A complete working example of the test application developed in this chapter is contained in the disk included with this book.

Exercises

Exercise 4-1. What characteristics, other than those discussed on page 4-5, could be tested with this DUT?

Exercise 4-2. Design and code a version of `getFreqMaxVoltage` that performs fewer instrument measurements, but still achieves the desired accuracy.

Exercise 4-3. Implement the `sourceSetFreq`, `sourceEnableOutput`, and `sourceDisableOutput` functions.

Exercise 4-4. Implement the `getFreqSpecVoltage` function, this is the function that implements the *Get frequency that matches specific voltage* function.

Exercise 4-5. Implement the `testw0` function (Module: *Test* ω_0).

Exercise 4-6. Implement the `testw1` and `testw2` functions (Modules: *Test* ω_1 and *Test* ω_2).

Part II

Object Oriented Programming and Design

5. Object Oriented Programming

Topics Covered:

Traditional Programming vs. Object Oriented Programming

Classes and Objects

Methods

Inheritance

Multiple Inheritance

Dynamic Binding

Sequential programming involved writing a series of instructions for a computer to execute. These instructions were executed sequentially, one after the other, from beginning until end. The sequential program execution was interrupted only by "branch" instructions, instructions that directed the execution of a program to continue from a new location. Such programming was simple to understand, simple to write, and simple for a computer to execute. A program would typically consist of the following types of instructions:

- **Sequential Instruction**. A simple instruction that is executed, then flow of control continues with the instruction immediately following the current instruction.
- **Conditional Execution Instruction**. An instruction that is executed only if a given condition holds true. This allows a program to make decisions and change its actions based on these decisions. This is a classic "if" statement.
- **Loop Instruction**. An instruction that causes a series of other instructions to be executed over and over again until either a given condition occurs, or a given number of iterations occur. This allows sequential instructions to be executed repetitively. This is typically a "for" or "while" statement.
- **Subroutine Execution Instruction**. An instruction that causes a sequence of code, called a *subroutine* to execute. After the subroutine has finished, execution control returns to the instruction immediately following the subroutine call. This allows common code to be shared, rather than duplicated over and over again. This is the "gosub" statement.
- **Branch Instruction**. An instruction that directs execution to continue at a new location. This is typically a "goto" statement.

This sequence-sensitive style of programming is often called *linear* or *classical* programming. BASIC and Fortran are examples programming languages that were designed for this style of programming.

Soon, however, programs written in this style became unwieldy. While these unwieldy programs are still easy for a computer to understand, they tend to be difficult for humans to understand. This is because this programming methodology forced no requirements on style, and it was unclear how particular segments of code were executed, who executed them, and what the code assumes has already happened. These programs were sometimes called *spaghetti code*, as they were as easy to figure out as a plate of spaghetti.

As time went on, a new style of programming became popular. *Modular programming* forced a more rigid structure on the style of code generated. While these programs were harder for computers to understand, they were much easier for humans to understand.

The basic component of a modular program is a *procedure*. A procedure is a section of code that is called like a subroutine, but is passed data for the code to act on (called *input parameters*), and generates data as a result (called *output parameters*). The procedure can also update or modify its environment (called *side effects*). A procedure also has *local variables* that allow the procedure to perform operations without affecting its environment. A procedure is a well modularized piece of code that is small enough to understand and performs an action that is well understood. By defining code into these sorts of pieces, documentation of the code and design of the code became much easier and much more straightforward.

Modular programming is sometimes called *structured programming*, because of the rules, requirements, and "structure" this programming style forces on its users. It is also sometimes called "goto-less" programming, as this style of programming removes the branch or "goto" instruction, which historically contributed greatly to spaghetti code.

Modular programming was a great improvement over linear programming in code readability and code design. *Top-down* and *bottom-up* layered program design became the norm, as outlining and structure of programs became more uniform. Pascal and C are example programming languages that use a modular programming model.

However, more was still needed. Modular programming was still sequence-sensitive in that it still focused on the sequence of instructions that had to be executed to complete a task. It typically ignored the data that programs manipulated. Since processing data was becoming increasingly the central focus of programming, a new style of program design was needed.

The new style of program design was called *data-flow design*. It differed from previous design methodologies (such as top-down design, and bottom-up design) as it focused on the data that a program was to manipulate rather than the code and its sequence. Program design became more abstract and higher-level as the mind-set of the program design got away from sequential instructions. This style of programming is popular for data-base systems, data acquisition, and other data-centric applications. While there are some programming languages that encourage a data-flow design methodology (such as APL), typically data flow design was implemented using modular programming languages such as Pascal and C.

Data-flow programming was a great leap in program abstraction, but too much it ignored the instructions needed to manipulate data.

Finally, data and code were merged in design with the introduction of the "object." An *object* is a set of data, and the code that operates on that data. By combining both the data and the code into a single design concept, more complete modular designs were possible. The object is completely isolated from its environment, and all the effects of an object can be hidden within the constructs of the object. This information hiding removed many of the complexities and bug-ridden problems with other programming methodologies.

Newer languages, such as Smalltalk and C++ were created to allow use of this new style of *object oriented programming*.

Classes and Objects

The basic element in object oriented programming is the class. A class is a container that encapsulates related data and the operations (code) that manipulate the data. A class is an abstraction of a collection of things that together perform a well-known function.

A simple example of a class is a *complex number.* A complex number class could contain the following elements:

Data:
- Real part of the complex number
- Imaginary part of the complex number

Operations:
- add and subtract complex numbers
- multiply and divide complex numbers
- store a value into the complex number
- return the real portion of a complex number
- return the imaginary portion of a complex number
- return the polar angle of a complex number in polar coordinates
- return the polar radius of a complex number in polar coordinates

As you can see, the complex number class contains related data (the real and imaginary part of a complex number), along with the code that manipulates the data (the operations that perform actions, or return portions of a complex number).

In order to make use of a class, it must be *instantiated.* There can be one or more than one *instance* of a class within a running system. Each instance of a class is called an *object*, and all objects exist independently of each other.

The relationship between a class and an object is identical to the relationship between a data type and a variable in many programming languages, such as C. A variable is an instantiated version of a data type. All variables exist independently of each other, but are related to other variables instantiated from the same data type in that they support the same actions and act in a similar way. The same is true with classes and objects. Objects exist independently of each other, but are related to other objects instantiated from the same class in that they support the same actions and operations.

So, *complex number* is a class, while the complex number `data1` and `x`, and `y` are objects. So close is the correlation between classes and data types that in C++ they are treated identically. A class is nothing more than a user-defined data type. Figure 5-1 shows the relationship between a class and its objects.

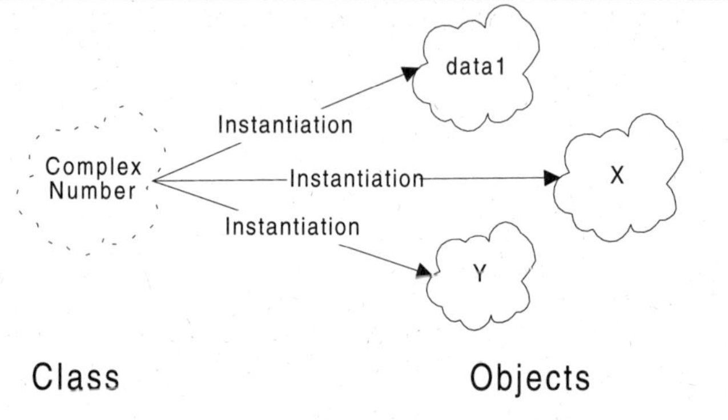

Figure 5-1: Relationship Between Class and Objects

Methods

Once a class has been instantiated into an object, it must be manipulated. This is accomplished by performing operations on the object. These operations are called *methods*.

Figure 5-2 shows a typical process of executing a method on an object. Here, we use the earlier complex number example. In picture A, an object of type complex number is shown containing the value "2+3i." In picture B, a method is executed on the object which "adds 3+5i" to the value of the object. The result is shown in picture C, where the object now has the value "5+8i."

Figure 5-3 shows methods that access data within the object. Using the complex number example again, the method in picture A is trying to get the rectangular coordinate version of the complex number stored in the object. The value returned is, as expected "5+8i." The method in picture B is trying to get the polar coordinate version of the complex number stored in the object. In this case, the method "get polar value" converts the value "5+8i" stored within the object to return the value "|9.4| + 58°."

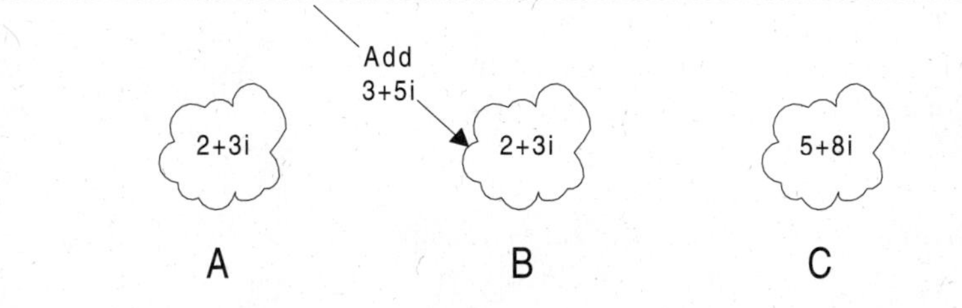

Figure 5-2: Executing a Method on a Complex Number Object

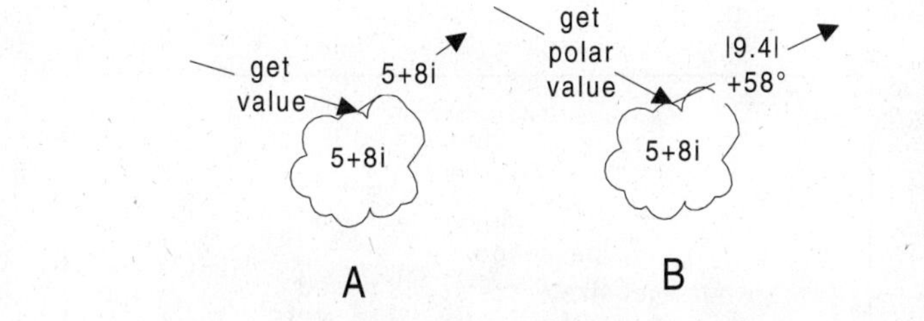

Figure 5-3: Example Access Methods

A method is a function that operates on the specified object. A method can:

- Set the value (or a portion of the value) of an object in one of many different forms
- Return the value (or a portion of the value) of an object in one of many different forms
- Perform mathematical operations on the object
- Perform other actions on the object

Inheritance

One of the powers of object oriented programming is the concept of *inheritance*. Inheritance is the ability for one class to take on the characteristics of another class, while adding characteristics of its own. Used correctly, inheritance can add substantial power to your ability to leverage and re-use programs, as well as modularize your programs to make them easier to use.

Let us start by assuming we have a class representing a `Vehicle`. A `Vehicle` might have the following data associated with it:

- Speed
- # of seats
- color
- size

In addition, the `Vehicle` class may have the following methods:

- change speed
- add/remove passenger
- get size of vehicle
- start/stop vehicle

Figure 5-4 shows the data and methods of this class.

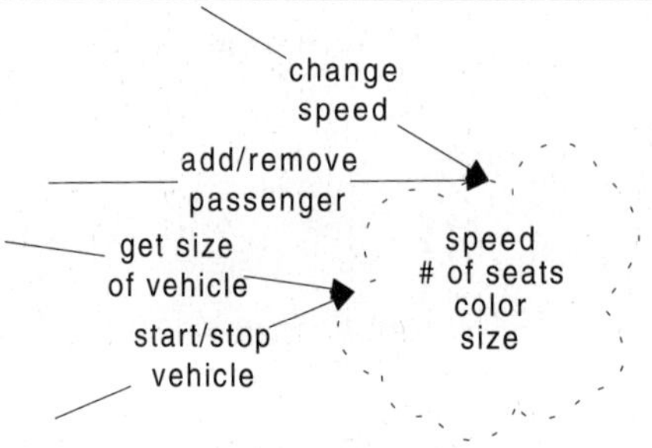

Figure 5-4: Data and Methods of Vehicle Class

Now, let us assume that we want to create a class called `Plane`. What would the characteristics of this class be? First, the data associated with the class:

- speed
- # of seats
- color
- size
- current altitude
- maximum altitude
- # of engines

And the methods associated with the class:

- change speed
- add/remove passenger
- get size of plane
- start/stop plane

- change altitude
- get maximum altitude
- takeoff/land

Figure 5-5 shows the data and methods of the `Plane` class.

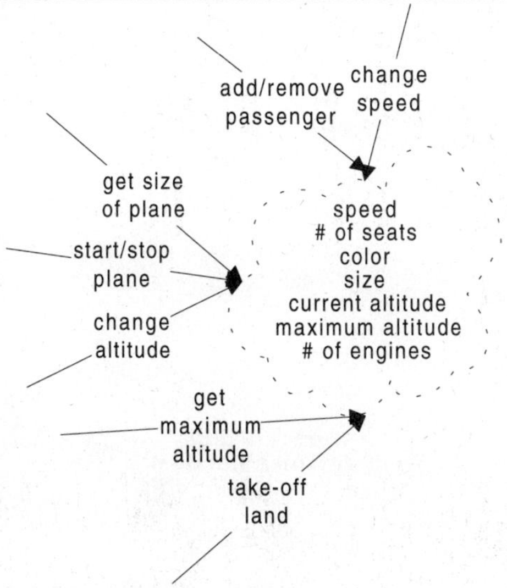

Figure 5-5: Data and Methods of the `Plane` Class

Notice that the `Plane` class has the same characteristics as the `Vehicle` class, plus a few more. Rather than creating a whole new class with all new implementations of these characteristics, the `Plane` class instead can *inherit* the common characteristics from the `Vehicle` class. Then the `Plane` class will only have to implement the characteristics that are specific to a `Plane` class.

If `Plane` inherits from `Vehicle`, then the `Plane` class only needs the following data:

- current altitude
- maximum altitude
- # of engines

and the following methods:

- change altitude
- get maximum altitude
- takeoff/land

Figure 5-6 shows how inheritance works. The `Vehicle` class is the same class as shown in Figure 5-4. The `Plane` class is shown as inheriting all the features of the `Vehicle` class, plus the additional data and methods shown. The net result of this is a `Plane` class with the exact same set of data and methods as shown in Figure 5-5, while only implementing the additional functionality needed for a `Plane`.

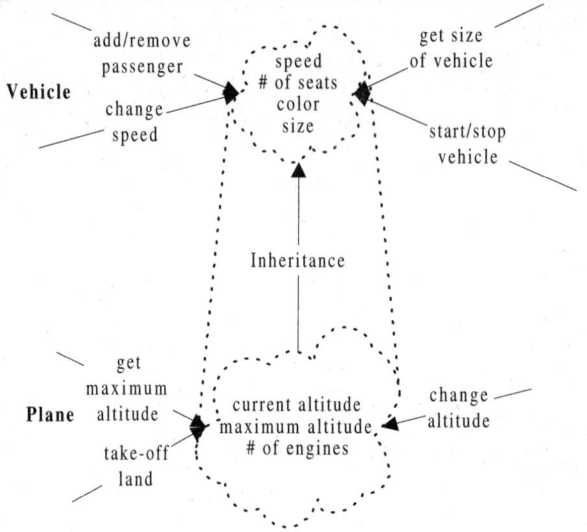

Figure 5-6: Inheriting characteristics from the `Vehicle` class

In object oriented terms, the `Vehicle` class is known as a *base class* and the Plane class is known as a *derived class*. These terms will be used throughout this book.

This concept of inheritance can be continued. Let's say we wanted a class called `PropPlane` (a Plane powered by a propeller). Let us assume it has all the same characteristics as a `Plane` class, plus the following data:

- diameter of propeller
- current RPM of propeller
- maximum RPM of propeller

and the following methods:

- increase propeller RPMs
- decrease propeller RPMs
- get prop diameter

This can be represented by Figure 5-7. Here, the `PropPlane` is shown inheriting from `Plane`, which inherits from `Vehicle`. The `PropPlane` has all the characteristics of a `Plane`, all the characteristics of a `Vehicle`, plus all the extra characteristics of a `PropPlane`.

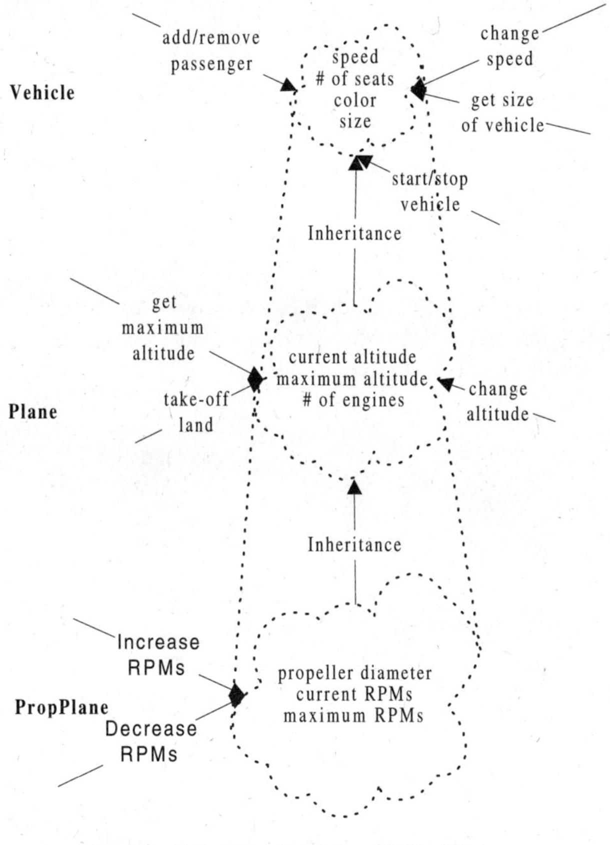

Figure 5-7: Two Levels of Inheritance

In this example, Vehicle is a base class, `PropPlane` is a derived class, and Plane is both a derived class and a base class. It is a base-class to `PropPlane`, and it is a derived class to `Vehicle`.

Multiple Inheritance

Sometimes it makes sense for a class to derive from more than one base class. Let us assume that in addition to the base class `Vehicle`, we have a base class called `Asset`. An `Asset` has the following characteristics.

Data elements of an `Asset`:

- value of asset (in dollars)
- owner of asset
- mortgage holder
- mortgaged amount (in dollars)

Methods of an `Asset`:

- get value
- get name of owner
- make mortgage payment

Now, let us assume that we want to think of our `Plane` as not only a `Vehicle`, but also as an `Asset`. So, we make `Plane` inherit from both `Vehicle` and `Asset`. When we are done, the following characteristics will exist for a `Plane`.

Data elements of a `Plane`:

- speed
- # of seats
- color
- size
- current altitude
- maximum altitude
- # of engines
- value (in dollars)
- owner
- mortgage holder
- mortgaged amount (in dollars)

Methods of a `Plane`:

- change speed
- add/remove passenger
- get size of plane
- start/stop plane
- change altitude
- get maximum altitude
- takeoff/land
- get value
- get name of owner
- make mortgage payment

Figure 5-8 shows this `Plane` class and its two base classes. In this example, `Plane` is a derived class from two base classes, `Vehicle` and `Asset`. As such, a `Plane` has the characteristics of both a `Vehicle` and an `Asset`, while the characteristics of a `Vehicle` and an `Asset` are very different and unrelated.

In object oriented terms, this is called *multiple inheritance*.

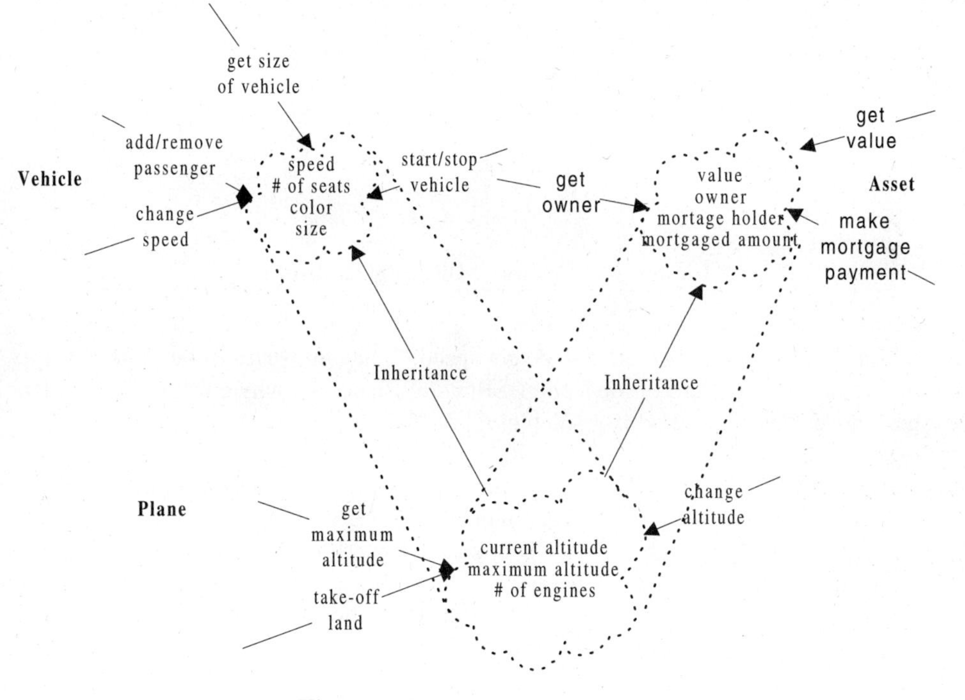

Figure 5-8: Multiple Inheritance

Dynamic Binding

Sometimes, a method may make sense in both a base class and a derived class, but the actions of the method may be different in each class. In this case, you want to guarantee that the correct version of the method gets called at the appropriate point in time.

Using a slightly different version of the previous example, let us imagine a hierarchy as shown in Figure 5-9. In this example, `Vehicle` is the base class, and there are two classes that derive from it, `Plane` and `Boat`.

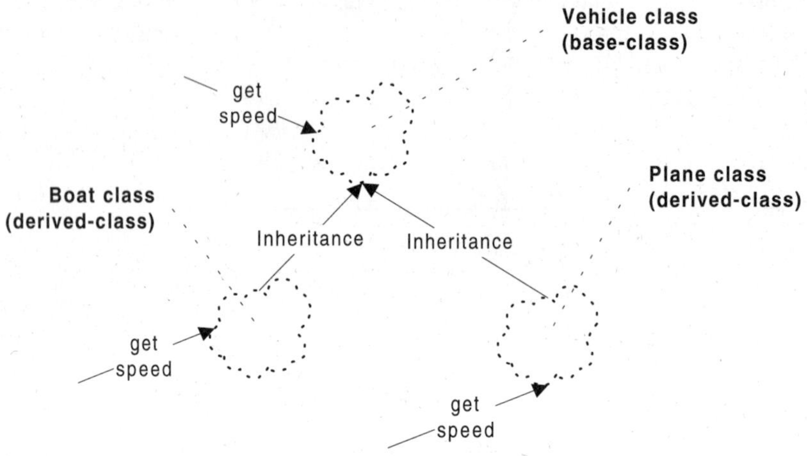

Figure 5-9: Dynamic Binding Example

Each of the three classes has a method called "get speed." They all perform the same general action, they get the current speed of the Vehicle, Boat, or Plane. So, why don't Boat and Plane simply inherit the get speed method from Vehicle?

Let us assume that the calculations that the method "get speed" has to perform in order to calculate the speed is different for a generic `Vehicle`, than it is for a `Boat`, and different again from that for a `Plane`. This makes sense, since a `Boat` may need to perform a very different calculation than a `Plane`, or any other `Vehicle`. In the case of the `Plane`, there may even be a different type of speed needed (air speed versus ground speed), so the thought of a different calculation needed to calculate the same value is not unreasonable.

Since each of the classes in Figure 5-9 has a get-speed method and an implementation for that function, the question that comes to mind is which get-speed method is called? The answer is simple, when a derived class implements a method that is already implemented in the base class, the new version of the method in the derived class takes precedent over the base-class method. In the case of the `Boat` class, the version of get speed in `Boat` is used over the version in `Vehicle`.

So, the basic rule is, whatever type the object is decides which version of an overridden method is used. If you have an object of type `Boat`, then the `Boat`'s get-speed method is used. If you have an object of type `Plane`, then the `Plane`'s get-speed method is used. If you have an object of type `Vehicle`, then the basic `Vehicle`'s get-speed method is used. In object oriented terms, this is called *polymorphism*.

What happens, however, if you do not know whether the `Vehicle` you have is a `Boat` or a `Plane`? Consider Figure 5-10. Here we have four objects,[1] two `Boats` and two `Planes`. Now, Lee and Beth can only use one of these four Vehicles at any one point in time, so we have a variable called "active" that points to the `Vehicle` that is currently being used. So, what type should "active" be? It can not be a pointer to a `Boat` or a `Plane`, since not all objects it can point to are either a `Boat` or a `Plane`. So, the pointer should point to a `Vehicle`, since all four objects, both `Boats` and `Planes`, are `Vehicles`. In Figure 5-10, the active `Vehicle` is Lee's Boat.

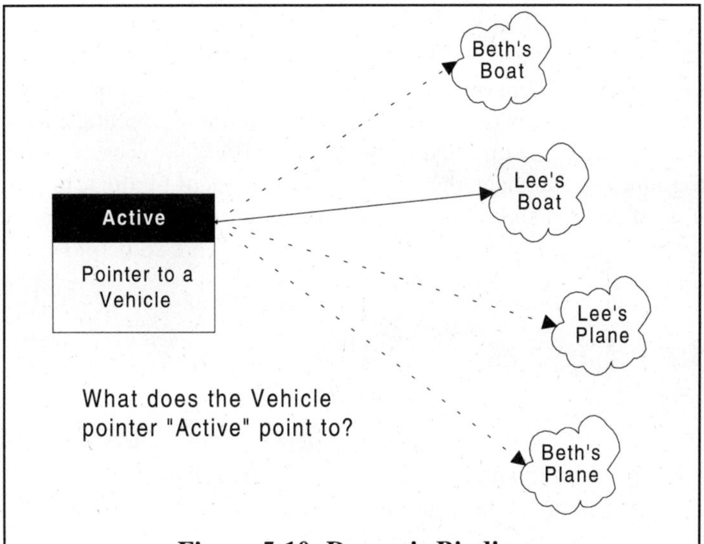

Figure 5-10: Dynamic Binding

Now, if you want to find the current speed of Beth's Boat, you would call the get-speed method on Beth's Boat. The same thing is true for Lee's Boat and both Lee's and Beth's Planes. However, what if you want to find the speed of whatever `Vehicle` is active? You would then call the get-speed method on `active`. Since, however, `active` is a `Vehicle`, this would cause the `Vehicle` version of get speed to be called, not either the `Boat` or the `Plane` version. Since `active` is always pointing to either a `Boat` or a `Plane`, calling the `Vehicle` version of get speed is incorrect.

---

[1] Remember, an object is an *instance* of a class. So Figure 5-10 can be referred to as an *instance diagram*, since it shows objects interconnected. The previous diagrams in this chapter are called *inheritance diagrams*, since they show how classes are interconnected. This will be discussed further in a later chapter.

Why has this happened? This is because the decision as to which version of get speed is called is made at compile time. At compile time, the compiler has no idea as to whether `active` refers to a `Vehicle`, a `Boat`, or a `Plane`. All it knows is that it *is* a `Vehicle`, so it uses the `Vehicle` version of get speed. This is called *static binding*.

There is another type of binding that can be used called *dynamic binding*. In this case, the decision as to which version of a method (such as get speed) is used is made at run-time. Therefore, the program can determine that `active`, in fact, points to "Lee's boat" (a `Boat`), and therefore call the `Boat` classes version of get speed. This is the desired behavior.

Since normally dynamic binding is the desired method of binding for object method execution, some object oriented languages support *only* dynamic binding, and do not support static binding. However, since dynamic binding is often more time-consuming to execute, and sometimes static binding is acceptable, some object oriented languages support both types of binding. C++ is an object oriented programming language that supports both types of binding. In order to determine which type of binding a method should use, the keyword "virtual" is used before the method name to signify dynamic binding. Thus, dynamically bound methods are sometimes called *virtual methods* or *virtual functions*.

Abstract Base Classes

Let us go back to Figure 5-9 for a minute. What happens if the only classes we want to instantiate are `Boats` and `Planes`? What if we never want to instantiate an object of class `Vehicle`? This makes sense, since we would never have just a `Vehicle`, we would have either a `Boat` or a `Plane`.

In this case, we can make the `Vehicle` class, an *abstract base class*. An abstract base class is a special type of base class that can not be instantiated, so you can never have an object of just this type. It only serves as a place-holder for other derived classes to use. Classes such as `Plane` and `Boat` can derive characteristics from the abstract base class `Vehicle`, and these new derived classes can be instantiated.

If we made the `Vehicle` class in Figure 5-9 an abstract base class, and used dynamic binding for the method get speed (i.e., made it a virtual method), then why would the `Vehicle` class itself need an implementation for get speed? Since `Vehicle` could never be instantiated, there can never be an object of type `Vehicle` in the system, so the `Vehicle`'s implementation of get speed can never be called.

This is correct. The get-speed method would not have to be implemented in `Vehicle`. Instead, the get-speed method can be marked as a *pure-virtual* method. A pure-virtual method is a virtual (dynamically bound) method that has no implementation. It can only be used in abstract base classes. In fact, making a method pure-virtual makes the class it is contained in an abstract base class and uninstantiatable.

Adding Inherited Classes Later

What happens if later we get a car? It is a simple matter to make another class inherit from `Vehicle` and add new data and methods to the new derived class. This can all be done without changing anything in either the base class `Vehicle`, or either of the derived classes `Boat` or `Plane`. The characteristics of a car can be added completely within the class `car`. However, once we are done, we have another new type of `Vehicle` that we can instantiate. And, using the model of Figure 5-10, we can instantiate a "Lee's Car" or a "Beth's Car" and make it "active" as well.

Summary

This chapter described general object oriented programming principles. This is the first exposure to object oriented concepts in this book. The chapter described object oriented concepts without the use of a particular programming language. Diagrams and real-world (non-programming) examples were shown to explain the principles.

Exercises

Exercise 5-1. What are the advantages of object oriented programming compared to modular programming?

Exercise 5-2. Do the concepts of "top-down" and "bottom-up" apply to OOP? If so, how?

Exercise 5-3. Can you implement some of the OOP concepts presented here using a traditional programming language such as C or Pascal? What OOP principles could you not implement this way?

Exercise 5-4. Add a `JetPlane` class to the diagram shown in Figure 5-7. What base class would you inherit from? What characteristics of what classes would you want in your class? What new characteristics would you add? What characteristics would you inherit, but implement differently?

Exercise 5-5. Sometimes in object oriented programming languages such as C++, it is advantageous to avoid multiple inheritance. Can you think of another way, without using multiple-inheritance, to implement the Plane class shown in Figure 5-8?

Exercise 5-6. What other methods in our `Vehicle` and `Vehicle` derived classes can take advantage of dynamic binding?

6. Object Oriented Programming in C++

The previous chapter described object oriented programming in generic terms. This chapter takes the concepts learned in that chapter and applies them to the C++ programming language.

Topics Covered:

Class Implementation

Public vs. Private

"this" Pointer

Constructors/Destructors

Copy Constructors

Inheritance

Protected Elements

Virtual Functions

Abstract Base Classes

Pure Virtual

Friend Functions

Operators

Classes

In C++, the basic object oriented feature is a *class.* A class describes the basic structure for objects within C++. A class contains:

- a series of data elements
- a set of functions for manipulating these objects (the *methods* that a class defines)
- a set of restrictions on the access of these elements

A class has a very similar syntax to a struct in C, except methods and access restrictions may also be listed. The following is a simple class declaration in C++:

```
class Vehicle {
   private:
      /* Data Elements of the Class */
      int speed;
      int numOfSeats;
      int numOfPassengers;
   public:
      /*Methods (functions) for accessing class*/
      void changeSpeed(int newSpeed);
      void addPassengers(int num);
      void removePassengers(int num);
      void start();
      void stop();
      int getSpeed();
};
```

Listing 6-1: Vehicle Class Declaration

This class contains the following elements:

- A data element, an integer called `speed` representing the current speed of the vehicle.
- A data element, an integer called `numOfSeats` representing the number of seats in the vehicle.
- A data element, an integer called `numOfPassengers` representing the current number of passengers in this vehicle.
- A function (method) for changing the speed of the vehicle (`changeSpeed`).
- Methods for adding and removing a passenger (`addPassenger` / `removePassenger`).
- Methods to start and stop the vehicle (`start/stop`).
- A method that returns the current speed of the vehicle (`getSpeed`).
- Protection for the data elements which prevents them from being accessed outside of the methods of this class (the methods must be used instead).

The "private:" keyword marks the data elements as private to the class itself. This means that only methods that are part of the `Vehicle` class (such as `changeSpeed`, `addPassenger`, etc.) may access these data variables. No one other than these methods may get or set these values. Any attempt to access these variables generates a compile-time error.

The "public:" keyword marks the methods as public. This means that anyone, either other methods within the class or any function not part of the class, may legally call these methods.

Instantiating Classes

The above class declaration creates a new user-defined type called `Vehicle`. To use this class, you must instantiate the class to create an object of type `Vehicle`. This is exactly the same, and is done exactly the same way as instantiating any other type of variable in C (such as an `int`, or a `float`). Once an instance of the class is created, the member functions may be called on that instance to operate on the class. For example:

```
Vehicle leeBoat; // Instantiates a Vehicle named leeBoat

leeBoat.addPassengers(2);
leeBoat.start();
leeBoat.changeSpeed(30);
leeBoat.changeSpeed(50);
printf("Current speed is: %d MPH\n",leeBoat.getSpeed());
leeBoat.removePassengers(1);//Not such a good idea at 50
leeBoat.changeSpeed(30);
leeBoat.stop();
```

Listing 6-2: Usage of Vehicle Class

This code segment produces the following results:

```
Current speed is: 50 MPH
Passenger thrown out at 50 MPH
```

More than one instance of the class may exist. Each instance has its own set of data values that operate independently. So:

```
Vehicle leeBoat,bethPlane;

leeBoat.start();
bethPlane.start();
leeBoat.changeSpeed(30);
bethPlane.changeSpeed(150);
leeBoat.stop();
bethPlane.changeSpeed(200);
printf("Speed of Beth's Plane is %d MPH\n",
          bethPlane.getSpeed());
printf("Speed of Lee's Boat is %d MPH\n",
          leeBoat.getSpeed());
bethPlane.changeSpeed(100);
bethPlane.stop();
```

Listing 6-3: Usage of Multiple Vehicle Objects

This code segment produces the following results:

```
Speed of Beth's Plane is 200 MPH
Speed of Lee's Boat is 0 MPH
```

Using new/delete

Classes may also be instantiated dynamically using a mechanism similar to the `malloc` procedure in traditional C. It uses special functions called `new` and `delete`. The following code segment illustrates its use:

```
Vehicle *pBoat;
// Create an instance of a Vehicle,
//    and return a pointer
pBoat=new Vehicle;

// Use the pointer, as you would any C pointer
pBoat->start();
pBoat->changeSpeed();
pBoat->stop();

// Delete the Vehicle and remove the memory used
delete pBoat;
pBoat=0;
```

Listing 6-4: Usage of Multiple Vehicle Objects

Class Implementation

A class declaration must also be combined with an implementation, of the given method functions. The following are example implementations for the Vehicle example.

```
void Vehicle::changeSpeed(int newSpeed){
    speed=newSpeed;
}

int Vehicle::getSpeed(){
    return speed;
}

void Vehicle::stop(){
    speed=0;
}

void addPassengers(int num){
    numOfPassengers+=num;
}
```

Listing 6-5: Implementation of Vehicle Methods

The syntax for these functions is almost the same as any other C-style function, with a few differences. First, since the functions are "owned" by a specific class, the class name `Vehicle`, must appear before the function name. The function name and the class name are separated by "`::`". So, for example, the function name `Vehicle::changeSpeed` means the `changeSpeed` method that is a member of the class `Vehicle`. Next, all data elements of the class are available as variables within the member function. In this example, the data elements `speed` and `numOfPassengers` are available for use within all the member functions.

Public vs. Private

The class declaration in Listing 6-1 shows two other keywords used commonly in class declarations that are not available in C. These are the `public:` and `private:` keywords. These keywords mark a given member variable or method to indicate whether they can be accessed outside the environment of the class or only within the class itself.

The `public:` keyword is used to signify member variables or methods that may be accessed by: member methods of this class, member methods of other classes, or any other global function or procedure. For data members of the class, use of the `public:` keyword is identical to data members of a C-style `struct`. If you have an instance of the class, you may use that instance to directly access these data members. For class methods, the `public:` keyword means these methods may be called by anyone who has an instance of the class.

The `private:` keyword is used to signify member variables or methods that may be accessed only by methods of this class. Access to these member variables or methods by any other classes or global functions results in a compile-time error. These member variables and methods are private to the class.

Both public and private elements (either data members or methods) may be available within a single class. The `public:` and `private:` keyword applies to all elements that occur immediately after the keyword until the next `public:` or `private:` keyword appears. Then, that keyword applies until the next, and so forth. Any number of `public:` and `private:` keywords may appear in any number and any order anywhere in the class declaration. If no keyword is specified, then `private:` is assumed.

A typical class will have both publicly accessible and private elements. The public elements constitute the class interface – the interface used to access the class. The private elements are used by the public elements to implement internal functionality of the class.

Good programming practice dictates that only those methods that need to be accessed externally from the class be made public, all functions that need only be accessed from within the class itself should be made private. In addition, all data members should be private. If the data members need to be accessed externally from the class, they should be accessed via access methods that are public. The data members themselves should not be accessible directly. This practice allows the structure of the class and the format of the data used to represent the object to be changed without affecting the external interface to the class.

The Hidden `this` Pointer

Looking once again at Listing 6-5, you may notice that implementations of class methods have direct access to data variables within the class. It looks to the method that these are global variables, but in fact they are not. They are members of the class and are "instance" variables of that class.

When a method is called, there is a hidden parameter to the method that is always passed to the method. It is called the `this` pointer. It is a pointer to an instance of the given class, in particular to the instance of the class that was used to call this method. Whenever a variable that is a member of the class is accessed, the `this` pointer is implicitly used to access the instances of the member variables used. For example, the following method (from Listing 6-5):

```
void Vehicle::changeSpeed(int newSpeed){
    speed=newSpeed;
}
```

is equivalent to the following method with the implicit `this` pointers added:

```
void Vehicle::changeSpeed(int newSpeed){
    this->speed=newSpeed;
}
```

This method is similar to the following function, which uses straight C-style syntax:

```
void Vehicle_changeSpeed(Vehicle *this,int newSpeed){
    this->speed=newSpeed;
}
```

Normally, the `this` pointer need never be used explicitly, since the C++ language takes care of this for you. There are cases, however, where it must be used explicitly. In those cases, it is available to use.

Constructors/Destructors

There are several standard methods available to most classes. They are used during the creation, destruction, and duplication of classes.

Constructors

A *constructor* is a special method that is called during the creation of an instance of a class. The constructor is a member method that has the same name as the class itself. The following is an example of a constructor declaration:

```
class Vehicle {
    ...
    public:
        Vehicle(); // Constructor of class Vehicle
    ...
};
```

Listing 6-6: Default Constructor Declaration

The constructor, in this example called `Vehicle`, never has a return value. The constructor is called whenever an instance of the Vehicle class is instantiated. Typically, data elements in the class are initialized by the constructor, as can be seen in the following example implementation of the constructor:

```
Vehicle::Vehicle()
    : speed(0)    // Initialization of speed

{
    numOfSeats=0;
    numOfPassengers=0;
}
```

Listing 6-7: Default Constructor Implementation

This example shows the method variables `speed`, `numOfSeats`, and `numOfPassengers` all being initialized to the value 0.

Note: Technically, there are two ways to initialize data elements in a constructor. The first is that shown by the `speed` variable in Listing 6-7. The second is shown by `numOfSeats` and `numOfPassengers`. Technically, the former is *initializing* speed to 0, while the latter is *assigning* the value of 0 to those variables. The difference is subtle, but occasionally important. The actual explanation is outside the scope of this chapter.

A class may have 0 or more constructors. By default, if no constructor is specified, a constructor that performs no operations (no-op) is assumed. A class may specify a constructor as above, but may also specify constructors that take one or more parameters. The following is an example showing constructors (declaration and implementation) that specifies one or more parameters:

```
class Vehicle {
    ...
    public:
        Vehicle(int defNumOfSeats);
        Vehicle(int defNumOfSeats,
                    int defNumOfPassengers);
    ...
}

Vehicle::Vehicle(int defNumOfSeats)
{
    speed=0;
    numOfSeats=defNumOfSeats;
    numOfPassengers=0;
}
Vehicle::Vehicle(int defNumOfSeats,
                 int defNumOfPassengers)
{
    speed=0;
    numOfSeats=defNumOfSeats;
    numOfPassengers=defNumOfPassengers;
}
```

Listing 6-8: Constructors with Parameters

The two constructors both allow specifying a default `numOfSeats` value. The second also allows specifying a default `numOfPassengers` parameter. In order to make use of these constructors, a special mechanism for instantiating the class is used. At the time the variables are instantiated, the desired parameters are passed as if it was a procedure call. The following example illustrates this:

```
Vehicle boat; // Boat w/ 0 seats and 0 passengers
Vehicle leeBoat(2); // Boat w/ 2 seats
Vehicle car(4,2); // Boat w/ 4 seats and 2 passengers
Vehicle *pVeh;

pVeh=new Vehicle(2); // Vehicle w/ 2 seats
```

Listing 6-9: Use of Constructors with Parameters

Here, the vehicle `boat` is created using the default constructor, which initializes both `numOfSeats` and `numOfPassengers` to 0. The vehicle `leeBoat`, however, uses the constructor that is passed a single integer. This uses the constructor that sets the `numOfSeats` variable to the value of the parameter, in this case 2. The vehicle `car` uses the constructor that is passed two integers. In this case, this causes the `numOfSeats` to be set to 4 and the `numofPassengers` to be set to 2. Finally, `pVeh` is initialized using the `new` operator that creates a vehicle using the single integer constructor, that sets the `numOfSeats` to 2 and `numOfPassengers` to 0, just like `leeBoat` was.

A class can have an arbitrary number of constructors used to create various types of objects from the class. The only requirement is that each constructor have a unique *signature*. A *constructor signature* is the number, type, and order of the parameters passed to the constructor. As long as each constructor has a different number, or type, or order of the parameters, the constructors can be uniquely identified at the time they are used.

Destructors

A *destructor* is a special method that is called during the destruction of an instance of a class. The destructor is a member method that has the same name as the class itself, but is prefixed with a tilde (~) character. The following is an example of a destructor declaration:

```
class Vehicle {
    ...
    public:
        ~Vehicle(); // Destructor of class Vehicle
    ...
};
```

Listing 6-10: Destructor Declaration

The destructor, in this example called `~Vehicle`, never has a return value. The destructor is called whenever an instance of the `Vehicle` class is destroyed. Typically, the destructor will perform whatever actions are necessary to clean up an instance of a class, such as freeing memory that may have been allocated during the use of the class. The following is an example destructor implementation:

```
Vehicle::~Vehicle()

{
    if(dataPtr!=0)
        delete dataPtr;
    if(data2Ptr!=0)
        delete data2Ptr;
}
```

Listing 6-11: Destructor Implementation

Unlike the constructors, a class may have at most one destructor. However, it may also have no destructor.

Copy Constructor

A *copy constructor* is a special type of constructor. It has a very specific signature. It is passed exactly one parameter, and the type of that parameter is a *reference to the given class*.

```
class Vehicle {
    ...
    public:
        // Copy Constructor
        Vehicle(const Vehicle &v);
    ...
};
```

Listing 6-12: Copy Constructor

A *reference* parameter is a parameter that is passed-by-reference, rather than passed-by-value. In the Vehicle example shown, the parameter `v` is not copied onto the stack when the constructor is called, rather a reference to the original variable is passed instead. This generates the same code as passing a pointer to `v` does, but the syntax for using the parameter is the same as if it were a normal pass-by-value parameter.

The copy constructor is used to create a duplicate of a given class. The copy constructor initializes itself (the class being created) to be an exact duplicate of the class passed as a parameter to the constructor. The following is an example implementation of the above copy constructor:

```
Vehicle:: Vehicle(const Vehicle &copyVeh)
{
    speed=copyVeh.speed;
    numOfSeats=copyVeh.numOfSeats;
    numOfPassengers=copyVeh.numOfPassengers;
};
```

Listing 6-13: Copy Constructor Implementation

The copy constructor is called in several instances where a temporary copy of an object is needed. A simple example is when an instance of an object is passed-by-value to a calling procedure, such as shown in the following example:

```
sampleFunction(Vehicle name)
{
    name.changeSpeed(20); // Operating on copy of car,
                          // not the original
};

main(){
    Vehicle car;

    // Call sampleFunction w/ car
    sampleFunction(car);
};
```

Listing 6-14: Copy Constructor Use

In this example, `car` is passed-by-value to `sampleFunction`. In `sampleFunction`, the `Vehicle` copy constructor is called to create `name`, an exact copy of `car`. Once the procedure `sampleFunction` is complete, `name` is destroyed and its destructor is called.

Inheritance

In the last chapter, inheritance was defined as the ability for one class to take on characteristics of another class, while adding characteristics of its own. In C++, this is implemented during the declaration of a class as follows:

```
// Base class
class Vehicle
{
    private:
        int speed;
        int numOfSeats;
        int numOfPassengers;
    public:
        void changeSpeed(int newSpeed);
        void start();
        void stop();
        int getSpeed();
};

// Derived class
class Plane
    : public Vehicle //Inherit Vehicle characteristics
{
    private:
        int altitude;
        int maxAltitude;
    public:
        void takeOff();
        void land();
        void changeAltitude(int newAltitude);
};
```

Listing 6-15: Inheritance Declaration

This code shows the creation of a class called Plane, that inherits capabilities from Vehicle. Using the code shown in Listing 6-15, the following code makes use of these declarations:

```
Plane bethPlane;
bethPlane.start();
bethPlane.changeSpeed(200);
bethPlane.takeOff();
bethPlane.changeAltitude(2000);
bethPlane.land();
bethPlane.changeSpeed(0);
bethPlane.stop();
```

Listing 6-16: Use of Inherited Plane Class

In Listing 6-15, the declaration of the `Plane` class shows the inheritance from the `Vehicle` class by specifying ": public Vehicle" after the class name in the declaration syntax. The colon (`:`) specifies inheritance, the word `Vehicle` specifies the base class from which to inherit functionality, and the keyword `public` specifies the type of inheritance.

By specifying `public` inheritance, all public elements of `Vehicle` become public elements in `Plane`, while all private elements of `Vehicle` are inaccessible to `Plane` (because private elements are only accessible from the class that declares them, `Vehicle` private elements are inaccessible from `Plane`).

Rather than specifying public inheritance, you may specify private inheritance by using the keyword `private`. With private inheritance, all public elements of `Vehicle` become private elements of `Plane`, while, all private elements of `Vehicle` are (as before) inaccessible to `Plane`.

Protected Elements in Base Classes

In addition to specifying elements in a base class as either private or public, a class that is destined to be used as a base class may specify elements as protected, by using the `protected:` keyword in identically the same way as the `private:` or `public:` keyword. The `protected:` keyword, within the base class, has exactly the same meaning as the `private:` keyword. However, during inheritance, `protected:` elements are accessible privately from elements of the derived class. The following code illustrates this functionality:

```
class BaseClass
{
    private:
        void methA();
    protected:
        void methB();
    public:
        void methC();
};

class DerivedClass
    : public BaseClass;
{
    private:
        void methD();
    public:
        void methE();
};
```

Listing 6-17: Use of Protected in Base Class

In the `DerivedClass` class, the method `methD` is private, and `methE` is public, as expected. In addition, base method `methC` is public and `methA` is inaccessible within `DerivedClass` (as expected). However, `methB` is available for use within `DerivedClass`, but only as a private method. It is inaccessible outside of `DerivedClass`. This is an example use of protected elements.

Table 6-1 lists the various combinations of access available. Along the top of the table are the types of inheritance supported (private, protected, or public). Along the left edge is the type of access available to elements in the base class (private, protected, or public).

The middle of the table lists the access that is given to the elements in the derived class (private, protected, public, or no access).

Access in Base Class	Type of Inheritance: private	protected	public
private	no access	no access	no access
protected	private	protected	protected
public	private	protected	public

Table 6-1: Access Under Derivation

Virtual Functions and Dynamic Binding

The concept of dynamic binding was discussed in Chapter 5. Dynamic binding in C++ is implemented using *virtual functions*. To make a method virtual means use of that function will cause binding to the specific implementation of the method to be done at run-time. Virtual methods are implemented by specifying the `virtual` keyword. An example is shown below:

```
class Vehicle
{
    ...
    public:
        virtual int getSpeed();
    ...
};
class Boat
    : public Vehicle;
{
    ...
    public:
        virtual int getSpeed();
    ...
};
class Plane
    : public Vehicle;
{
    ...
    public:
        virtual int getSpeed();
    ...
};
```

Listing 6-18: Use of Virtual Keyword

Other than the use of the `virtual` keyword in the declaration, the declaration and implementation of virtual methods is identical to non-virtual methods. The only difference is the type of binding used.

Abstract Base Classes and Pure Virtual Functions

Abstract base classes are base classes that are not instantiatable without the use of a derived class. Making a base class abstract involves making one or more of the virtual functions in the base class a pure virtual function. A *pure virtual function* is a function that has no implementation of its own, and therefore requires re-implementation in a derived class.

To make a virtual function a pure virtual function is simply a matter of specifying "=0" after the declaration, as shown below:

```
class Vehicle
{
    public:
        virtual int getSpeed()=0; // Pure Virtual
};

class Plane
    : public Vehicle;
{
    public:
        virtual int getSpeed(); // Derived version is
                                // implemented
};
```

Listing 6-19: Use of Virtual Keyword

In this code segment, the `Vehicle` version of `getSpeed` is pure virtual and therefore needs no implementation. However, the derived class `Plane` has a `getSpeed` function that needs implementation. Given the above declaration, `Vehicle` is an abstract base class and not instantiatable, while `Plane` is a derived class that is instantiatable.

Inline Functions

When you make a call to a function or a method, overhead work is needed to perform the call. In particular, register states have to be stored, a stack frame has to be generated, and a return address and return value have to be stored on the stack. Occasionally, it is desirable for a method to execute without all this overhead. This is usually the case for simple, extremely short methods, such as methods that simply return the value of a member variable. In these cases, the method can be marked as *inline*, which means the code is inserted directly into the code of the calling routine, rather than generating a procedure call. The net result is faster execution of the code at the cost of potentially larger code size.

The following is an example use of an inline function:

```
inline int sum(int a,int b){
    return a+b;
}

void proc1(){
    int c,d;

    c=sum(2,3);
    d=sum(c,4);
}
```

When the compiler sees this code segment, it replaces it with code that performs the following:

```
void proc1(){
    int c,d;

    c=2+3;
    d=c+4;
}
```

This is different then the #define macro mechanism, in that a #define macro is simply a textual substitution, while with an inline method all the rules and parameter passing (pass by value, reference, etc.) are observed as if it were a regular non-inline function.

Both methods (class member functions), and standalone functions can be made inline. In the case of class member methods, there are two ways to mark a method as inline, the first is similar to the above method. This involves using the inline keyword in either the definition or declaration of the method, as shown below:

```
class sample{
    public:
        inline int func1();
        int func2();
        int func3();
};

int sample::func1(){
    // This is an inline method, because the
    // inline keyword appears in the declaration
}
inline int sample::func2(){
    // This is an inline method, because the
    // inline keyword appears in the definition
}
int sample::func3(){
    // This is not an inline method
}
```

The second method involves simply putting the body of the method within the declaration of the method. In this case, the inline keyword is assumed:

```
class sample{
    public:
        int func1(){
            // This method is an inline method, because
            // the body of the method is contained
            // within the class declaration
        }
};
```

Friend Functions

Sometimes it is necessary to have no-nmember functions have access to private and protected data within a class. These non-member functions may perform actions that require intimate knowledge of the class, but not be members of the class.

In order to have access to non-public data from outside the class, functions must be marked as *friend* functions. A friend function has complete access to all private and protected elements of the class, as shown below:

```
class example{
    friend void extFunc1();
    private:
        int val;
        void func();
    public:
        void func2();
};

void extFunc1(){ // Friend Function
    example x;

    // Legal, because extFunc1 is a friend
    x.val=1;
    x.func();
    // Legal anywhere
    x.func2();
}
void extFunc2(){
    example x;

    // Illegal, because extFunc2 is not a friend
    x.val=1;
    // Illegal, extFunc2 is not a friend
    x.func();
    // Legal anywhere
    x.func2();
}
```

Listing 6-20: Friend Functions

Operators

One of the powers of C++ is the ability to overload the standard language operators, such as +, -, +=, and so forth in order to provide these functions to C++ user created classes.

Let us assume we have created a new C++ class called "Complex," which represents complex numbers, and we want to write code such as the following:

```
void func(Complex a, Complex b){

    Complex c;

    // Add two complex numbers and store into a third
    c=a+b;
}
```

Listing 6-21: Complex Number Operator +,= Example

In order to implement this functionality, the Complex class must support the operators + and =. User-defined operators are essentially regular functions with the name "operator *op*", where *op* is replaced by the specific operator. So, for example, the following code shows an example of a + operator function that takes two Complex numbers and returns a third:

```
Complex operator +(Complex lhs,Complex rhs){
    // Code to implement a + operator
    Complex tmp;

    tmp.real  = lhs.real + rhs.real;
    tmp.imagin = lhs.imagin + rhs.imagin;

    return tmp;
}
```

Some operators are good candidates for friend functions. In particular, if the left hand side of the operator is not of the same type as the class itself, then the operator cannot be a member of the class. A simple example is the following function prototype:

```
Complex operator +(int lhs,Complex rhs);
```

Here, the left hand side of the operator + expects an integer, even though the operator is part of the Complex class. Since the above function is itself not a member of the Complex class, but the implementation may very well need access to the private data and functions of the class, it must be a friend function of the class Complex.

The number of parameters required by an operator + is fixed. It requires exactly two parameters. All binary operators (+, -, etc.) require two parameters, the first representing the left-hand side of the operation and the second representing the right-hand side of the operation. Unary operators, however (such as ~) only expect one parameter. The return value of all of these operator functions is the return value of the given operator, as expected.

Many definitions of "operator +" may exist within a single application, as long as the first and second parameter types combined are unique. For example, the following operator + functions may exist within the same application:

```
Complex operator +(int lhs,Complex rhs);
Complex operator +(Complex lhs,int rhs);
Complex operator +(Complex lhs,Complex rhs);
```

Each of these functions requires a different implementation and may perform different actions. The first two allow adding a normal integer to a complex number, while the third allows adding two complex numbers.

Some operator functions may be implemented as methods of a class, rather than as separate friend functions. For binary operators, if the first parameter is of the same type as the class, then the operator may be made a method of the class. In this case, however, only one parameter is specified (the right-hand side of the operator), while the left hand side is used as the instance of the class. The following is an example declaration of the three operator + using member methods where possible:

```
class Complex {
    ...
    friend Complex operator +(int lhs,Complex rhs);
    public:
        // Complex + int
        Complex operator +(int rhs);
        // Complex + Complex
        Complex operator +(Complex rhs);
    ...
};

// Friend, non-member
// int + Complex
Complex operator +(int lhs,Complex rhs);
```

Any of the standard operators may be defined in either of the ways specified. Table 6-2 shows most of the standard operators that may be overloaded this way.

<table>
<tr><th>Operator</th><th>Meaning</th><th>Operator</th><th>Meaning</th></tr>
<tr><td>+</td><td>addition</td><td>&</td><td>bit-wise AND</td></tr>
<tr><td>-</td><td>subtraction</td><td>|</td><td>bit-wise OR</td></tr>
<tr><td>*</td><td>multiplication</td><td>~</td><td>bit-wise NOT</td></tr>
<tr><td>/</td><td>division</td><td>^</td><td>bit-wise XOR</td></tr>
<tr><td>%</td><td>modulus</td><td>&&</td><td>logical AND</td></tr>
<tr><td>++</td><td>auto increment</td><td>||</td><td>logical OR</td></tr>
<tr><td>--</td><td>auto decrement</td><td>!</td><td>logical NOT</td></tr>
<tr><td>==</td><td>equality</td><td>></td><td>greater than</td></tr>
<tr><td>!=</td><td>inequality</td><td><</td><td>less than</td></tr>
<tr><td>=</td><td>assignment</td><td>>=</td><td>greater than or equal</td></tr>
<tr><td>+=</td><td>add and assign</td><td><=</td><td>less than or equal</td></tr>
<tr><td>-=</td><td>subtract and assign</td><td>*=</td><td>multiply and assign</td></tr>
<tr><td>/=</td><td>divide and assign</td><td>...=</td><td>etc.</td></tr>
</table>

Table 6-2: Operators

Summary

This chapter discussed how C++ can be used to write object oriented programs. This chapter takes the same abstract example used in Chapter 5, and applies C++ syntax to the problem. This chapter discussed private and public data elements and methods. The C++ hidden `this` pointer was introduced. The concept of constructors and destructors was discussed. Inheritance was described using C++ terms, which introduced the concept of protected data elements and methods. Friend functions and their use was introduced. Finally, the concept of creating new operators was discussed.

Exercises

Exercise 6-1. Describe the advantages and disadvantages between initializing a variable in a constructor, and assigning a value to a variable. Why is this difference important? You may have to consult a general C++ programming book to answer this question.

Exercise 6-2. Using the concepts of constructors, how could you convert an object of type "int" to an object of type "Vehicle". What semantics could you give to this conversion?

Exercise 6-3. Create declarations for operators of type += and -= that take the right-hand side of an integer that increases and decreases the speed of the Vehicle. Create implementations of these methods.

Exercise 6-4. Discuss the advantages and disadvantages of friend functions. When would you want to use them? When are they dangerous to use?

Exercise 6-5. What meaning could you assign to the operators >, <, >=, and <= when applied to Vehicles on the left-hand side, and either integers or Vehicles on the right-hand side.

Exercise 6-6. Create declarations and implementations for the operators discussed in Exercise 6-5.

Exercise 6-7. How can you make a base class an abstract base class without making use of pure virtual functions? This abstract base class must generate a compile-time error if an attempt is made to instantiate the class. Hint: What can you do to the constructors (all of them) to make them inaccessible, while still accessible to derived classes?

7. Object Oriented Design

Topics Covered:

OOD Process

Identifying Classes

Designing for Inheritance

Connecting Classes

Defining Data Needs

Class Interfaces

Virtual Functions

Private vs. Public

OOD Diagrams

This chapter discusses the object oriented design process. Building object oriented applications is very different than designing procedural based non object oriented applications. The object oriented design process is often referred to as the *OOD process*.

Developing object oriented applications requires a mind-set shift that does not come overnight. Many OOD experts agree that experimenting with sample object oriented applications that are eventually thrown away is a good idea. Your first one or two major object oriented applications should not be used. By the time you've designed and built one or two major applications, you should be proficient enough with the OOD process that it almost becomes second nature.

It should also be noted that there are as many OOD processes as there are object oriented programmers. There are many useful books describing a variety of OOD processes. In this book, we will discuss a rather basic OOD process that can easily be used to get a new object oriented programmer started. However, if you are interested in learning more about the object oriented design process, then you should get a book that specifically discusses object oriented design.

The basic steps in designing an object oriented application are as follows:

1. **Identify your classes**. Deciding what classes will exist up-front is fundamental to a good OO design. This involves determining what your "nouns" are.

2. **Design for inheritance**. Deciding what classes inherit functionality from other classes is imperative for a good OO design and affects every step of the design. Deciding the inheritance hierarchy consists of creating *is-a* relationships.

3. **Connect objects**. Next, you must decide how your classes are connected and how they interact with each other. Deciding how classes are connected consists of creating *has-a* relationships and *uses-a* relationships.

4. **Define your data needs**. This involves deciding what data will be stored in each of your classes.

5. **Define your class interface**. This involves deciding on the public methods and access functions for each of your classes. These are your "verbs."

6. **Define your internal interfaces**. This involves deciding on the private methods and data elements used within your classes.

Identifying Classes

The first step in the object oriented design process is identifying your classes. There are many things to look for when deciding what your classes should be. Look at the problem you are trying to solve. Then, try to find "things," or "objects" in your problem. These will often become classes in your design. There are several ways to come up with a list of "things" in your problem:

1. Explain your problem to someone using a white-board. Blocks you draw are good candidates for classes in your design.

2. Look for nouns in your problem. These are good candidates for classes in your design.

3. Look for "real" objects in your problem (things like cards, boxes, displays). These are good candidates for classes in your design.

In a test & measurement problem, typical examples of "things" that can become classes are:

- Instruments
- Voltmeters
- HP E1410A Multimeter
- Device Under Test
- Switches
- Tests
- Frequency Response Test
- Measurements
- Voltage Measurement
- Data
- Complex Number
- Signal
- Cards/Boxes

- GPIB Interface Card
- Displays
- Disk Drives

You will notice that some objects are more specific descriptions of other objects. For example, a "Frequency Response Test" is a specific type of "Test," and a "Signal" is a specific type of "Data." This is normal and desirable. As you come up with your list of potential classes, keep this in mind and consciously think of these sorts of generalized objects along with the specific objects. You will see in the next section how this is put to use.

Be careful not to confuse nouns and verbs. For example, the word "test" could have been both a noun and a verb in the problem description:

"Test the DUT using a voltmeter for correct voltage on pin 5." (verb)

"This test determines whether the DUT has a correct voltage on pin 5." (noun)

As you go along with the rest of the design, you will likely add to and remove from the list of classes in your design. This is normal and expected. You will probably go through several iterations of your class list before you are done. Again, the more object oriented designs you do, the better you will get at identifying classes in your system.

In C++, these "things" discussed above become classes. Particular instances of the "things" above become objects (instantiated classes).

Designing for Inheritance

The next step is determining which classes inherit from other classes. Inheritance is best described as is-a relationships. An object that can be said is-a second object can becomes a class that inherits from the second class. Since class A that inherits from class B takes on all the characteristics of class B, class A is-a class B.

Using the previous list of potential classes used in T&M, the following are some example is-a relationships and, therefore, potential inheritance points:

- A "voltmeter" **is-a** "instrument."
- A "HPE1410 Multimeter" **is-a** "voltmeter."
- A "HPE1410 Multimeter" **is-a** "instrument."
- A "switch" **is-a** "instrument."
- A "frequency response test" **is-a** "test."
- A "voltage measurement" **is-a** "measurement."

- A "complex number" **is-a** "data."
- A "signal" **is-a** "data."
- A "GPIB interface card" **is-a** "card."
- A "disk drive" **is-a** "data store."

So, therefore:

- A voltmeter class can inherit from an instrument class.
- A hpe1410 class can inherit from a voltmeter class.
- A switch class can inherit from a instrument class.
- A frequency-response-test class can inherit from a test class.
- A voltage-measurement class can inherit from a measurement class.
- A complex-number class can inherit from a data class.
- A signal class can inherit from a data class.
- A GPIB-interface-card class can inherit from a card class.
- A disk-drive class can inherit from a data-store class.

Write down a picture showing how your different classes inherit from each other. When you are done, examine your inheritance picture and see if it is complete. Ask the following questions:

1. Are classes of similar scope at the same level? For example, do the "hpe1410" class and the "hpe1426" class inherit from the same base class, or do their base classes inherit from the same class? Do the "voltmeter" class and the "switch" class and the "scope" class inherit from the same base class (or its base class, etc.).

   At some point, all similar scope classes should inherit at the same level from the same base class.

2. Do you have all the specific classes necessary to implement the functionality needed? For example, if you have an hpe1410 class in your system, do you also have an hpe1426 class (if you will be using an HPE1426 instrument) and a hpe1411 (if you will be using an HPE1411 instrument)?

   Do you have a specific class for each test you plan on performing (such as a "Frequency Response Test," a "Temperature Variance Test," a "Voltage Deviation Test," or whatever specific tests your application needs)?

   Your class picture should be "filled in," it should have all classes needed at a given level specified.

3. Do you have the appropriate base classes defined? Typically, if you have many classes that derive from one base class, you should look to see if another level of base classes should be inserted.

   For example, assume you have an "hpe1410," a "hpe1426," a "hp82554," and a "hp26254" instrument all deriving from the "instrument" base class. If the first two instruments are VXI instruments and the last two are HP-IB instruments, maybe it makes more sense to have two new classes called "VXI instrument" and "HP-IB instrument" that both derive from "instrument." Then the "hpe1410" and "hpe1426" class could derive from "VXI instrument," and the "hp82554" and "hp26254" classes could derive from "HP-IB instrument."

Connecting Objects

The next step is determining how objects of a given type are connected to each other. The interconnection of objects is best described as has-a or uses-a relationships. An object A that has-a object B means that object A contains a pointer, reference, or copy of object B. This is since object A needs some facilities of object B, or uses some methods of object B, or contains collections of object B's.

Using the above list of potential classes used in T&M, the following is some example has-a and uses-a relationships.

- A "frequency response test" **uses-a** "voltage measurement."
- A "frequency response test" **has-a** "signal."
- A "signal" **has-a** "complex-number" (actually, more accurately "has-some").
- A "voltage measurement" **uses-a** "voltmeter."
- A "voltmeter" **uses-a** "Device Under Test."
- A "data store" **has-a** "data."

Be careful with how you set up these has-a and uses-a relationships, as you can easily confuse a "noun has-a noun" with a "noun-verb" relationship. For example, you could say:

A "voltage measurement" **uses-a** "voltmeter" (noun uses-a noun relationship).

But you might also be tempted on saying:

A "voltmeter" **has-a** "voltage measurement" (noun has-a noun relationship).

Which can easily be confused with:

A "voltmeter" "measures-voltage" (noun verb relationship).

In this case, the verb "measures-voltage" is a method of the "voltmeter" class. This is not one object connected to another this is a method of an object, which is discussed later in this section.

In C++, when class A has-a or uses-a class B, then class A will have a data member that is a pointer or reference to an instance of class B, or will contain a complete instance of class B within class A. Methods of class A may, therefore, call methods of class B.

Differences Between Has-a and Uses-a Relationships

Usually, has-a and uses-a relationships are treated very similarly. But they can be used to represent distinct relationship types. The difference is probably subtle at this point, but may be more important as you continue through this book and get more experience with object oriented designs:

- A has-a relationship means the first object contains a copy of the second object that it uses to implement its functionality. When we say "Object A has-a Object B," this typically means that the existence of Object B is completely contained within Object A. Object B can be said to be owned by Object A.

- A uses-a relationship means the first object has a pointer or reference to the second object. When we say "Object A uses-a Object B," this typically means that the existence of Object B is independent of Object A, but Object A is a user of some facility that Object B provides.

As we go through a sample object oriented design process, this difference should become clearer.

Defining Data Needs

The next step in our design process is determining the data that is needed for each class. Remember, since each instance of a class will have a separate copy of all data members within the class, the data that is stored in the class is called *instance data.* This means there is a copy of the data for each instance of the object in the system.

As an example, there will be one instance of an "hpe1410" class for each HPE1410 voltmeter in the system. If your test system has two such voltmeters, then there will be two instances of an hpe1410 class. If each hpe1410 class has a variable called, for instance, `timeout`, then each HPE1410 voltmeter in the system will have its own `timeout` variable.

There are several steps in determining the data needs for a class:

1. Deciding what data elements are needed within the class.

2. Determining whether the data should be static, or instance data.

3. Determining whether the data should be in a given class, or one of its base classes.

These steps must be repeated for each class in the system repetitively until all data needs for all classes have been identified. Since the process of identifying the data for one class can affect the data needs of another class, this process is iterative. Each of these steps will be discussed in turn.

Decide Data Elements Needed

For a given class, decide the types and names for the data needed. The data needed by a class can consist of several types of things. It can be variables representing the state of the object, it can be variables representing attributes or options assigned to the object, or it can be values associated with readings or measurements.

Sometimes, the has-a relationships discussed above are not interconnections between objects, but describe data needs of an object. For example, a "Signal" class has-a (or many) "Complex Numbers" may not mean that the Signal has a connection to Complex Number objects, but instead may mean that the Signal class contains one or more Complex Numbers as data elements within the class. Remember, that a class is nothing more than a user-defined type mechanism within C++, so that a "Complex Number" class may be a data element just as easy as a `float`, `double`, or `int` can be.

As an example, some of the types of data that might be needed for T&M classes include:

Instruments:

Bus Address of the instrument (Logical Address, GPIB Primary Address, etc.)
State variables containing the state of the instrument (DCV 2V Range, etc.)
Status of instrument (idle, power-off, measuring, etc.)
Environmental information (ambient temperature in room, etc.)

Switches:

Current state of the switch card (a switch setting)
Status of switch settling (settled, not settled, unsure, etc.)

Switch Setting:

List of switches that are open/close (R1C2 Closed, R3C5 Closed)
Route List (DUT Pin 5 to DMM Pin 1)

Measurements:

Status of measurement in progress (idle, in-progress, results ready)
Data contents of the measurement (3.5467 Volts)
Date and time of last measurement

Tests:

Status of test in progress (idle, in-progress, results ready)
Passed/Failed status of test
Date and time of last run of test
Attributes necessary for performing the test (voltage applied to DUT Pin 3, etc.)

GPIB Interface Card:

State of the GPIB bus (talkers, listeners)
Active Controller State

Determine if Data is Static or Instance

Next, we must determine if the data is static or instance data. *Static data* is shared (global) to all instances of a class. *Instance data* is local to a given instance of a class.

Examples of static data might include:

- Constant data (such as text strings, etc.) that cannot change value.

- Data that is needed when an instance of a given class is not available for use. An example may be the list of possible switch settings available. Such a list may be needed before an instance of a switch setting is identified.

- Data that, when changed in one class, should be changed in all classes of the same type. An example is the ambient room temperature. This may be a data element of the instrument class that is needed by several instrument functions (or measurement functions). Since the temperature can change over time, it can not be a constant, but the same ambient temperature may apply to all instruments in the system (if they are in the same room, for instance).

Examples of instance data might include:

- State variables
- Object status (idle, working, etc.)
- Attributes of a particular object (time-out values, etc.)
- Any data that varies from one instance of a class to another

Almost all data in a class is instance data. If you are not sure whether it is instance data or not, it is probably instance data.

Determine Whether Data Should be in Derived or Base Class

Think of the following example, should the variable "Bus Address of Instrument" be associated with the "HPE1410" class, or with the base class "voltmeter," or the base class "instrument"?

Let us assume, for this example, we have a class hierarchy similar to the following:

Derived Class	→	Base Class
Instrument	→	Object
VXI Instrument	→	Instrument
VXI Voltmeter	→	VXI Instrument
hpe1410	→	VXI Voltmeter

Table 7-1: Inheritance Structure for Example hpe1410 class

Now, let us assume we are deciding where the "voltage range" variable should be located. Let us assume that this variable is a state variable containing the current voltage range of the instrument.

- Should the variable go in the hpe1410 class? Well, maybe. But since a "voltage range" is relevant to voltmeters other than the hpe1410, this may be too specific a location for the variable.

- Should the variable go in the instrument class? No. Not all instruments have a "voltage range" variable, and as such would not be relevant in non-voltmeter instruments.

- Should the variable go in the VXI instrument class? No. Same argument as for the instrument class.

- Should the variable go in the VXI Voltmeter class? Yes. It is a variable that may apply to all voltmeters, not just the hpe1410, but not to non-voltmeter classes.

A general rule: Put a class member in the most general class that it still belongs to, without being too general.

Let us try another example, how about a "VXI Logical Address" variable. This variable gives the bus address of the hpe1410 voltmeter on the VXI backplane.

- Should the variable go in the hpe1410 class? No. Since this variable applies to more than just the hpe1410 instrument, it should go into a more general class.

- Should the variable go in the VXI Voltmeter class? No. Since this variable applies to more than just VXI voltmeters, it should go into a more general class.

- Should the variable go in the instrument class? No. Not all instruments have a "VXI Logical Address." For example, HP-IB instruments do not have a VXI Logical Address.

- Should the variable go in the VXI Instrument class? Yes. It is a variable that applies to all VXI instruments, but not necessarily all instruments.

It is important to make sure variables get into the appropriate class. This is true for two reasons:

1. The more generalized class you put the variable into, the more classes can make use of code written to use that variable.

   Think of the "VXI Logical Address" variable. If this variable was in the "hpe1410" class, then another "VXI instrument," such as a "hpe1426," would not be able to use code written for that variable, since a "hpe1426" would inherit from "VXI instrument", not from "hpe1410."

2. If a variable is put into a too-generalized class, then code written that uses that variable will not be usable in all classes that inherit from that class. This may cause errors or misuse of data in classes that do not need the data.

   Think of the "VXI Logical Address" variable. What use would this variable have to an HP-IB instrument? This could be the case if the variable was in the "instrument" class, since a class such as "HP-IB Instrument," which likely would also inherit from "instrument", would not know what to do with a "VXI Logical Address" variable.

Defining Class Interface

Finally, the interface to the class must be created. The class interface is the list of public methods that are used to manipulate instances of this class.

The following steps are involved in determining the methods needed for a class:

1. Decide what methods are needed within the class.

2. Determine whether the functions are static or not.

3. Determine whether the function applies to a given class, a base class, or both.

4. Determine whether base class functions should be virtual or not, and determine whether they should be inherited or re-implemented in a derived class.

What Methods are Needed?

Determining the methods a class needs involves determining the actions that a class needs to implement to perform the functions it must provide.

There are several types of methods that a class may have:

- Methods that read and modify variables, or attributes of the class. Examples include setting a time-out value, or getting an instrument's address.
- Methods that perform actions on behalf of an object. An example is taking a measurement from an instrument.
- Methods that create, assign, and destroy instances of the class.
- Methods that determine the type of an object.

There are several mechanisms that can be employed to come up with a class's methods:

- If classes are nouns, then methods are verbs. Think of verbs that can be applied to a class, these will likely be methods.
- Think of variables or states that may need to be read or changed. Typically, methods for reading or setting these variables are needed.

As an example, let us take the "hpe1410" class. First, what verbs can be applied to the noun "hpe1410"? How about:

→ measure
→ reset
→ trigger

Next, what states must be updated in a "hpe1410"? How about:

→ set range
→ set function
→ get range
→ get function
→ set trigger line
→ get trigger line
→ get status (idle, measuring, waiting for trigger, etc.)

What about other variables that might be read or written?

→ set time-out
→ get time-out
→ get result (of a measure)

Each of these items is a potential method of the class.

Static vs. Non-Static Methods

Next, it must be determined if the method should be static or not. Static methods are methods that may be implemented without having an instance of a class (an object) available. Non-static methods may only be called with an instance of a class.

The following guidelines should be followed in determining if a method should be static or not:

- If the method must access a variable of the class that is not static, then the method must not be static. Static methods are not allowed to access non-static data. This is a hard and fast rule and overrides all other concerns listed below.

- If the method must be called when an instance of a class is not available, then the method should be static. Static methods may be called when no instance of a class is available (as if they are "normal" functions).

- Methods that, when called, must act on behalf of **all** objects of the same class, should be static. An example is a function that informs all instruments of the ambient room temperature.

In general, almost all methods in a class are **not** static. If you are not sure whether a method should be static or not, it probably should not be.

Examples of non-static methods might include:

- measure
- set/get range
- set/get time-out
- get bus address
- get status
- get measure results

Examples of static methods might include:

- get ambient room temperature

Define in Derived Class, Base Class, or Both?

This question is very similar to the question asked earlier "where does data belong, base class or derived class?" Here, the question is "what class should first define the method?" The key here is "first define", as will be seen later.

The rules for deciding what class should first define a method is similar to the rules for data:

1. A method should be defined in the most generalized class possible. For example, a method that sets an instrument time-out should be defined in an "instrument" class versus an "hpe1410" class.

2. A method should be defined in no more a generalized class than make sense. For example, a "Trigger on VXI Trigger Line" function should be defined in a "VXI instrument" class, versus an "instrument" class.

Which Classes Implement the Methods? -- Virtual Functions

Now that you have decided what class should first define a method, next you must determine which classes (the base class and/or the derived classes) should implement this method. The following situations should be considered:

1. *The base class (the class that first defines the method) should implement the function.* This is often the case for methods that get and set values and attributes that are simply variables in the class and do not require any other functions than getting and setting the variable. In this case, the method is implemented in the base class as a non-virtual method. All of the derived classes simply inherit this version of the method for their use.

2. *The base class does not implement the method, but each derived class does.* This is often the case for methods that have the same action for different classes, but the implementations are different in each class. An example is the "measure" method. This method would have the same action for all voltmeters (it makes a measurement of the given range and function), but the implementation of the command may be very different for a "hpe1410" voltmeter as for a "hpe1411" voltmeter. In this case, the method is defined in the base class as a pure virtual method with no implementation. Each of the derived classes must then provide an implementation of this method. In this case, the base class becomes an abstract base class.

3. *The base class implements the method, in addition some derived classes also implement it.* This is often the case for methods that have the same action for different classes, and many implementations for different classes are the same, but some classes need a different implementation. A good example is a "set time-out" function. The "instrument" class may have a default implementation that simply sets a class variable, which will work for most specific instrument classes, but the "hpe1411" voltmeter may need to perform some additional functionality in order to set the instrument time-out. In this case, the method is defined and implemented in the base class as a virtual method. Each derived class that needs a different implementation than the base class must also implement the method.

Other Standard Functions

Sometimes it is useful to determine, at run time, the type of an object. Is this object an instrument or a test? Is it a voltmeter or a switch card?

An easy way to implement this functionality is to define a pure virtual function that is implemented in each derived class. The derived class implementations simply return the type of object that it is.

For example, let us assume you have a base class called "instrument" and you want a function that returns what type of instrument it is. Consider the following code:

```
enum InstType {voltmeter, switchInst, scope}; // etc.
class instrument {
    ...
    public:
        virtual InstType instType()=0; // Pure Virtual
    ...
};

class voltmeter : public instrument {
    ...
    public:
        virtual InstType instType(){return voltmeter;}
    ...
};

class switchInst : public instrument {
    ...
    public:
        virtual InstType instType()
                {return switchInst;}
    ...
};

class scope : public instrument {
    ...
    public:
        virtual InstType instType(){return scope;}
    ...
};
```

Listing 7-1: Creating an `instType` Method

Now, if you have a pointer to an instrument, you may call the `instType` method to determine what type of instrument this is:

```
instrument *inst;

inst=...;

if(inst->instType()==voltmeter){
    ...
}
```

Listing 7-2: Use of `instType` method

As another example, let us say you have an object, and want to determine if it is an instrument, a measurement, a test, a DUT, and so forth. You may implement an `objType` method as a pure-virtual function in "object" and have all of the classes that inherit from "object" (such as "instrument," "measurement," "test," etc.) implement the method and return an appropriate value. This would be very similar in implementation to the `instType` method above.

A completed class hierarchy may have one or more than one version of the `*Type` methods to identify appropriate pieces of the hierarchy.

Another useful method that a class may want to implement is the "dump" method. This is a method that is implemented in all classes in the system. What it does is print to a file a human-readable version of all the data stored in the object. It then calls the dump function to all objects that it is connected to. The result is a file that contains a human readable version of all the objects instantiated in a given system.

Finally, many systems implement a method in every class called `myName`. This is a virtual method that is implemented in all non-abstract base classes in the system. What it does is return a constant, human-readable string, that represents the name of this instance of the object. Additionally, you could implement an equivalent method that returns a constant, human readable string, that represents the class name of this object.

Any or all of these ideas may be helpful in a given system, and should be considered and designed into the system from the beginning.

Constructors, Destructors, Operators

Finally, the constructors, destructor, and standard operators for a class should be designed. These are methods too and should be designed into the object from the beginning. Questions to ask yourself include:

1. Does the class have any data elements that must be initialized?
2. Does the class have any other initialization tasks that must take place when an object is created?
3. Is the default constructor acceptable, or do I need constructor(s) that accept parameters?
4. What about the copy constructor? Is the default copy constructor acceptable or do I need my own? Do I want to specifically disallow the use of a copy constructor? Typically, if any constructor allocates memory, then the default copy constructor is not acceptable.

5. Do I need a destructor? Typically if any constructor allocates memory, then a destructor is needed to free that memory. Depending on what other initialization tasks the constructor does, a destructor may also be needed.

6. What about the assignment operator? Is the default assignment operator acceptable or do I need my own? Do I want to specifically disallow the use of the assignment operator? Typically, if any constructor allocates memory, then the default assignment operator is not acceptable.

Private vs. Public Elements

Finally, you must decide which data variables and methods are to be private, protected, or public. The following guidelines should be followed:

1. All variables should be private or protected. Typically you do not want someone modifying your data variables other than by using your class methods. If you want to give users of the class access to your variables, provide public access methods. This is a programming style issue. If you want derived classes to access variables in your class, make them protected, otherwise make them private.

2. All methods that describe the interface to the class (callable by users of the class) should be public.

3. All methods that are used only internally within the class to implement functionality should be private.

4. All methods that are used only by derived classes to implement functionality should be protected.

Diagramming

Diagrams are useful tools in visualizing an object oriented design. There are several different formal methodologies for diagramming object oriented designs. Some are more complicated than others. However, no single methodology is in wide use in the industry yet.

Rather than using a complicated diagramming process, this book describes a simple but effective approach to diagramming an OO design. It involves creating two or three types of diagrams:

- An Inheritance Tree
- An Instantiation Diagram
- A Uses-A Diagram (optional)

Together, these diagrams completely describe the object oriented design of a system to such a level that fairly complex object oriented designs can be visualized in a small amount of space. Each of these types of diagrams will be discussed in turn.

Inheritance Tree

An inheritance tree is nothing more than a diagram that shows the class inheritance structure between the C++ classes in a system. It shows the is-a relationships. It contains the following elements in the diagram:

- **Labeled Ovals/Clouds**. Ovals or "clouds" represent individual C++ classes. The label on the oval or cloud represents the name of the C++ class.
- **Arrows**. Arrows connect C++ classes and show the inheritance structure. The tail of the arrow points to the derived class and the head of the arrow points to the base class.
- **Call-outs**. Call-outs (free text with lines attached) are comments. They are not part of the diagram and don't represent any part of the OO design, but are useful for commenting or explaining different aspects of the design. The line points to the object that the free text is commenting about.

Figure 7-1 shows a very simple inheritance tree diagram showing the inheritance between a voltmeter and an instrument class:

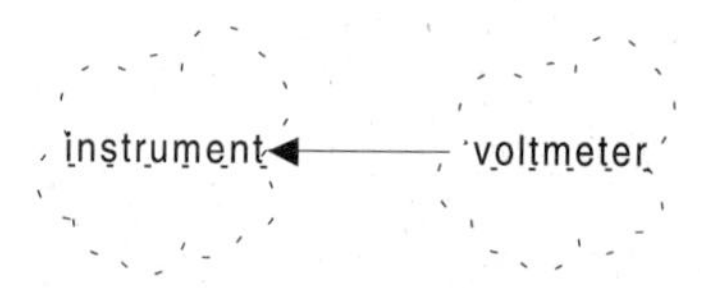

Figure 7-1: Simple Inheritance Tree

In this diagram, the instrument is the base class and the voltmeter is the derived class. Since a base class can itself be derived from another base class, and since one base class can serve as the base class for multiple different derived classes, the structure you get often will look like a tree, as shown in Figure 7-2. This diagram uses ovals instead of clouds to represent classes. The choice is a matter of personal preference.

In a single-inheritance system (one where each derived class inherits from only one base class), the diagram will always look like a tree. In a multiple-inheritance system (one where each derived class inherits from more than one base class), the diagram will no longer look like a tree. Single-inheritance systems are by far the most common (and all we talk about in this part of the book), that is why these diagrams are often called "inheritance trees."

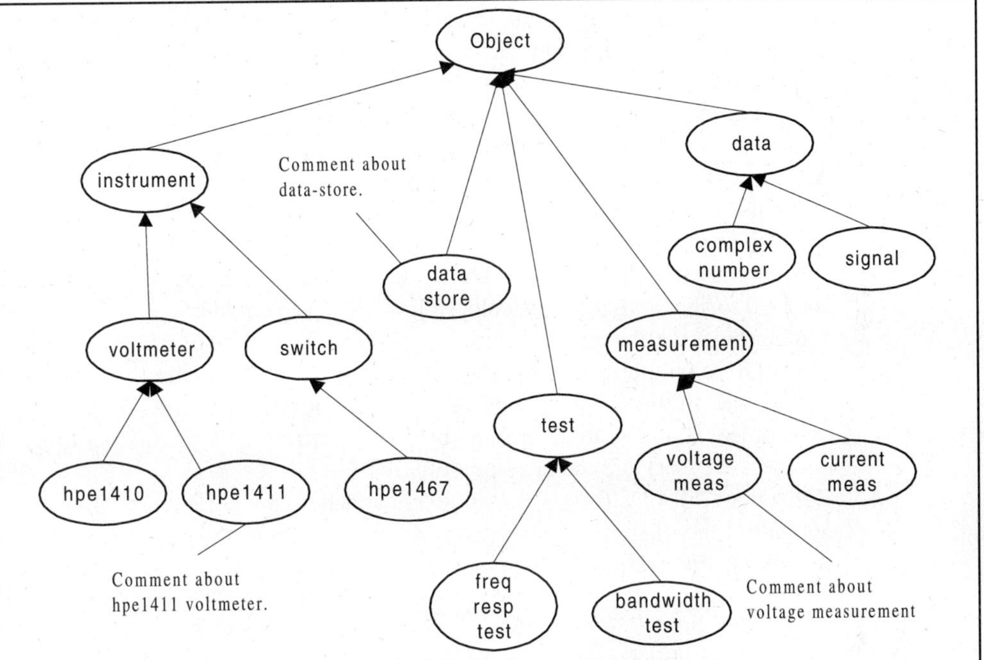

Figure 7-2: Sample Inheritance Tree

Instantiation Diagram

An instantiation diagram is a diagram that shows how objects (instances of classes) connect in a object oriented design. This diagram shows objects (instances of classes), rather than classes themselves.

The connections between objects in the instantiation diagram shows the has-a and uses-a relationships. It contains the following types of elements:

- **Labeled Circles/Ovals/Squares/Rectangles/Clouds**. Any of these elements represent individual **instances** of C++ classes. There may be more than one of each type of C++ class on the diagram. It is sometimes useful to categorize different types of objects and use one shape for each type (ovals for instruments, circles for data, rectangles for tests, etc.). The label on the object represents an identifier for the instance, which may or may not be related to the C++ class name. If necessary, the C++ class name can be put in parenthesis after the object identifier. Alternatively, the cloud approach can also be used for instantiation diagrams. Typically, clouds used in instantiation diagrams are solid instead of dotted, to show that they represent objects instead of classes.
- **Arrows**. Arrows connect objects and show has-a and some uses-a relationships. The object at the tail of the arrow contains a data member that refers to or uses the object at the head of the arrow.
- **Dotted Arrows**. Dotted arrows show uses-a relationships exclusively. They are used to show when a particular objects does not contain a pointer to another object, but uses the other object during the course of its work. This can be, for example, when an object A is passed as a parameter to a method of object B. In this cases, B uses-a A, but does not contain an A. In this case, object B and A are connected by a dotted arrow with the tail pointing to object B (user) and the head pointing to object A (use-e).
- **Call-outs**. Call-outs (boxes with pointers attached) are comments. They are not part of the diagram and do not represent any part of the object oriented design, but are useful for commenting or explaining different aspects of the design.

Figure 7-3 shows a very simple instantiation diagram showing an instance of a "voltage measurement" using an instance of a "voltmeter":

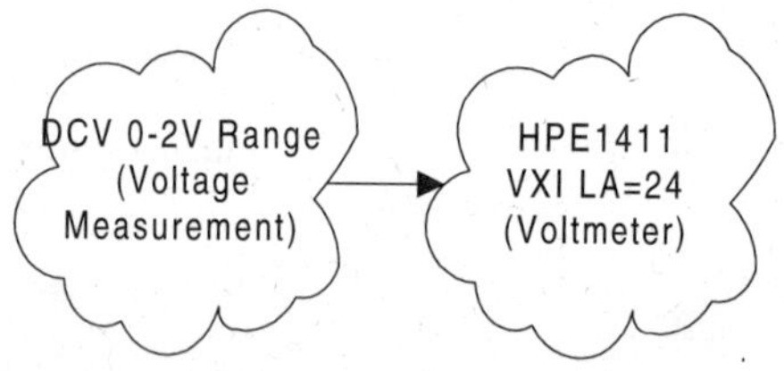

Figure 7-3: Simple Instantiation Diagram

In this diagram, the "DCV 0-2V Range" is an instance of a voltage measurement that takes a DC Voltage measurement in the 0-2V range. In order to implement its functionality, it uses-a HPE1411 voltmeter (which happens to be at VXI Logical Address 24).

Figure 7-4 is a slightly more complicated example showing a "voltage measurement" using an instance of a "voltmeter" and a "switch" card. However, in order to use the switch card, the voltage measurement must pass the switch card a "switch-setting" object, which tells the switch card which pin of the DUT to connect.

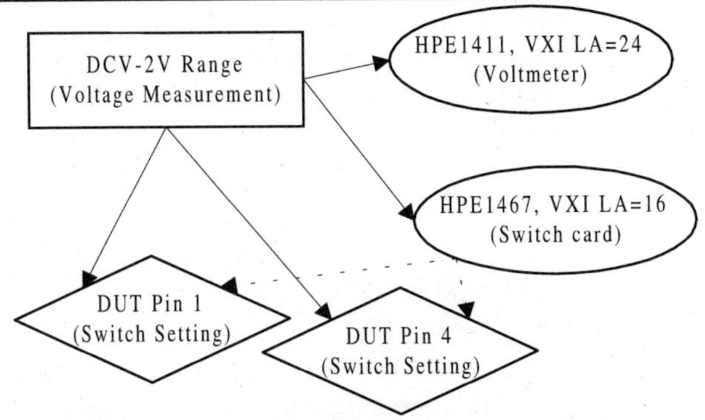

Figure 7-4: Instantiation Diagram with Switch Settings

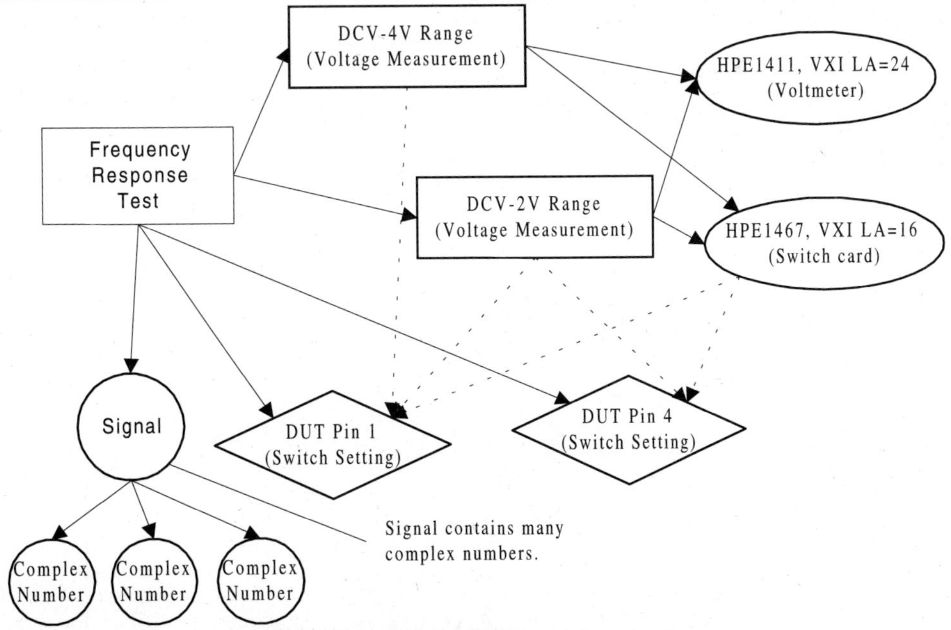

Figure 7-5: Sample Instantiation Diagram

In this case, the voltage measurement has-a switch setting, and uses-a switch card. The voltage measurement passes the switch setting to the switch card, so that the switch card uses-a switch setting (but does not has-a).

Figure 7-5 shows a more complete example instantiation diagram. In this version, the "source" of the switch settings is the frequency response test. In order for the test to perform its work, it must call the "DCV-4V Range Measurement" and the "DCV-2V Range Measurement". Each of these must be passed a switch setting which specifies the DUT pin from which to measure the voltage. In order for the measurement routines to perform their work, they need a voltmeter and a switch card. The switch setting is passed to the switch card, which needs the switch setting to close the appropriate contacts. Notice also in this example that the frequency response test requires a "Signal" data element. The Signal data element requires the use of three (or perhaps more) "Complex Numbers".

Uses-A Diagram

Occasionally, a third diagram is used called a *uses-a diagram.* Essentially, a uses-a diagram is the same thing as an instantiation diagram, except classes are shown instead of objects. Sometimes, a uses-a diagram can present the same sort of information as an instantiation diagram without the complexity. An example uses-a diagram is shown in Figure 7-6.

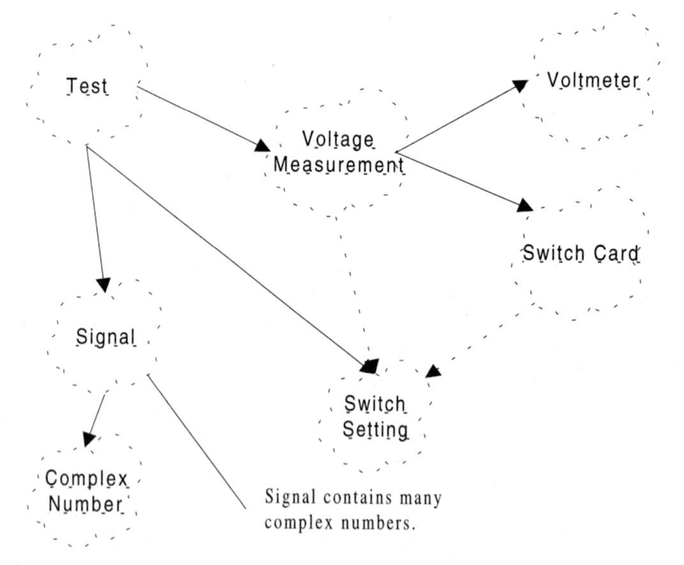

Figure 7-6: Sample Uses-A Diagram

Summary

This chapter discussed the process of creating an object oriented design. There are many philosophies for the OOD process. This chapter gives an introduction to one process. Variations of this process will be used in object oriented designs throughout the rest of this book. Other OOD processes exist and there are entire books dedicated to this topic.

This chapter discussed identifying classes, design-for-inheritance and *is-a* relationships, connecting objects and *has-a* and *uses-a* relationships, nouns and verbs, defining data needs, and class interfaces.

Exercises

Exercise 7-1 Take a real-world problem, and start an object oriented design by identifying what classes exist in the problem.

Exercise 7-3. Discuss how inheritance can be used between classes in this problem. What are the *is-a* relationships between your classes?

Exercise 7-3. Create your *uses-a* and *has-a* relationships between your classes.

Exercise 7-4. Create diagrams showing your high-level design. Show your inheritance structure in one diagram, and your connecting objects structure in another diagram.

Exercise 7-5. Create your data and interfaces for your classes.

Part III

Object Oriented Test & Measurement Systems

8. High-Level OO Design of a T&M System

This chapter uses the object oriented design principles presented in Chapter 7, and applies them to a typical T&M test system. For this chapter, we will use the example test system presented in Chapter 4. As you may recall, the test system presented in that chapter used traditional programming techniques (procedural based programming, top-down modular design, etc.). This chapter will take the same problem and apply an object oriented design.

Topics Covered:

Example Object Oriented Design

T&M Application of OOD

Identifying Classes

Inheritance

Uses-a Relationships

Class Data Needs

Class Interface

Instantiation

The Problem

The problem that we described in Chapter 4 is to build a test station to test a simple band-pass filter to make sure it satisfies a specific set of conditions. This test application is the basis for a production test system where a continuous supply of band-pass filters are passed by the test station on the assembly line and tested. Filters that pass the tests are sent on their way, while filters that do not pass the test are discarded.

The following values are of interest in this test system:

- ω_0 **- The center frequency**. This is the frequency at which the output voltage is maximized.
- ω_1 **- The low frequency**. This is the frequency where the output voltage is $1/\sqrt{2}$ of the voltage at ω_0. Lower frequencies have a lower voltage, higher frequencies have a higher voltage. This is the low-end of the passband.
- ω_2 **- The high frequency**. This is the frequency where the output voltage is $1/\sqrt{2}$ of the voltage at ω_0. Lower frequencies have a higher voltage, higher frequencies have a lower voltage. This is the high-end of the passband.
- β **- The bandwidth**. This is the width of the frequency response between ω_1 and ω_2.

- V_o - **The output voltage at a given frequency**. The value V_{om} is the maximum output voltage, which is the output voltage at frequency ω_0.

For the band-pass filter that will be tested by this example test application, the following characteristics are desired:

$$\omega_0 = 2250Hz$$
$$\omega_1 = 1455Hz$$
$$\omega_2 = 3045Hz$$
$$\beta = 1590Hz$$
$$0.5V \leq V_o \leq 1.0V$$

DUT

As you will remember, the DUT being tested is a simple RLC circuit. The RLC circuit is repeated again in Figure 8-1. For this DUT, the following values for were chosen:

$$R = 50\Omega$$
$$L = 5mH$$
$$C = 1\mu F$$

This gives the following results:

$$\omega_0 = 14142 \tfrac{rad}{\sec} = 2251Hz$$
$$\omega_1 = 9142 \tfrac{rad}{\sec} = 1455Hz$$
$$\omega_2 = 19138 \tfrac{rad}{\sec} = 3046Hz$$
$$\beta = 9996 \tfrac{rad}{\sec} = 1591Hz$$

These values are within .1% of the desired values.

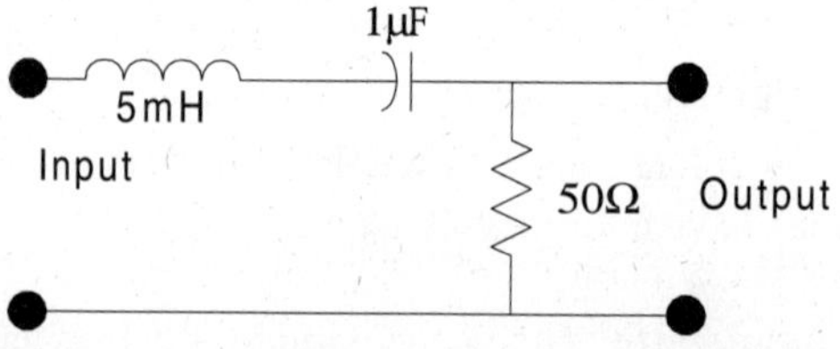

Figure 8-1: DUT - RLC Band-pass Filter

Test Criteria

The test criteria will be identical to those in Chapter 4. The following tests will be performed for V_i=0.5V, V_i=1.0V or V_i=1.5V:

Verify ω_0 is within expected limits (2025Hz $\leq \omega_0 \leq$ 2475Hz).
Verify ω_1 is within expected limits (1310Hz $\leq \omega_1 \leq$ 1600Hz).
Verify ω_2 is within expected limits (2741Hz $\leq \omega_2 \leq$ 3349Hz).
Verify β is within expected limits (1431Hz $\leq \beta \leq$ 1749Hz).
Verify V_{om} is within expected limits (V_i*95% $\leq V_{om} \leq V_i$*105%).
Verify I_{om} is within expected limits (I_{exp}*95% $\leq I_{om} \leq I_{exp}$*105%).
Verify V_L is within expected limits ($V_L \leq V_i$*20%).
Verify V_H is within expected limits ($V_H \leq V_i$*50%).

Object Oriented Design Principles

In Chapter 7, we discussed the steps involved in creating an object oriented design. For reference, they are:

1. **Identify your classes**. Deciding what classes will exist up-front is fundamental to a good object oriented design.

2. **Design for inheritance**. Deciding what classes inherit from what other classes consists of creating is-a relationships.

3. **Connect classes**. Deciding what classes are connected to other classes consists of creating has-a relationships and uses-a relationships.

4. **Define your data needs**. This involves deciding what data will be stored in each of your classes.

5. **Define your class interface**. This involves deciding on the public methods and access functions for each of your classes.

6. **Define your internal interfaces**. This involves deciding on the private method and access functions used within your classes.

7. **Instantiation**. This involves deciding how classes will be instantiated into objects and used within the system. In some cases, this is a direct outcome of the "connect classes" step, but sometimes more thought is needed.

These steps will be followed one by one in each of the next sections until a complete object oriented design for this test system is created.

Identifying the Classes

First, let us brainstorm our classes. We will start by looking at these two things:

1. Look for nouns in the problem description.
2. Look for "real" objects (like "boxes") in the system.

From our description, we come up with the following list:

Nouns:

- band-pass filter
- test station
- center frequency
- low frequency
- high frequency
- bandwidth
- output voltage
- load current
- measure
- test
- instrument
- frequency response

Real Objects:

- DUT
- I/O interface
- Frequency source
- Multimeter (DMM)
- Switch card

This is a good start, but let us try characterizing and categorizing these better. First, let us talk about real devices in the system. We have the following:

1. *The DUT for the system.* This is the band-pass filter being tested. We will make this a class in our system and call it `DUT`.

2. *I/O interface.* This is the interface card used to talk to the test instruments from the test controller. This will typically be an HP-IB interface card, a VXI interface, or RS-232. We will make this a class in our system and call it `IOIntf`.

3. *Frequency source.* This is a test instrument that generates sine-wave signals of various frequencies at various voltages. We will make this a class in our system and call it `Source`.

4. *Multimeter.* This is a test instrument that measures voltage at the output of the DUT, and the current through load R. This could be broken down into two classes, one to measure voltage and one to measure current. But, for this example, we will use one instrument class and call it `DMM`.

5. *Switch card.* This is a physical test device that connects the frequency source and multimeter to various points of the DUT. This will be a class in our system called `Switch`.

Next, let us talk about the nouns in the system:

1. *Band-pass filter.* This is the DUT and is identical to the DUT class identified above.

2. *Test station.* The real question here is what role does the test station have in our test application? It could be a class that handles telling the mechanical assembly line system whether the DUT connected passed or failed the test. It could also provide feedback to an operator of the system. As such, we should probably make this a class. We can clarify its operations later. We will call it `TestStation`.

3. *Center/low/high frequency.* These were nouns in our original problem. We will be measuring these things in order to determine if the DUT passed or failed. We will combine all of these into one class and call it `FrequencyMeasurement`.

4. *Bandwidth.* This is a function of the frequency measurements. As such, we decide not to make this a class, but an operation on other classes (the frequency classes). We can revisit this decision later in the design, if we desire.

5. *Output voltage/load current.* These nouns actually take on multiple flavors in the original problem description. First, the output voltage and load current at a given frequency is of importance. Second, the maximum output voltage and load current are important.

For the first flavor (output at a given frequency), we will make this into a class called `ReadAtFreqMeasurement`. For the second flavor (maximum outputs), we will create a class called `MaxValMeasurement`.

6. *Measure/test/instrument*. These nouns are generalized terms for other classes in this system. Even though they are generalized, it still important to recognize their existence. We will create classes called `Measurement`, `Test`, and `Instrument`. How are these used in our system? This will be explained in the discussion on inheritance, below.

7. *Frequency Response*. This is a thing to be tested in our system. We will create a class called `FrequencyResponseTest`.

This is a good start. We probably have identified over 90% of the classes we need. We may have identified classes that we do not need, but we can weed these out later.

Now, we need to talk about how to organize and structure these classes.

Design for Inheritance -- Inheritance Tree

Next, we must brainstorm the is-a relationships that exist in our system. This will be the first step in creating our inheritance tree. While we do this, we may even identify more classes that are needed. These classes may become real classes, or possibly abstract base classes. Let us start with the following:

A `DMM` *is-a* `Instrument`.

A `Source` *is-a* `Instrument`.

A `Switch` *is-a* `Instrument`.

These are all relationships between a particular test instrument and the class `Instrument`. Probably, `Instrument` will be an abstract base class, but we are not sure yet.

Now, let us look at measurements:

A `FrequencyMeasurement` *is-a* `Measurement`.

A `MaxValMeasurement` *is-a* `Measurement`.

These are all relationships between specific types of measurements and the class `Measurement`. Like `Instrument`, `Measurement` will probably be an abstract base class. We can do the same with tests:

A `FrequencyResponseTest` *is-a* `Test`.

So far, that is all we have for tests.

Now, how about physical devices? We already have all of our instruments characterized, but is there a further characterization for all physical devices? How about:

An `Instrument` *is-a* device.

An `IOIntf` *is-a* device.

A `DUT` *is-a* device.

A `TestStation` *is-a* device.

Here, we have taken all of our physical devices and created *is-a* relationships with a new thing, called a device. This is a good candidate for a new class, and we will create one called `Device`.

Let us create an inheritance tree from these relationships. Figure 8-2 shows the tree as it currently exists. Here, it is actually three separate trees, one with `Device` as a root, one with `Measurement` as a root, and one with `Test` as a root.

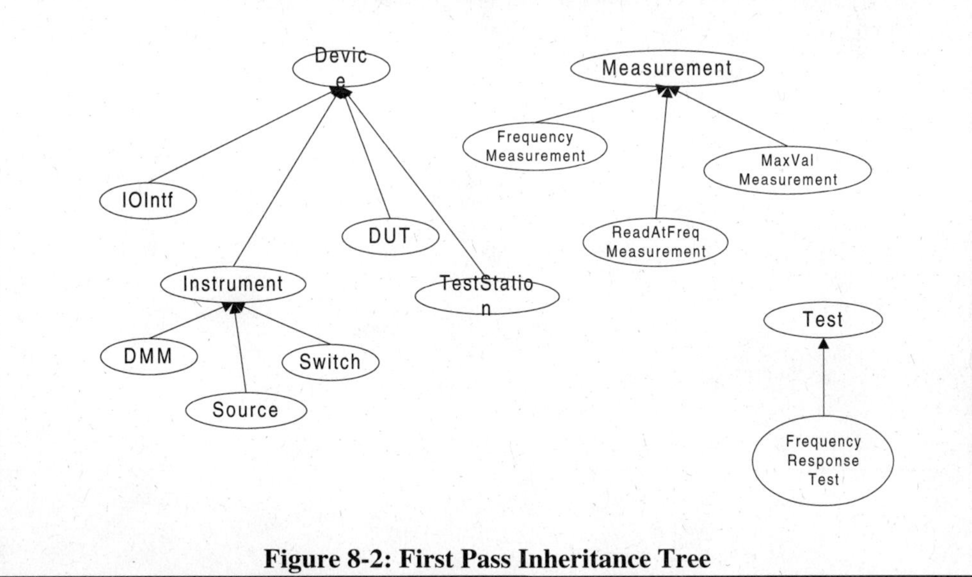

Figure 8-2: First Pass Inheritance Tree

There are a few things to notice about this tree. First, while having several root classes (base of the trees, in this case `Device`, `Measurement`, and `Test`) is acceptable in an object oriented design, sometimes it is convenient to have one base class that everything derives from. We will create a new abstract base class called `Object`, and create the relationships:

A `Device` *is-a* `Object`.

A `Measurement` *is-a* `Object`.

A `Test` *is-a* `Object`.

Next, look at the `Test` inheritance tree. It is hard to believe that the only "Test" we have to perform is a frequency response test, perhaps we are missing some classes from our hierarchy. We probably will have a test for each of the potential measurements we will take. So, let us add a new class to our `Test` hierarchy, and let us call it `OutputAtFreqTest`. This class will be used to test the output voltage and load current at various frequencies.

Figure 8-3 shows an updated inheritance tree for our system. It shows the inclusion of the `Object` relationships and the additional `Test` subclass.

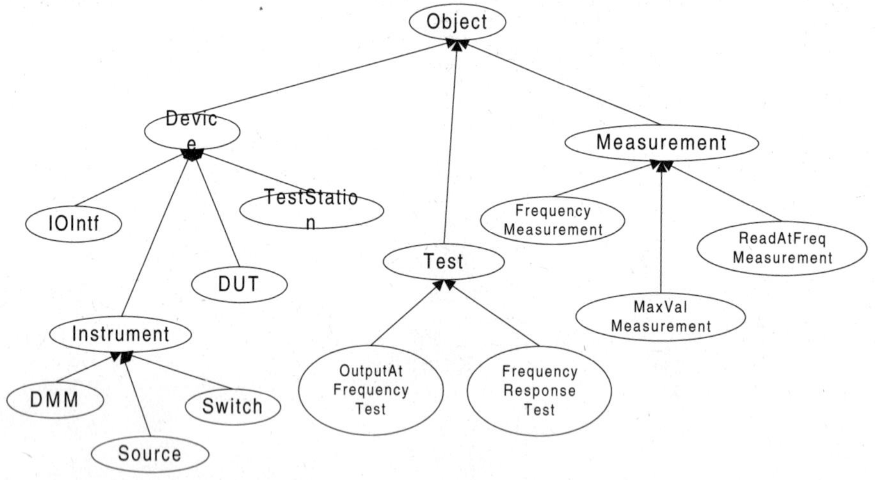

Figure 8-3: Final Inheritance Tree

This is a fairly complete inheritance tree. We have most, if not all of our classes defined and shown in our inheritance tree. We will leave this tree alone for now, and move on to the next step in the design process.

Connect Classes

The next step is deciding how instances of our classes will interact with instances of other classes. The first step in this process is determining has-a or uses-a relationships between classes. For example, the following are some of the relationships that exist between classes that we have created for our system:

A `FrequencyResponseTest` *uses-a* `FrequencyMeasurement`.

A `FrequencyMeasurement` *uses-a* `ReadAtFreqMeasurement`.

A `ReadAtFreqMeasurement` *uses-a* DMM.

A `ReadAtFreqMeasurement` *uses-a* `Source`.

These relationships say the following:

1. In order to test the frequency response of a DUT (`FrequencyResponseTest`), you must measure key frequencies, namely ω_0, ω_1, and ω_2 (`FrequencyMeasurement`).

2. In order to measure key frequencies (`FrequencyMeasurement`), you must be able to read voltages at various frequencies (`ReadAtFreqMeasurement`), in order to "close in" on the correct frequencies.

3. In order to measure the voltage output at a given frequency (`ReadAtFreqMeasurement`), you must be able to read a voltage from the DUT (`DMM`) and set the DUT input frequency (`Source`).

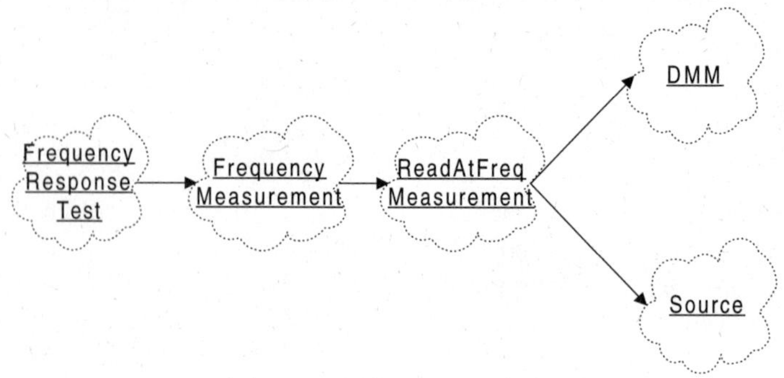

Figure 8-4: Sample Uses-A Relationships

Figure 8-4 shows graphically these *uses-a* relationships. Showing these relationships graphically makes it easier to see how the various classes interact with each other. As you create all of the *uses-a* relationships, care must be taken to make sure that you maintain the "noun uses-a noun" and "noun has-a noun" relationships and do not create "noun-verb" relationships.

Next we need to come up with as many of the *uses-a* and *has-a* relationships as we can. The easiest way to do this is, for each class, to think about what classes it uses directly or indirectly. Direct relationships become connected classes in the uses-a relationship diagrams, while indirect relationships usually have another class between them on the diagrams.

Here are some of the *uses-a* relationships that make sense in this design:

A `OutputAtFrequencyTest` *uses-a* `MaxValMeasurement`.

A `OutputAtFrequencyTest` *uses-a* `ReadAtFreqMeasurement`.

In order for the `OutputAtFrequencyTest` to test the output voltage and load current at ω_0, ω_1, and ω_2, it must first determine the output voltage and load current at ω_0 (`MaxValMeasurement`), then determine the output voltage and load current at other frequencies (`ReadAtFreqMeasurement`), namely ω_1 and ω_2.

A `MaxValMeasurement` *uses-a* `FrequencyMeasurement`.

A `MaxValMeasurement` *uses-a* `ReadAtFreqMeasurement`.

In order for the `MaxValMeasurement` to determine the output voltage and load current at ω_0, it must first determine what ω_0 is (`FrequencyMeasurement`), then it must determine the voltage at that frequency (`ReadAtFreqMeasurement`).

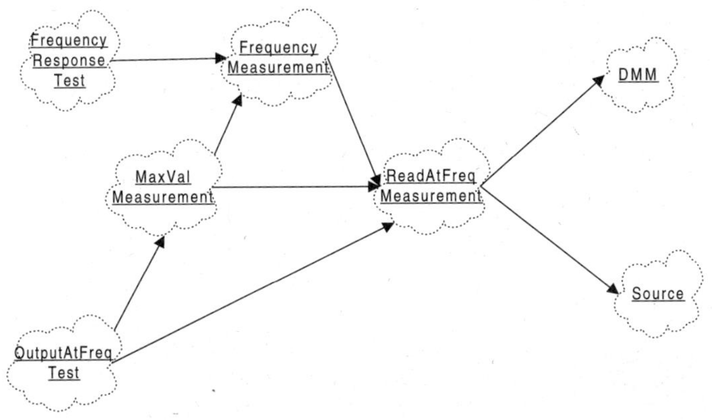

Figure 8-5: First Pass Uses-A Relationships

Figure 8-5 shows the uses-a relationships we have created up until this point. Notice that the diagram basically shows "flow of relationships" to be from left to right. While this is not necessary, it tends to make the diagram more readable.

What is missing from this figure? Well, look back at our list of classes. Are there any classes that are in our system that are not presented on this graph? While not everything needs to be represented on this diagram, missing classes can be viewed as suspect.

The following derived classes are present on our inheritance tree diagram (Figure 8-3), but not in Figure 8-5:

- `IOIntf`
- `DUT`
- `TestStation`
- `Switch`

The following base classes are present on our inheritance tree diagram, but not in Figure 8-5:

- `Instrument`
- `Device`
- `Object`
- `Test`

- `Measurement`

There are some obvious relationships that come from this information, when combined with previous relationships:

A `Instrument` *uses-a* `IOIntf`

A `DMM` *uses-a* `IOIntf`

A `Source` *uses-a* `IOIntf`

A `Switch` *uses-a* `IOIntf`

A `DMM` *uses-a* `Switch`

Adding these relationships, we get Figure 8-6.

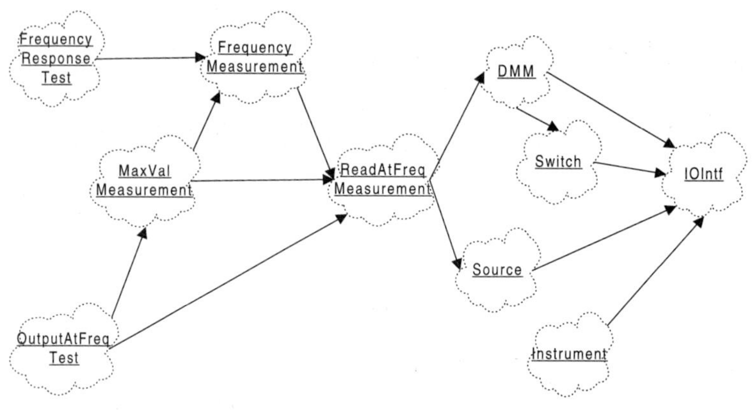

Figure 8-6: Second Pass Uses-A Relationships

There are some things to observe about Figure 8-6:

1. The class `Instrument` is the first base class shown in this diagram. Since three classes on this diagram (`Source`, `Switch`, and `DMM`) all derive from `Instrument`, it would be nice to show that derivation on this diagram. Since this relationship is a *is-a* relationship instead of a *uses-a* relationship, we will use a different type of arrow to differentiate it from the *uses-a* relationships.

2. All classes that derive from `Instrument` (`Source`, `Switch`, and `DMM`) have a *uses-a* relationship with `IOIntf`, including `Instrument` itself. This implies that we can show just the *uses-a* relationship from `Instrument` to `IOIntf`, and all the other three derived classes (`Source`, `Switch`, and `DMM`) can inherit the *uses-a* relationship from `Instrument`.

We also do not have relationships for the derived classes `DUT` and `TestStation`. How should these classes interact with the rest of the system? Actually, there are probably many different acceptable ways, but let us try this out:

A `TestStation` *uses-a* `DUT`.

A `TestStation` *uses-a* `DMM`.

A `TestStation` *uses-a* `Source`.

A `TestStation` *uses-a* `FrequencyResponseTest`.

A `TestStation` *uses-a* `OutputAtFrequencyTest`.

This is an interesting set of relationships. We choose this set for the following reasons:

1. The role of the `TestStation` in this system is to control the entire testing process. This means connecting a **DUT** (both physically and logically, in all likelihood) to the test station. Therefore the `TestStation` class *uses-a* `DUT`.

2. The `TestStation`, once it has connected the `DUT`, is responsible for creating and running the individual tests. Therefore, the `TestStation` *uses-a* `FrequencyResponseTest` and an `OutputAtFrequencyTest`.

3. While the tests (and the measurements they depend on) must change as the `DUT` is changed (the measurement values and therefore the test results are per-`DUT`), the instrumentation itself does not change. Therefore the `TestStation` must also *use* the `DMM` and `Source` so that, when a new `DUT` is inserted into the system, the new tests can be connected to the instrumentation. Therefore, the `TestStation` *uses-a* `DMM` and a `Source`.

Figure 8-7 shows these changes inserted in the *uses-a* relationship diagram.

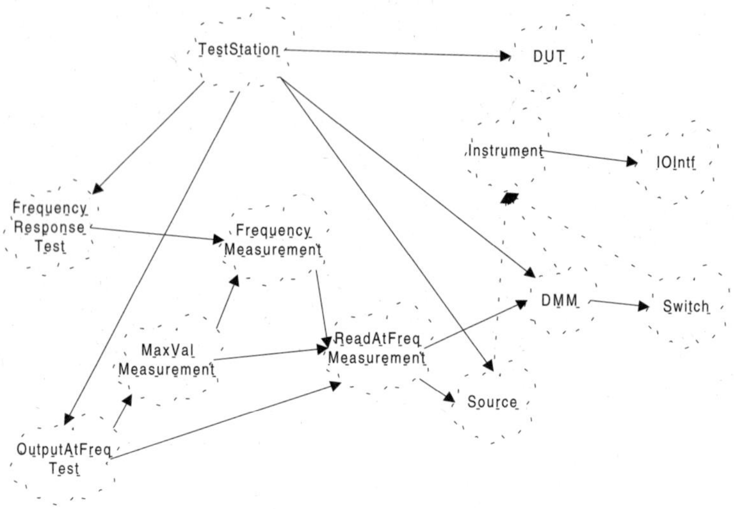

Figure 8-7: Third Pass Uses-A Relationships

This diagram is starting to get complicated. Sometimes it is not possible or practical to put all *uses-a* relationships on one diagram. However, we probably have not gotten to this point yet with our diagram.

Let us look at Figure 8-7 some more. There is still an interesting complexity presented on this diagram. This complexity is the `TestStation` class. It has a relationship with each and every test in the system. What if we add new tests? We need to update `TestStation` to show these new tests. How can we accomplish this? The answer is quite simple, we will have `TestStation` simply *use* a list of `Tests`. There is no reason why `TestStation` needs to know anything about the particular tests it runs, only if they pass or fail. To accomplish this, we will change the `TestStation` relationships with the tests to one simple one:

A `TestStation` *uses-many* **Test**s.

This, of course, is the same as a *uses-a* relationship. We will put `Test` in this diagram in the same way that we inserted `Instrument`.

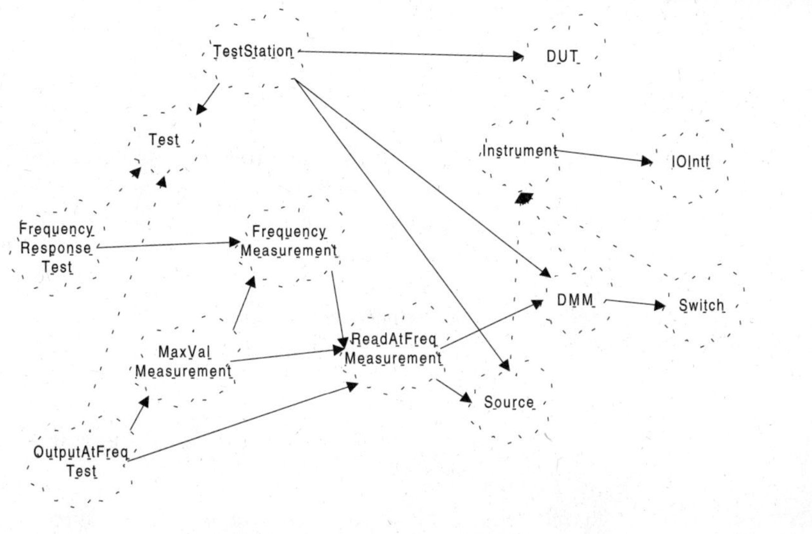

Figure 8-8: Final Uses-A Relationships

Notice that we did not make the same change for the `Instrument`'s relationships with `TestStation`, as we did with the `Test`'s relationships with `TestStation`. This is because, while the `TestStation` should not necessarily have any knowledge about the particulars of the `Tests` that it runs, it probably should have knowledge of the individual `Instrument`'s in the system. This, of course, is a fairly arbitrary decision at this point. However, later you will see the advantages of this decision.

Figure 8-8 is our final attempt at the *uses-a* diagram. Again, just like the instantiation diagram, we may need to update this as we continue our design.

Define Data Needs Within Each Class

Next, we need to decide what data is needed within each of our classes. Let us look at each class, one by one, and see what data is needed for that class. We will not discuss every class, or go into significant details, as this will be discussed in more detail in later chapters.

`Instrument`

The `Instrument` class needs to have a pointer to the `IOIntf` instance that is used to communicate with the real instrument. This pointer must be a non-static member of

`Instrument` class, since potentially different `Instrument` instances can point to different `IOIntf` instances.

Are there other data elements needed that are common to all instruments? How about the power-on status? How about the ready state? These are all possibilities for state variables needed within the `Instrument` class. We will stop here for now. As we do the more detailed design, we will need to decide once and for all what, if any, of these things will be used within our `Instrument` class. Chapter 10 discusses implementation of the `Instrument` class and its derivatives in more detail.

Remember, information stored in the `Instrument` class is inherited by each of the specific instrument classes that derive from `Instrument`, namely `DMM`, `Source`, and `Switch`.

IOIntf

The `IOIntf` class will need data that refers to the state of the interface control hardware (HP-IB, VXI, etc.), the address of the instrument that this instance of `IOIntf` is communicating with, the locking state of this device or interface, and so forth. Chapter 9 discusses implementation of generic `IOIntf` classes in substantially more detail.

TestStation

The `TestStation` has a fair amount of data associated with it:

- A pointer to the `DUT`. The `TestStation` uses the `DUT` characteristics to decide what tests need to be run on this device.
- A list of `Test` objects, one for each test that needs to be run on this `DUT`.
- A pointer to the `DMM`. This is used by the `TestStation` when a request is made to talk to the `DMM`. This request will probably be made by one of the `Measurement` objects, since they need the `DMM` to perform their tests.
- A pointer to the `Source`. This is used by the `TestStation` when a request is made to talk to the `Source`. This request will probably be made by one of the `Measurement` objects, since they need the `DMM` to perform their tests.

DUT

The `DUT` will need a flag telling its status. The flag should be allowed to contain one of three values:

- Untested -- this `DUT` has yet to be tested.
- Passed -- this `DUT` has passed all tests.

- Failed -- this `DUT` has failed one or more tests.

In addition, information as to why the `DUT` has failed may be needed. Tracking information, failure analysis data, and so forth may be useful in determining why a given `DUT` failed. Finally, a reference number that is used to physically identify the **DUT** will make correlating test data with the actual `DUT` possible. This reference number could be a serial number, or a barcode (UPC) symbol.

DMM

The `DMM` itself will have variables that track the state of the `DMM` itself, such as:

- Setting -- DC Volts, AC Volts, DC Current, etc.
- Range -- 2V, 20V, 200V, etc.
- Error values, failure modes, etc.

The exact details could vary depending on which `DMM` is chosen.

> **Virtual Instrument.** It is possible that rather than having a DMM, we have a voltmeter and an ammeter. In this case, the `DMM` class could be a pseudo instrument that would not talk to any real instrument. Instead, it would have pointers to a `Voltmeter` and an `Ammeter` class, which would communicate with the real instruments. In this case, the `DMM` class would be an example of a *Virtual Instrument.*

Source

The `Source` will have variables, similar to the `DMM`, that track the state of the real, physical `Source` itself. Examples include:

- Function -- sine wave, square wave, etc.
- Frequency -- 200Hz, 2000Hz, etc.
- Amplitude -- 4.2V, 10V, 25V
- Error values, failure modes, etc.

Switch

The `Switch` card would contain variables showing the state of all the switch elements in the array. When a request is made to change the switch to a different state, the new state could be compared to the old state, and only the appropriate changes need be communicated to the switch card itself.

Test

The Test class itself will probably have a state variable showing the status of this test:

- Not Run Yet -- This test has not yet been run on this DUT.
- Passed -- This test has passed with the given DUT.
- Failed -- This test failed with the given DUT.

In addition, information as to why a given DUT has passed or failed may be stored.

Remember, the data stored in the Test class is inherited by each of the specific tests, namely OutputAtFrequencyTest and FrequencyResponseTest.

OutputAtFrequencyTest

This test needs a MaxValMeasurement object and a ReadAtFreqMeasurement object. It may need other data, depending on how the test is implemented.

MaxValMeasurement

This measurement needs a FrequencyMeasurement object and a ReadAtFrequencyMeasurement object in order to implement this measurement.

ReadAtFreqMeasurement

This measurement needs a pointer to the DUT and the Source in order to implement its measurement. It acquires this by asking the TestStation for a pointer to them.

Object

Object is an interesting class. Remember we inserted it more to make the inheritance tree a single tree instead of multiple trees. Now that we have it, what good is it? Here is one practical use for it:

> During the course of the execution of a test or measurement in this system, an element in the system (Test, Measurement, Instrument, etc.) may need to communicate with the TestStation. This may be needed for many reasons, but in our test system, one use immediately comes to mind. How does a Measurement, such as ReadAtFrequencyMeasurement, get a pointer to the Instruments, such as the DMM? The answer can be via

the `TestStation`, since the `TestStation` maintains a relationship to each instrument in the system.

In order to talk to the `TestStation`, each element in the system needs a pointer to `TestStation`. Since all elements in the test system derive from `Object`, `Object` seems like the natural spot to put this pointer. That way, every class that derives from `Object` (which is every class) will have a pointer to the `TestStation` for it to use. This creates a *uses-a* relationship between `Object` and `TestStation`, which can be shown on our *uses-a* diagram.

Define Class Interfaces

Now, we need to decide the external interface to our classes. We will look at each class, one by one, and see what interface is needed. We will not discuss every class, or go into significant details, as this will be discussed in more detail in later chapters.

Instrument

Depending on how we implement the `Instrument` class, we may need methods to perform the following actions:

- `IsOffLine` -- Is this instrument turned off or is it off line and unavailable?
- `IsReady` -- Is this instrument ready to perform a measurement, or is it in the process of performing a measurement or performing some action?

As we do the more detailed design, we can change this interface as necessary, finalize this list, and create a syntax for these calls. Chapter 10 discusses implementation of the `Instrument` class and its derivatives in more detail.

Remember, methods implemented in the `Instrument` class are inherited by each of the specific instrument classes that derive from `Instrument`, namely `DMM`, `Source`, and `Switch`.

IOIntf

The `IOIntf` class will need methods for communicating to the real physical instruments themselves. Methods such as the following may be needed:

- `write/read` -- Read and write data to/from the given instrument.
- `printf/scanf` -- Format data and send to/from the given instrument.
- `readStatus` -- Read the status of the given instrument.

- `trigger` -- Send a trigger command to an instrument.
- `peek/poke` -- Directly talk to I/O registers on the instrument.
- `lock/unlock` -- Lock and unlock this interface or instrument.
- interrupts -- Handle interrupts received from the instrument, such as command complete, error occurred, and so forth.

Chapter 9 discusses implementation of generic `IOIntf` classes in substantially more detail.

TestStation

The `TestStation` will need some main entry points for controlling the system:

- `InitializeSystem` -- Initialize the entire system.
- `ConnectDUT` -- Connect a DUT to the test system, and create the `Test` objects needed to talk to it.
- `DisconnectDUT` -- Disconnect the DUT from the test system.
- `TestDUT` -- Run all tests available on the installed DUT.

In addition, Other `Objects` in the system need to talk to the `TestStation` to perform actions, some of the methods needed are:

- `GetDMM` -- Get a pointer to the `DMM`.
- `GetSource` -- Get a pointer to the `Source`.
- `LogResults` -- Log the results of a test run.
- `IdentifyDUT` -- Get the identification number of this `DUT`.

DUT

The `DUT` will need methods to perform the following actions:

- `GetStatus` -- Get the test status of this `DUT` (passed, failed, untested).
- `Passed` -- Mark this `DUT` as having passed all tests.
- `Failed` -- Mark this `DUT` as having failed at least one test.
- `GetIdentifier` -- Get the serial number, or barcode number for this `DUT`.
- `StoreResults` -- Store the detailed test results for later analysis.
- `GetResults` -- Retrieve the detailed test results for analysis.

DMM

The `DMM` will need methods to perform actions such as the following:

- `MeasureACVolts` -- Measure the AC Voltage using the given range from the specified `DUT` pins. This routine will set up the `DMM`, set the switch card to the appropriate settings, and perform the measurement.
- `MeasureACCurrent` -- Measure the AC Current using the given range from the specified `DUT` pins.

Source

The `Source` will need methods to perform actions such as the following:

- `EnableSource` -- Enable the output of the source to the input of the `DUT`.
- `DisableSource` -- Disable the output of the source.
- `SetSineSource` -- Set the source to generate a sine wave of the specified amplitude at the specified frequency.

Switch

The `Switch` will need to specify which `DUT` output pins should be connected to which `DMM` input pins. In addition, it may need to specify which `DUT` input pins should be connected to which `Source` output pins.

Test

The `Test` class will probably have methods such as the following:

- `HasTestRun` -- Has this test been run on this `DUT` yet?
- `RunTest` -- Run this test on this `DUT`, and return the results.
- `GetResults` -- If a test has already been run on this `DUT`, return the results.

Measurement

The `Measurement` class will need methods such as:

- `HasMeasurementBeenDone` -- Has this measurement been performed on this `DUT` yet?
- `DoMeasurement` -- Do the measurement on this `DUT`.
- `GetResult` -- Return the results of the measurement.

The `GetResult` is an odd one. If all the measurements in the system return data of the same format (such as doubles, etc.), then we can probably have a generic `GetResult` method in the `Measurement` class. If, however, each measurement needs a different type of data format for the result, then we probably should not implement `GetResult()`

here, but in each of the specific `Measurement` classes (such as `ReadAtFrequencyMeasurement`, etc.). We will need to make this decision later, as we get more information. Specifically, we will discuss this in Chapter 11.

`Object`

`Object` probably does not need an external interface. The only data it contains (a pointer to the `TestStation`), is only used internally and needs no external interface.

A possible method needed within `Object` is a `log` method. Since all classes derive from `Object`, a `log` method implemented in `Object` will be available for use within all other classes.

Instantiation

Now, we must create our instantiation diagram. The instantiation diagram will look like a further qualified version of the *uses-a* diagram. It will contain an oval for each instance of each class used in the system.

To create the instantiation diagram, start with the *uses-a* diagram, then determine how individual classes will be instantiated. For our system, we will try the following:

1. We will have exactly one `TestSystem` in our system.
2. We will have several `DUT`s in our system, each ready to be tested. However, only one of them at a time will be associated with the `TestSystem`.
3. We will have one `DMM`, one `Source`, and one `Switch` in our system.
4. When we install our `DUT` in the `TestSystem`, we will have the `TestSystem` create one each of the `Tests` that will be run on that `DUT`.
5. When each `Test` gets instantiated, it will instantiate all the necessary `Measurements` it needs to perform its job.
6. The `Measurements` will get a pointer to the `Instruments` by talking to the `TestSystem`.

Each object oriented design will have its own set of instantiation rules. Even for this test system, a different design could have different instantiation rules. Given this list of instantiation rules, we can create our instantiation diagram. It is shown in Figure 8-9.

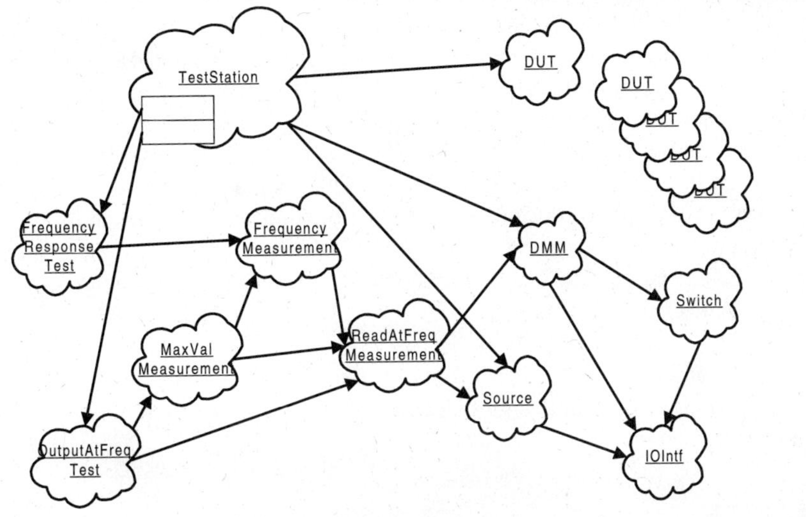

Figure 8-9: Instantiation Diagram

What if...

What if, for performance reasons, we want to test multiple DUTs at the same time? Assume we have additional `DMM`s, `Switch`es, and `Source`s in our system.

There are two ways we could accomplish this without fundamentally changing our design:

1. **Add more `TestSystem` instances.** Each `TestSystem` instance would have a `DMM`, a `Switch`, and a `Source`. Also, each `TestSystem` would test a different `DUT` simultaneously.

2. **Enhance the one `TestSystem` instance.** Alternatively, we could still have one `TestSystem` that knew how to manage multiple `DUT`s and multiple sets of instruments. It could instantiate a new array of `Test`s for each `DUT`, and associate a set of instrumentation to each `Test` array.

The second alternative to our instantiation design is more complicated than the first and requires changes to `TestSystem`, but has some other advantages. Let us say, for example, that we have multiple `DMM`s, but a fewer number of `Source`s. Also, we have a single switch array that lets us connect any `DMM` and any `Source` to one of several different `DUT`s. Now, it is possible to build the test system in such a way that the

`TestSystem` class could execute several tests at the same time. Then, when a given measurement was needed, a `DMM` and `Source` could be assigned to the measurement and the `Switch` could be set as appropriate. With this mechanism, the `TestSystem` could be made more intelligent to determine system needs. If two `Measurements` for two different `DUT`s need the same `Source` setting, then both `Measurements` could share a `Source`, assuming of course, the source could be connected to the multiple DUTs without causing interference between the DUTs. This is an advanced mechanism that becomes fairly straightforward to implement, without dramatic changes to the `Measurements`, `Tests`, or `Instruments`. This is an example of how a good object oriented design can be used to make fairly complex changes to the behavior of a system with fairly simple changes.

Doing this type of what-if analysis is often useful at this stage in the design. Often, it can uncover shortcomings in your design that can be corrected now much more easily than they can later in the construction process.

Summary

This chapter showed an example high-level design of a typical T&M test system. The test system designed is the same system we built using traditional procedural programming techniques back in Chapter 4. The next several chapters discuss the more detailed design and construction of various components in this test system.

The completed high-level design is contained in the following locations in this chapter:

Table 8-2: Design Elements

Design Element	Location
Inheritance Tree	Figure 8-3
Uses-A Diagram	Figure 8-8
Data Needs	Pages 15 through 19
Class Interface	Pages 19 through 22
Instantiation Diagram	Figure 8-9

Exercises

Exercise 8-1. What other items in the T&M application designed in this chapter could become Classes? Why would these things make good classes?

Exercise 8-2. In the design in this chapter, we decided not to make bandwidth a class. What are the pros and cons with making bandwidth a class?

Exercise 8-3. We decided to make the `DUT` into a class in our system. What are the pro's and con's with making `DUT` a class?

Exercise 8-4. If we did not make `DUT` a class, how could we deal with issues of logging test results?

Exercise 8-5. What are some of the advantages and disadvantages of making `Object` a class in our inheritance hierarchy?

Exercise 8-6.What are some of the advantages and disadvantages of making `Device` a class in our inheritance hierarchy?

Exercise 8-7. What are some of the problems with the inheritance tree shown in Figure 8-3 and what would you do to improve this hierarchy?

Exercise 8-8. Philosophically, what is the difference between "X *uses-a* Y-Measurement," and "X Measures Y"? How would these two statements differ in an object oriented design?

Exercise 8-9. Discuss the issues associated with `MaxValMeasurement` and `FrequencyMeasurement` both using a `ReadAtFrequencyMeasurement`, especially since `MaxValMeasurement` uses a `FrequencyMesurement`? How can these be solved in the instantiation design phase? *Hint*: How do you avoid having more than one `ReadAtFrequencyMeasurement` for a given DUT, and therefore have the measurement performed more than one time?

Exercise 8-10. Does the problem in Exercise 8-9 occur with any other classes/objects in our design? How might we solve the problem in these cases too?

Exercise 8-11. Is there an effective way to show all three of our design diagrams (inheritance, uses-a, and instantiation) in a single diagram? What are the advantages and disadvantages of doing this?

Exercise 8-12. How does our design change if we do not use a `DMM`, but instead use a separate voltmeter and ammeter? What is the impact on the rest of our system?

Exercise 8-13. Describe the changes needed to our design in order to support multiple `DUT`s by using the "multiple `TestStation`" approach.

Exercise 8-14. Describe the changes needed to `TestStation` in order for it to support multiple `DUT`s with multiple instrumentation using the "single `TestStation`/multiple `DUT`" approach described in this chapter.

Exercise 8-15. Discuss design issues associated with supporting testing multiple `DUT`s with fewer test instruments. How can test instrumentation be shared in testing multiple `DUT`s?

9. Building an Instrument I/O Class

This chapter describes the object oriented design and construction of a generic instrument I/O class. This class provides the functionality needed to communicate with test instrumentation in a generic object oriented way.

Topics Covered:

`IOIntf` Class Definition

Subclasses Needed

Adding C++ Interface to VISA

I/O Class Inheritance

I/O Class Instantiation

Data Needs

Error Handling

I/O Class Implementation

In Chapter 3, we discussed software needs for test and measurement systems. One of the software needs we discussed was I/O software, which is used to control interface hardware that connects the computer to the test instrumentation. We discussed two different I/O software products available, SICL, and VISA. While both of these packages provide a variety of options and mechanisms to control test instrumentation, neither of them provides a C++ object oriented interface for I/O control. This chapter describes the creation and implementation of such an interface. We will build this class interface on top of the existing VISA I/O interface. This chapter assumes familiarity with this I/O library. If you are not familiar with this library, a copy of the specification may be obtained from the VXI*plug&play* Systems Alliance or from Hewlett-Packard.

We will begin this chapter with a high-level design of an instrument control class, then we will finalize this design and describe the implementation of this interface.

High-Level Design

In Chapter 8, we discussed the object oriented design of a complete T&M system. One of the components of this design was an `IOIntf` class. We will use this as the starting point for the design of our interface, but several questions remain in the implementation of this class:

1. Is this the only class needed for this interface, or do we need additional classes?

2. How do the `IOIntf` classes interact with each other?

3. How do we instantiate `IOIntf` classes? What does an instance of an `IOIntf` class correspond to?

4. Do we need any supporting classes?

5. How do we handle data being sent to and from the I/O system? How do we convert data from internal formats to formats that are typically used in T&M instrumentation?

Defining Classes

Let us start with the first question, since the answer to that affects the answers to several other questions. Let us brainstorm potential classes:

- We could have a separate class for each type of instrument.

  This is not appropriate at this layer since the `IOIntf` layer should be able to communicate with any instrumentation, and therefore not have any instrument specifics embedded. This is best left for the `Instrument` class, which is also included in our sample T&M system design.

- We could have a separate class for each type of `IOIntf` supported (GPIB, VXI, RS-232, etc.).

  This allows us to have functionality specific to each type of interface (such as peek/poke for VXI, etc.).

- We could have one `IOIntf` class only, and provide all functionality through this class.

  This allows us to have functionality that is independent of interface type, which allows a level of abstraction away from the hardware. This level of abstraction is also supported by both VISA and SICL, so this independence has some value.

- We could have one `IOIntf` class as a generic base class, then provide sub-classes for each interface type supported (`GPIBIOIntf` for GPIB interfaces, `VXIIOIntf` for VXI interfaces, and `AsrlIOIntf` for RS-232 interfaces).

  This allows us to have generic functionality in `IOIntf`, and interface-specific functionality in the sub-classes.

We decide on the latter structure.

Inheritance Tree

Using the classes described above, we create an inheritance tree that looks as shown in Figure 9-1.

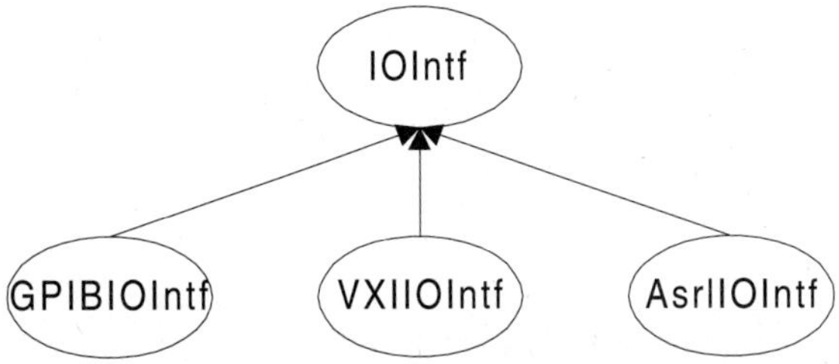

Figure 9-1: `IOIntf` Inheritance Diagram

Operations common to any interface (such as write or read) will be provided in the `IOIntf` class, while operations specific to GPIB (such as `passControl`) will be provided in `GPIBIOIntf`, operations specific to VXI (such as `peek/poke`) will be provided in `VXIIOIntf`, and operations specific to RS-232 (such as `setBAUDrate`) will be provided in `AsrlIOIntf`.

Instantiation

Next, we need to decide how the `IOIntf` class and its derivatives are to be instantiated. Three choices come immediately to mind:

1. Instantiate one instance of the class per interface in the system. If there is one GPIB card and one RS-232 port, then there would be one instance of `GPIBIOIntf` and one instance of `AsrlIOIntf`.

2. Instantiate one instance of the class per device in the system. If you have three GPIB instruments, an RS-232 instrument, and 4 VXI instruments, you would have three instances of `GPIBIOIntf`, one instance of `AsrlIOIntf`, and four instances of `VXIIOIntf`.

3. Instantiate one instance of the class per session to a device. This is slightly different than #2. It is possible to have a session to fewer than all of the

instruments, and it is possible to have multiple sessions to the same instrument.

We choose option #3. This option allows us to easily instantiate objects and the objects will have a one-to-one correspondence with open sessions in either of the underlying I/O layers (SICL or VISA). The advantages of #2, that is being able to have complete control over who and how access to a device is provided, is not important in this layer, as the locking model of the underlying I/O layers provides this control. The same can be said for option #1.

Therefore, the creation of an instance of an `IOIntf` (or one of its derivatives) corresponds to the opening of an I/O session, and the destruction of an instance of an `IOIntf` corresponds to the closing of an I/O session.

Class Interface

There are some obvious interfaces that a user would expect from an instrument I/O class:

- Write raw data to an instrument.
- Read raw data from an instrument.
- Read status information from an instrument.
- Trigger an instrument to perform some action.
- Clear an instrument.

There are others that are interface-specific:

- Peek/poke/block-copy from memory (VXI).
- Set BAUD rate, parity, stop bits, etc. (RS-232).
- Fire a TTL trigger line (VXI).

There are others that may be needed for more advanced applications:

- Set a trigger protocol for TTL trigger lines (VXI).
- Handle modem control and status lines (RS-232).
- Send command bytes to the bus (GPIB).
- Send data to/from commander.
- Process service requests from an instrument.

In addition, methods are needed to:

- Locate devices
- Create/destroy sessions

- Format Data to/from the internal computer format and the instrument's format
- Set time-outs.

Design Details

Next, we will transform the high-level design discussed in the previous section into C++ header files, then we will fill in the details missing. For starters, let us look at the basic class hierarchy:

```
class IOIntf {
};

class GPIBIOIntf : public IOIntf {
};

class VXIIOIntf : public IOIntf {
};

class AsrlIOIntf : public IOIntf {
};
```

Listing 9-1: Basic Class Hierarchy

Now, let's create method prototypes for each of the basic interfaces described in the last section:

- Write raw data to an instrument.

```
void write(char *data,long dataLen,int end);
```
[1]

- Read raw data from an instrument.

```
void read(char *data,long maxDataLen,long
*actualLen);
```

- Read status information from an instrument.

```
void readSTB(unsigned char *stb);
```

---

[1] Errors will be returned using the C++ exception handling mechanism, which will be discussed later.

- Trigger an instrument to perform some action.

```
void trigger();
```

- Clear an instrument.

```
void clear();
```

And, the interface-specific functionality:

- Peek/poke/blockcopy from memory (VXI).

```
void poke16(
        unsigned short data16,
        int space,
        unsigned long address
        );[2]
void peek16(
        int space,
        unsigned long address,
        unsigned short *data16
        );
void blockCopy(
        int space,
        unsigned long address,
        void *localData,
        int increment,
        int direction,
        int size,
        long count
        );[3]
...
```

- Set BAUD rate, parity, stop bits, etc. (RS-232).

```
void setBaud(int baud); // baud is bits/sec
void setParity(int parity);//0=none,1=odd,2=even,etc.
void setStop(int stop); //10=1bit,15=1.5bits,20=2bits
```

---

[2] There are other peek/poke functions needed, 8 bit, 16 bit, 32 bit, and blockcopy. This is just a representation. The `space` parameter is 16, 24, or 32 for representing the device's memory in A16, A24, or A32 space. The `address` parameter is offset in the given address space relative to the location of the device's memory in that address space.

[3] `localData` is the local memory to transfer data to/from. `increment` is 0 for VXI FIFOs and 1 is for VXI block copy. `direction` is 0 for reading from VXI, 1 for writing to VXI. `size` is 8 for 8-bit, 16 for 16-bit and 32 for 32-bit transfers. `Count` is number of blocks (8, 16, or 32 bit values) to transfer.

- Fire a TTL trigger line (VXI).

```
void ttlTrigFire(int trigLine); //0=TTL0,1=TTL1,etc.
```

We will not discuss here the features described above for advanced applications. Putting this information into the class structure, we have the following:

```
class IOIntf {
   public:
      void write(char *data,long dataLen,int end);
      void read(char *data,
                   long maxDataLen,
                   long *actualLen);
      void readSTB(unsigned char *stb);
      void trigger();
      void clear();
};

class GPIBIOIntf : public IOIntf {
   // Nothing in basic is GPIB Specific
};


class VXIIOIntf : public IOIntf {
   public:
      void poke16(
                unsigned short data16,
                int space,
                unsigned long address
                 );
      void peek16(
                int space,
                unsigned long address,
                unsigned short *data16
                );
      void blockCopy(
                int space,
                unsigned long address,
                void *localData,
                int increment,
                int direction,
                int size,
                long count
                );
      void ttlTrigFire(int trigLine);
};

class AsrlIOIntf : public IOIntf {
   public:
      void setBaud(int baud);
      void setParity(int parity);
      void setStop(int stop);
};
```

Listing 9-2: Classes With Basic Methods Added

Constructors and Destructor

Next, we need to create constructors and destructor for each of the classes to perform the necessary work to create and destroy sessions. Since the destructor is the easiest, we will show it first. We will define a public destructor for each of the interface classes:

```
class IOIntf {
    ...
    public:
        virtual ~IOIntf();
    ...
};

class GPIBIOIntf : public IOIntf {
    ...
    public:
        virtual ~GPIBIOIntf();
    ...
};

class VXIIOIntf  : public IOIntf {
    ...
    public:
        virtual ~VXIIOIntf();
    ...
};

class AsrlIOIntf : public IOIntf {
    ...
    public:
        virtual ~AsrlIOIntf();
    ...
};
```

Listing 9-3: Destructors

Constructors are more complicated. First, let us make a basic constructor for `IOIntf`. This constructor requires a string which represents the VISA Resource Name for the instrument you wish to connect to. So, the basic constructor to `IOIntf` looks like this:

```
class IOIntf {
    ...
    public:
        IOIntf(char *visaName);
    ...
};
```

The next constructor allows specifying a regular expression to look for an instrument:

```
class IOIntf {
    ...
    public:
        IOIntf(char *findStr,int cnt);
    ...
};
```

Here, the `findStr` parameter specifies a VISA regular expression to search for a given instrument name. If more than one instrument matches the search string, then `cnt` is used to specify which match to use. If `cnt` is 1, then the first match is used; if `cnt` is 2, then the second match is used, and so forth.[4]

The default constructor is not valid, since we don't know how to open a device without a specification (name) of that device, so we invalidate the default constructor by making it private:

```
class IOIntf {
    ...
    private:
        IOIntf();
    ...
};
```

What about the copy constructor? It would be useful to pass instances of `IOIntf` by value, without creating new VISA sessions. However, this will complicate our implementation.[5] For now we will add it to our class interface, we can always remove it later if it complicates our implementation too greatly.

```
class IOIntf{
    ...
    public:
        IOIntf(const IOIntf&);
    ...
};
```

What about constructors for the inherited classes? Here, we can perform more specialized opening of devices. For example, the `GPIBIOIntf` constructor can specify values representing the device, instead of a VISA string. For example:

---

[4] The VISA regular expression syntax is the syntax used in the `viFindRsrc` routine. See the VISA documentation for more information.

[5] For more information, look at the copy constructor for the `Data` class presented in Chapter 13.

```
class GPIBIOIntf:public IOIntf{
    ...
    public:
        GPIBIOIntf(int intfNum,int primAddr);
        GPIBIOIntf(int intfNum,int primAddr,
                   int secAddr);
    ...
};
```

This constructor allows specifying which GPIB interface to use (`intfNum`), and the primary GPIB address of the device. The second constructor also allows specifying a secondary GPIB address.

For VXI, there are a couple of options:

```
class VXIIOIntf:public IOIntf{
    ...
    public:
        VXIIOIntf(int intfNum,int logAddr);
        VXIIOIntf(int intfNum,int manfID,
                  int model,int cnt);
        VXIIOIntf(int intfNum,int cageNum,
                  int slotNum);
    ...
};
```

The first constructor is similar to the GPIB case, it allows specifying a VXI interface to use (`intfNum`), and the VXI logical address (`logAddr`) of the device. The second constructor is a little more unique. It searches for a given instrument with the specified manufacturer ID (`manfID`) and model code (`model`). If `intfNum` is -1, it looks on all VXI interfaces sequentially. Also, if more than one instance of a given instrument exists, `cnt` will specify which one to open. If `cnt` is 1, the first such instrument found is used; if `cnt` is 2, the second, and so forth. The third constructor allows specifying an instrument by location instead of logical address or identification. The location is specified by a card cage number (`cageNum`) and slot number (`slotNum`).

RS-232 is easy:

```
class AsrlIOIntf:public IOIntf{
    ...
    public:
        AsrlIOIntf(int intfNum);
    ...
};
```

For RS-232, there is only one device per interface, so the `intfNum` is all that is needed.

In addition, for each interface, we need constructors for creating the derived class instances using the VISA resource string (as in the base class). Plus, we need copy constructors for all the subclasses as well. So, the following constructors will exist:

```
class GPIBIOIntf : public IOIntf {
    ...
    public:
        GPIBIOIntf(char *visaName);
        GPIBIOIntf(char *findStr,int cnt);
        GPIBIOIntf(const GPIBIOIntf&);
    ...
};

class VXIIOIntf : public IOIntf {
    ...
    public:
        VXIIOIntf(char *visaName);
        VXIIOIntf(char *findStr,int cnt);
        VXIIOIntf(const VXIIOIntf&);
    ...
};

class AsrlIOIntf : public IOIntf {
    ...
    public:
        AsrlIOIntf(char *visaName);
        AsrlIOIntf(char *findStr,int cnt);
        AsrlIOIntf(const AsrlIOIntf&);
    ...
};
```

In summary, here are the constructors and destructors needed for the classes:

```
class IOIntf {
    private:
        IOIntf();
    public:
        IOIntf(char *visaName);
        IOIntf(char *findStr,int cnt);
        IOIntf(const IOIntf&);
        ~IOIntf();
    ...
};

class GPIBIOIntf : public IOIntf {
    private:
        IOIntf();
    public:
        GPIBIOIntf(int intfNum,int primAddr);
        GPIBIOIntf(int intfNum,int primAddr,
                   int secAddr);
        GPIBIOIntf(char *visaName);
        GPIBIOIntf(char *findStr,int cnt);
        GPIBIOIntf(const GPIBIOIntf&);
        ~GPIBIOIntf();
    ...
};
```

```
class VXIIOIntf  : public IOIntf {
   private:
      IOIntf();
   public:
      VXIIOIntf(int intfNum,int logAddr);
      VXIIOIntf(int intfNum,int manfID,
                int model,int cnt);
      VXIIOIntf(int intfNum,int cageNum,
                int slotNum);
      VXIIOIntf(char *visaName);
      VXIIOIntf(char *findStr,int cnt);
      VXIIOIntf(const VXIIOIntf&);
      ~VXIIOIntf();
   ...
};

class AsrlIOIntf  : public IOIntf {
   private:
      IOIntf();
   public:
      AsrlIOIntf(int intfNum);
      AsrlIOIntf(char *visaName);
      AsrlIOIntf(char *findStr,int cnt);
      AsrlIOIntf(const AsrlIOIntf&);
      ~AsrlIOIntf();
   ...
};
```

Listing 9-4: Constructors and Destructors

Data Needs

The data needs for the IOIntf class is quite simple. Since the IOIntf class simply uses VISA to provide the functionality desired, we need a data element that refers to the VISA session variables used. There are a total of three variables needed:

- devSess -- The session that refers to the VISA session opened to talk to the specified device.
- rmSess -- The session that refers to the VISA Resource Manager session used to open the devSess session. This resource manager session must remain opened as long as the devSess session is opened.
- refCnt -- A pointer to the number of opens that refer to these sessions.

Reference Counting. The refcnt variable is used to refer to the number of instances of the IOIntf class that refer to the given VISA session. Usually, the answer will always be 1. However, when the copy constructor is called, the VISA sessions are copied to a new instance of the IOIntf class. Without the refCnt variable, once one of these two IOIntf sessions is closed, the VISA session would be closed, and the other IOIntf session would refer to an invalid VISA session.

To avoid this, we apply a reference count. The primary constructor sets the reference count to one, when it opens the VISA sessions. When the copy constructor is executed, the reference count is incremented. Now, when the destructor is called, it first decrements the reference count variable. Only when the reference count reaches 0 is the VISA sessions actually closed. Thus, the desired behavior of the copy constructor is maintained.

This is a common technique for handling copy constructors and we use it in other spots within this book. For a complete description of this mechanism, and other issues associated with using reference counts, look at the Signal class presented in Chapter 13.

The following is the class definition needed to implement these variables:

```
class IOIntf {
    ...
    private:
        ViSession devSess;
        ViSession rmSess;
        int *refCnt;
    ...
};
```

The copy constructor will simply copy the variables and increment the refCnt. The other constructors will allocate a refCnt variable, set it to 1, and open the appropriate VISA sessions. The destructor will decrement the refCnt variable and, when it hits 0, deallocate the memory needed for refCnt and close the VISA sessions.

Error Handling

Next, we must decide how errors will be handled. We will use C++'s built-in error handling mechanism to handle errors. When an error occurs, we will *throw* the error, so that the caller may *catch* and handle the error. This allows creating code such as the following to handle errors from the IOIntf class:

```
try {
   IOIntf dmm("VXI0::24::INSTR");

   dmm.write(...);
   dmm.read(...);

}catch (...){
   // Handle errors here
}
```

Error handling is discussed in more detail in Chapter 14. We will leave the detailed error handling design for that chapter.

Complete Interface

The following is the complete interface for our `IOIntf` class and its derivatives:

```
class IOIntfError {
   private:
      ViStatus errorValue;

      IOIntfError();
   public:
      IOIntfError(
                  ViStatus errorValue,
                  ViSession vi,
                  char *routine
                );
      IOIntfError(const IOIntfError&);
      ~IOIntfError();

      ViStatus getErrorValue();
      const char *getErrorString();
      const char *routineName();
};


class IOIntf {
   private:
      // refCnt used for copy constructor
implementation
      int *refCnt;
      // Data variables used for VISA sessions
      ViSession devSess;
      ViSession rmSess;

      // Default constructor is not allowed
      IOIntf();
   public:
      IOIntf(char *visaName);
      IOIntf(char *findStr,int cnt);
      IOIntf(const IOIntf&);
      virtual ~IOIntf();
```

```
        void write(char *data,long dataLen,int end);
        void read(char *data,
                     long maxDataLen,
                     long *actualLen);
        void readSTB(unsigned char *stb);
        void trigger();
        void clear();
};


class GPIBIOIntf : public IOIntf {
    private:
        // Default constructor is not allowed
        GPIBIOIntf();
    public:
        GPIBIOIntf(int intfNum,int primAddr);
        GPIBIOIntf(int intfNum,int primAddr,
                   int secAddr);
        GPIBIOIntf(char *visaName);
        GPIBIOIntf(char *findStr,int cnt);
        GPIBIOIntf(const GPIBIOIntf&);
        virtual ~GPIBIOIntf();
};


class VXIIOIntf : public IOIntf {
    private:
        // Default constructor is not allowed
        VXIIOIntf();
    public:
        VXIIOIntf(int intfNum,int logAddr);
        VXIIOIntf(int intfNum,int manfID,int model,
                  int cnt);
        VXIIOIntf(int intfNum,int cageNum,
                  int slotNum);
        VXIIOIntf(char *visaName);
        VXIIOIntf(char *findStr,int cnt);
        VXIIOIntf(const VXIIOIntf&);
        virtual ~VXIIOIntf();

        void poke16(
                  unsigned short data16,
                  int space,
                  unsigned long address
                   );
        void peek16(
                  int space,
                  unsigned long address,
                  unsigned short *data16
                  );
```

```
          void blockCopy(
                    int space,
                    unsigned long address,
                    void *localData,
                    int increment,
                    int direction,
                    int size,
                    long count
                    );
          void ttlTrigFire(int trigLine);
};


class AsrlIOIntf : public IOIntf {
    private:
          // Default constructor is not allowed
          AsrlIOIntf();
    public:
          AsrlIOIntf(int intfNum);
          AsrlIOIntf(char *visaName);
          AsrlIOIntf(char *findStr,int cnt);
          AsrlIOIntf(const AsrlIOIntf&);
          virtual ~AsrlIOIntf();
          void setBaud(int baud);
          void setParity(int parity);
          void setStop(int stop);
};
```

Listing 9-5: Complete Interface

Implementation

Next, we discuss implementation of portions of the `IOIntf` class. Some of the pieces not discussed here appear as exercises at the end of this chapter.

Constructors

The primary purpose of all the constructors is to:

1. Set up the `refCnt` variable appropriately.
2. Open the VISA resource manager session.
3. Open the appropriate device session.

The primary constructor specifies a VISA resource name to open. This is the simplest constructor. Here is the implementation:

```
IOIntf::IOIntf(char *visaName){
   ViStatus err;

   devSess=VI_NULL; // Invalidate it for destructor
   rmSess=VI_NULL; // Invalidate it for destructor

   // Set up the refCnt variable and set it to 1
   refCnt = new int;
   if(!refCnt)
      throw ...6;
   *refCnt=1;

   // Open the VISA sessions
   err=viOpenDefaultRM(&rmSess);
   if(err<VI_SUCCESS)
      throw ...;
   err=viOpen(rmSess,visaName,VI_NULL,VI_NULL,
               &devSess);
   if(err<VI_SUCCESS)
      throw ...;
}
```

Listing 9-6: Constructor Implementation

The copy constructor is fairly straightforward, it must:

1. Copy the `refCnt` pointer, then increment it by 1.

2. Copy the `rmSess` and `devSess`.

Here is the implementation:

```
IOIntf::IOIntf(const IOIntf& cpy){
   refCnt=cpy.refCnt;
   (*refCnt)++;

   rmSess=cpy.rmSess;
   devSess=cpy.devSess;
}
```

Listing 9-7: Copy Constructor Implementation

---

[6] The throw call is a C++ mechanism for processing and reporting error conditions. It is discussed in more detail in Chapter 14. The complete syntax for the throw call is shown in that Chapter.

Destructor

The destructor must undo the affects of the regular constructors and the copy constructor. It must:

1. Decrement the `refCnt` variable.
2. If `refCnt` is not 0, simply return.
3. Otherwise, free the memory for `refCnt`.
4. Close the device session.
5. Close the resource manager session.

Here is the implementation:

```
IOIntf::~IOIntf(){
    if(refCnt){
        (*refCnt)--;
        if((*refCnt)!=0)
            return;
    }
    // Free up memory and close sessions
    delete refCnt;
    if(devSess!=VI_NULL)
        viClose(devSess);
    if(rmSess!=VI_NULL)
        viClose(rmSess);
}
```

Listing 9-8: Destructor Implementation

Write

The write method simply calls the VISA `viWrite` entry point, with the appropriate device session. The only complexity has to do with the "end" flag. This parameter is an attribute in VISA, so the `viSetAttribute` call must be made first.

```
IOIntf::write(char *data,long dataLen,int end){
    ViStatus err;
    ViUInt32 retCount;

    err=viSetAttribute(devSess,
                        VI_ATTR_SEND_END_EN,
                        end?VI_TRUE:VI_FALSE
                      );
    if(err<VI_SUCCESS)
        throw ...;
    err=viWrite(defSess,data,dataLen,&retCount);
    if(err<VI_SUCCESS)
        throw ...;
}
```

Listing 9-9: Write Method Implementation

We can improve this implementation by only calling `viSetAttirbute` if the END indicator status has changed from the last call. This can be implemented by adding a new data variable to our class:

```
class IOIntf{
    ...
    private:
        ViBoolean endEn;
    ...
};
```

This variable can be initialized in the constructors to the default value of the attribute:

```
endEn=VI_TRUE; // Default value
```

Then we only need to do work if the END indicator state changes. When it changes, we call `viGetattribute` and change the `endEn` variable to match. Here is the new write method implementation:

```
IOIntf::write(char *data,long dataLen,int end){
    ViStatus err;
    ViUInt32 retCount;
    ViBoolean myEndEn;

    myEndEn=end?VI_TRUE:VI_FALSE;

    // See if END indicator changed
    if(myEndEn!=endEn){
        err=viSetAttribute(
                                devSess,
                                VI_ATTR_SEND_END_EN,
                                myEndEn
                              );
        if(err<VI_SUCCESS)
            throw ...;
        endEn=myEndEn;
    }

    err=viWrite(defSess,data,dataLen,&retCount);
    if(err<VI_SUCCESS)
        throw ...;
}
```

Listing 9-10: Alternate Write Method Implementation

Notice that this change was made without changing the public class interface. All that changed was the private class interface and the actual `write` method implementation.

`VXIIOIntf` Constructors

Next, we will show implementation of constructors in a derived class. For example, here is the basic constructor for `VXIIOIntf`. The implementation is very simple, it simply calls the base class `IOIntf` basic constructor:

```
VXIIOIntf::VXIIOIntf(char *visaName)
    : IOIntf(visaName)
{
}
```

Listing 9-11: `VXIIOIntf` Constructor

This routine demonstrates how a constructor can call a base-class constructor and pass a parameter to that base class constructor. In this case, the `VXIIOIntf` constructor uses the `IOIntf` constructor that expects a single "char*" parameter. The parameter it passes to the `IOIntf` constructor is the `visaName`. The actual initialization of the `IOIntf` class variables is performed by the `IOIntf constructor.`

A more interesting version of this constructor is the one that allows specifying which instrument to open by type, instead of by name. This constructor must:

1. Open the resource manager session.
2. Create a search string to use for a `viFindRsrc` call.
3. Call `viFindRsrc`, verify that enough devices were found to satisfy the request (i.e., at least as many as specified in the `cnt` variable).
4. If `cnt` is not 1, then call `viFindNext` enough times until we have the correct match.
5. Open the session to the requested device.

Here is the implementation:

```
VXIIOIntf::VXIIOIntf(
    int intfNum,int manfId,
    int model,int cnt
)
    : IOIntf() // Protected Constructor sets up refCnt
{
    ViStatus err;
    ViFindList fList;
    ViUInt32 fCnt;
    int i;
    char name[VI_FIND_BUFLEN];
    char find[VI_FIND_BUFLEN];

    // Open the resource manager session
    err=viOpenDefaultRM(&rmSess);
    if(err<VI_SUCCESS)
        throw ...;

    // Create a find string for this given device
    // for example:
    //    VXI0?*INSTR  ((VI_ATTR_MANF_ID==0xfff)&&
    //           (VI_ATTR_MODEL_CODE==0x240))
    sprintf(find,
                "VXI%d?*INSTR"
                "((VI_ATTR_MANF_ID==0x%x) &&"
                "(VI_ATTR_MODEL_CODE==0x%x))",
                intfNum,manfId,model);

    // Ok, find all instruments that match that string
    err=viFindRsrc(rmSess,find,&fList,&fCnt,name);
    if(err<VI_SUCCESS)
        throw ...;

    // Make sure we have enough devices
    if(cnt>fCnt)
        throw ..;

    // If we want the first, return it, or keep
    // calling viFindNext until we have the name
    // we want
    for(i=1;i<cnt;++i){
        err=viFindNext(fList,name);
        if(err<VI_SUCCESS)
            throw ...;
    }

    // Close the find list
    viClose(fList);

    // Now, open this resource
    err=viOpen(rmSess,name,VI_NULL,VI_NULL,&devSess);
    if(err<VI_SUCCESS)
        throw ...;
}
```

Listing 9-12: Open by Type `VXIIOIntf` Constructor

The default IOIntf constructor is used to implement VXIIOIntf. This is because at the time the constructor is called, we do not know the address to open yet. As such, we need to use an IOIntf constructor that only sets up refCnt and leaves the opening of the VISA sessions for the derived class. For this we decide to use the IOIntf default constructor. The implementation of this constructor looks like this:

```
IOIntf::IOIntf(){
    // Set up the refCnt variable and set it to 1
    refCnt = new int;
    if(!refCnt)
        throw ...;
    *refCnt=1;

    // These must be set up by derived constructor!
    rmSess=VI_NULL;
    devSess=VI_NULL;
}
```

Listing 9-13: Default IOIntf Constructor

Since we previously said this constructor was not callable by anyone, we made it private so that any attempts to use it would fail. Since we now need this constructor to implement a derived class constructor, but we still do not want to expose it to everyone (because it does only a portion of the work needed for a constructor), we decide to make it protected:

```
class IOIntf{
    ...
    protected:
        IOIntf();
    ...
};
```

AsrlIOIntf setBaud

The setBaud method of AsrlIOIntf is an example interface-specific method. It has a very simple implementation:

```
void AsrlIOIntf::setBaud(int baud){
  ViStatus err;

  err=viSetAttribute(devSess,VI_ATTR_ASRL_BAUD,baud);
  if(err<VI_SUCCESS)
       throw ...;
};
```

Other methods need to be implemented, but will not be presented here.

Summary

This chapter discussed the design and construction of an I/O interface class layered on top of the VISA I/O Library. This design could as easily been built on top of SICL, VISA, or any other I/O library that was available and supported the I/O interfaces desired. This interface class is easily extensible. A more complete implementation is contained on the source disk included with this book. This implementation can be used as is, or modified to meet particular needs.

Exercises

Exercise 9-1. How would you implement the `IOIntf` constructor described by the following definition:

```
IOIntf(char *findStr,int cnt);
```

How does this constructor compare to:

```
VXIIOIntf(int intfNum,int manfId,
          int model,int cnt);
```

Exercise 9-2. Implement the following constructor:

```
VXIIOIntf(int intfNum,int cageNum,
          int slotNum);
```

Exercise 9-3. Implement the following constructor:

```
VXIIOIntf(int intfNum,int logAddr);
```

Exercise 9-4. Implement the destructors for each of the derived classes `GPIBIOIntf`, `VXIIOIntf`, and `AsrlIOIntf`. Are these destructors really needed, or is the destructor for `IOIntf` enough?

Exercise 9-5. What are the pros and cons of making the destructors virtual?

Exercise 9-6. Implement the `VXIIOIntf::ttlTrigFire` method. How can you increase the performance of this method by caching which trigger line was last used?

Exercise 9-7. How can you add time-out support to the `IOIntf` class? What methods will you add? What data elements will you add? What changes will need to be made to the rest of the `IOIntf` class? What about the derived classes?

10. Instrument Classes

In Chapter 8, we discussed the high-level design of our T&M system. We did a preliminary design of the instrumentation class hierarchy within that system. This chapter will take a closer look at that hierarchy. We will finish the design of this section of our T&M system, adding instrumentation specifics where needed.

Topics Covered:

`Instrument` Class OOD

Components of All Instruments

Instrument-Specific Functional Components

OO Design Diagrams

Figure 8-3 contains the inheritance tree of our high-level design. We will take this tree as the starting point for our design. The instrumentation specific portions of this inheritance tree are shown in Figure 10-1.

For the purposes of this chapter, we will focus on only the true instrumentation portion of this hierarchy. In particular, the portion shown in Figure 10-2.

This diagram shows a simple inheritance tree with a base class named `Instrument`, and derived classes for each of the test instruments we will be using, a `DMM`, a `Source`, and a `Switch`. For the remainder of this chapter, we will stick with this inheritance tree.

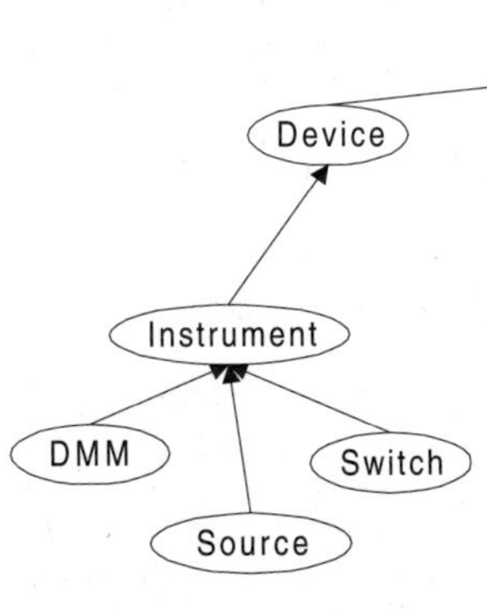

Figure 10-1: Instrument Inheritance Tree

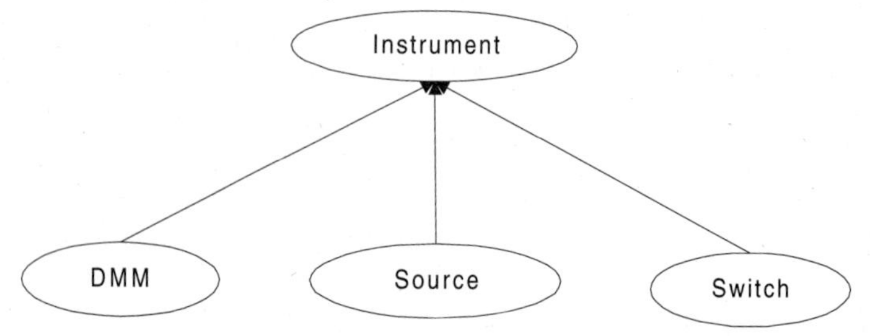

Figure 10-2: Primary Instrument Inheritance

The uses-a diagram for our T&M design was shown in Figure 8-8. The instrumentation specific portions of that are repeated in Figure 10-3.

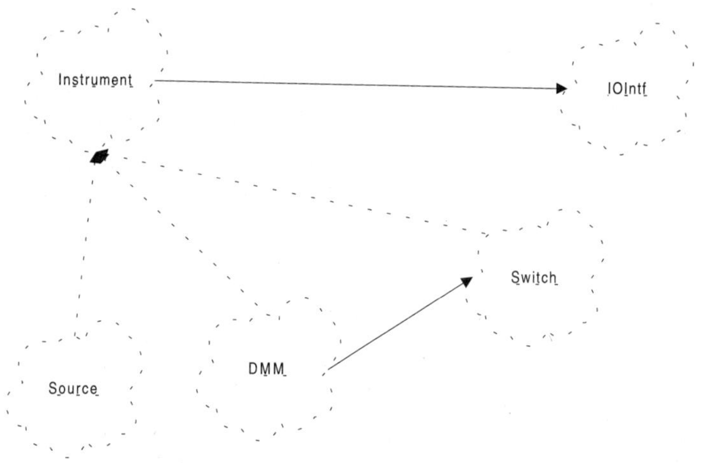

Figure 10-3: Instrumentation Uses-A Relationships

This diagram shows the same inheritance tree presented in Figure 10-2, plus the uses-a relationship between `Instrument` (and, thus, all the derived classes) and `IOIntf`, and the uses-a relationship between the `DMM` and the `Switch` card. The first uses-a (`Instrument` *uses-a* `IOIntf`) is used to communicate between the instrument objects and the real instrumentation hardware. The second uses-a (`DMM` *uses-a* Switch) is used to communicate which `DMM` pins to connect to which DUT pins using the switch card.

The final diagram of significance to our design is the instantiation diagram for our T&M system shown in Figure 8-9. The instrumentation portions of this relationship is shown in Figure 10-4.

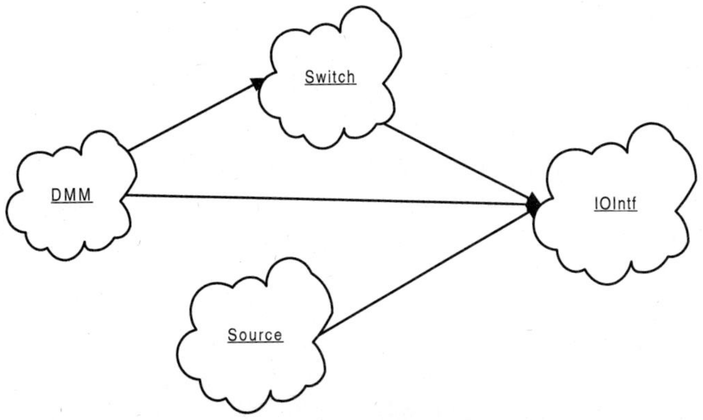

Figure 10-4: Instrumentation Instantiation Relationships

Here, we show one instance of each of our three instruments, each connected to a single instance of the `IOIntf` class. In this chapter, we will assume the `IOIntf` design as discussed in Chapter 9. As you remember from that design, there was one instance of an `IOIntf` object for each device we are using. Therefore, our instrumentation instantiation diagram should be changed to take that into account. Figure 10-5 shows these changes.

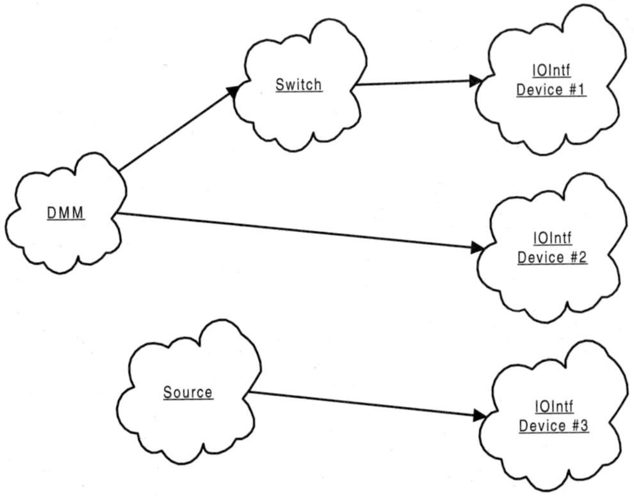

Figure 10-5: Modified Instantiation Relationships

Designing the Base Instrument Class

Let us first talk about building the base `Instrument` class. This is the class that all three of our instruments derive from. This class should contain things that are common to all instruments. Based on our design in Chapter 8, we come up with the following elements:

- **Reference to an `IOIntf` class**. This variable will be filled in with an instance of an appropriate `IOIntf` object that refers to an open session to the appropriate instrument.

  Since the specific type of `IOIntf` that needs to be instantiated (`GPIBIOIntf`, `VXIIOIntf`, etc.) and the actual address of the device we want to talk to is instrument specific, the derived instrument class (`DMM`, `Source`, etc.) will be responsible for creating the `IOIntf` object and filling in this variable. However, since the deletion of all the `IOIntfs` are the same, the base `Instrument` class destructor can do the deletion of this object.

- **Power-on status**. We will implement a method called `isOffLine()` which will always return false in our implementation (i.e., always on-line). Derived classes can implement this method to do more sophisticated status checking, if desired.

- **Ready state**. We will support two mechanisms by which a derived class can indicate whether the device is ready or not. The first way is to have the base class send the IEEE 488.2 *WAI command. The second way is to have the derived class set and reset a state variable in the base class indicating whether the instrument is ready or not.

Our declaration for this class will look something like this:

```
class Instrument {
   private:
      IOIntf *ioIntf;

      bool ready; // Is this device ready?
      bool suppWai; // Use *WAI instead?

      Instrument();
      Instrument(const Instrument&);
   protected:
      // Require a derived class to use
      // this constructor
      Instrument(IOIntf *);
      IOIntf *getIOIntf(); // Access IOIntf instance

      // Idle loop for waitReady()
      virtual void doIdleWork();

      // Touch the ready variables
      void setReady(bool);
      void setSuppWai(bool);
   public:
      virtual ~Instrument();
      virtual bool isOffLine();
      virtual bool isReady();
      virtual void waitReady(); // Wait until ready
};
```

Listing 10-1: Instrument Class Declaration

Listing 10-1 includes all the details mentioned above, plus a few other things. First, it includes a constructor that expects an `IOIntf` pointer that is filled in by the derived class constructor. Second, it includes an access method, `getIOIntf`(), that allows access from derived classes only to the `ioIntf` private variable. Third, it disallows two private constructors (the default constructor and the copy constructor), since these will not be needed. It disables them by making them private. Finally, it includes a public destructor. The implementation of most of these methods is trivial. In fact, many of them can be implemented inline within the class declaration itself:

```
class Instrument {
    private:
        IOIntf *ioIntf;

        bool ready; // Is this device ready?
        bool suppWai; // Use *WAI instead?

        Instrument(){};
        Instrument(const Instrument&){};
    protected:
        // Require a derived class to use
        // this constructor
        Instrument(IOIntf *intf)
            :ioIntf(intf)
        {
            ready=true;
            suppWai=true;
        };
        IOIntf *getIOIntf(){
            return ioIntf;
        };

        // Touch the ready variables
        void setReady(bool val){
            ready=val;
        };
        void setSuppWai(bool val){
            suppWai=val;
        };
    public:
        virtual ~Instrument(){
            delete ioIntf;
        };
        virtual bool isOffLine(){return false;};
        virtual bool isReady();
        virtual void waitReady();
};
```

Listing 10-2: Instrument Class With Inline Methods

All that remains is the basic implementation of the `isReady` and `waitReady` methods:

```
bool Instrument::isReady(){
    if(suppWai){
        int res;
        ioIntf->printf("*OPC?\n");
        ioIntf->scanf("%d%*t",&res);
        return (res!=0);
    }else{
        return ready;
    }
}

void Instrument::waitReady(){
    while(!isReady())
        doIdleWork();
}

void Instrument::doIdleWork(){
    // Do nothing -- we could sleep here instead
}
```

The `waitReady` method simply calls `isReady` in a loop until it returns success. While in the loop, an idle routine is executed that can either do nothing (as the default implementation does), or it can be implemented in a derived class to perform some functionality, such as instrument background tasks necessary to make the instrument ready.

The default `isReady` method sends the IEEE 488.2 `*WAI` command to the instrument. Alternatively, the `isReady` method can return the value of the `ready` class method. This choice depends on the value of the `suppWait` class variable that is set by the derived class. This method can be used as is, or re-implemented in the derived class.

Notice that, by itself, this class is not usable – it must have an instrument-specific class derive from it before it can be used. In the next section, we will discuss the derived classes used for each of our test instrumentation.

Functional Components for a Given Instrument

We have three test instruments in our design, each will correspond to a separate class derived from the `Instrument` base class.

Source

The `Source` class will have:

- state variables that track the state of the physical source itself
- access methods that change the source state based on user needs (source state variables, and real physical source state)

The state variables needed include:

- frequency in Hz
- output amplitude in Volts
- function (sine wave, square wave) -- the source will always be set to a sine wave, so we will not track this physical source state variable in software (it never changes)
- output enabled/disabled

The class declaration now becomes straightforward:

```
class Source:public Instrument {
    private:
        double frequency;
        double amplitude;
        bool outputEnabled;
    public:
        Source();
        ~Source();
        void setFrequency(double freq);
        double getFrequency();
        void setAmplitude(double ampl);
        double getAmplitude();
        bool isOutputEnabled();
        void enable();
        void disable();
};
```

Listing 10-3: Source Class Declaration

Each of the *get* methods can simply access the software state variables, as shown:

```
Source::getFrequency(){
    return frequency;
}
Source::getAmplitude(){
    return amplitude;
}
Source::isOutputEnabled(){
    return outputEnabled;
}
```

The set methods are more complicated. They must not only set the state variable, but also send the appropriate commands to the instrument to change its state. For example:

```
Source::setFrequency(double freq){
    getIOIntf()->printf("SOUR:FREQ %f\n",freq);
    frequency=freq;
}
```

While this is acceptable for a simple implementation, a complete implementation will probably provide error checking, parameter validation, and so forth. For example, is the frequency requested too high or too low for this particular source? How close do you want the actual frequency to be compared to the requested frequency (resolution)? What is the actual frequency? Should we set the frequency variable to the requested frequency or the actual frequency? All of these are valid questions and the answers depend on the design requirements of the particular problem being solved.

The constructor for the Source must instantiate a `IOIntf` object, then set the enable variables in Instrument such that Instrument will send *WAI to implement wait functionality:

```
Source::Source()
    // Instantiate a VXI device at:
    //          VXI0 interface
    //          Logical Address=8
    :Instrument(new VXIIOIntf(0,8))
{
    setSuppWai(true);
}
```

DMM

The DMM is somewhat more complicated. For this instrument we have to track the state of the DMM and the DUT connectivity requirements using the switch card, and perform appropriate measurements.

Here are the state variables we need:

- Setting. Are we set for DC volts, AC volts, or DC current?
- Range. Are we using 2V, 20V, 200V, or what?

In addition, we need a variable that points to the switch card, so that we may update it as necessary before taking the measurement.

Next, we need methods that perform the following measurements:

- Measure AC voltage. Parameters specify range. The setting is updated, if necessary, and the switch card is set to measure the output voltage
- Measure AC current. Parameters specify range. The setting is updated, if necessary, and the switch card is set to measure the output current.

Finally, we need private methods that update the setting and range as appropriate prior to taking a measurement.

Here is the class declaration for DMM:

```
enum DMMSetting {dcV,acV,dcC};
class DMM {
   private:
      DMMSetting setting;
      double range;
      Switch *sw;

      // Private Methods
      setRange(double);
      setSetting(DMMSetting);
   public:
      DMM();
      ~DMM();
      double measVoltAc(double range);
      double measCurrAc(double range);
};
```

Listing 10-4: DMM Class Declaration

This class will not need the `isReady()` or `waitReady()` methods, since the routines `measVoltAc` and `measCurrAc` never return until after the measurement is complete. Therefore, we can tell the Instrument base class that we are always ready. The constructor for DMM looks like:

```
DMM::DMM()
   :Instrument(new VXIIOIntf(0,16))
{
   setSuppWai(false); // Look at ready flag
   setReady(true);    // Ready flag is always true
   sw=???;
}
```

The variable `sw` must be filled in with a pointer to the switch instrument. Since only the DMM uses the switch card, the DMM can instantiate the switch card, if desired. If not, the DMM can query the `TestStation` to get the appropriate switch card and fill it in from that. We will leave this detail out of our design for now. We will look at it again in Chapter 12 as we put all the design pieces together into a working system.

The `measVoltAc` method must make sure the range and setting are correct, then set the switch card appropriately. Finally, it must take the desired measurement:

```
double DMM::measVoltAc(double range){
   double res;

   // Set DMM appropriately
   setRange(range);
   setSetting(acV);

   // Set switch card: measure voltage on DUT output
   sw->setState(swV);
   sw->waitReady(); // Wait until switch stabilizes

   // Do the measurement
   getIOIntf()->printf("MEAS:VOLT:AC?\n");
   getIOIntf()->scanf("%f",&res);
   return res;
}
```

The `setRange` routine will see if the requested range has changed from the current range. If it has, it updates the instrument range as appropriate:

```
void DMM::setRange(double r){
   if(r!=range){
      // Range has changed
      getIOIntf->printf("RANG:VOLT:AC %f\n",r);
      range=r;
   }
}
```

The `setSetting` method is similar.

Switch

The `Switch` class is very different than the `Source` or `DMM`: It makes no measurement and generates no output. All it does is reroute wires in the system by opening and closing switches (either relays or solid-state). One of the odd characteristics of the Switch card is that it can take a while for the switch state to actually change and settle down. So, the `isReady()` and `waitReady()` methods are important.

The class declaration for Switch looks like the following:

```
enum SwitchSetting {swV,swC,unKnown};
class Switch{
   private:
      SwitchSetting setting;
   public:
      Switch();
      ~Switch();
      setState(SwitchSetting set);
};
```

Listing 10-5: Switch Class Declaration

The constructor will simply set a default setting (unknown), then tell the `Instrument` constructor to use the *WAI command and instantiate an `IOIntf`:

```
Switch::Switch()
    :Instrument(new VXIIOIntf(0,24))
{
    setSuppWai(true);
};
```

Alternatively, we could supply our own `isReady` method that does instrument-specific functionality to determine if the switch has settled yet or not. For example, many VXI switch cards are register based. Given that, testing to see if the switch has settled or not could be reading a bit in a register instead of sending the *WAI command. In this case, we would override the `isReady` method in the switch card and have it test the appropriate bit:

```
class Switch {
    public:
        virtual bool isReady();
};

bool Switch::isReady(){
    unsigned short data;

    getIOIntf()->peek16(16,...,&data);
    return ((data&0x8000)!=0);
}
```

Notice that the `waitReady` method will continue to work with no change, even though what we do to determine if we are ready is drastically different.

The main method in our switch card is the routine that changes the switch setting to one of two known states, measure DUT output voltage (using DMM voltage pins), and measure DUT output current (using DMM current pins). The following is a skeleton implementation of this method:

```
void Switch::setState(SwitchSetting sw){
    if(sw!=setting){
        // It changed, so change it
        switch(setting){
            case swV:
                // Set switch to output voltage here
                ...
                break;
            case swC:
                // Set switch to output current here
                ...
                break;
        }
        setting=sw;
    }
}
```

Summary

This chapter discussed the detailed design and construction of the `Instrument` and `Instrument` derived classes necessary for our example test application. We discussed the data and methods needed for the `Instrument` class, and the `DMM`, `Source`, and `Switch` classes. We showed the complete design and some of the implementation. Some of the rest of the implementation will be left for exercises. The complete header file for the completed class declaration is contained on the enclosed disk.

Using the concepts presented in this chapter, it may be useful to create libraries of instrument classes to correspond to instruments you tend to use. Then, when a need to use a particular instrument arises, the corresponding class can be pulled out, updated as needed, and put to use.

In Chapter 12, we will put all of the pieces of this design together in building a complete object oriented test application. Also, in Chapter 15 we will discuss advanced topics related to the `Instrument` and `Instrument` derived classes.

Exercises

Exercise 10-1. Modify Listing 10-1 so that Instrument is not a base class, but instead derives from a class called Device, such as shown in Figure 10-1.

Exercise 10-2. How would the design, implementation, and use of the instrument classes change if there was no *uses-a* relationship between `DMM` and `Switch` (in other words, if `Switch` was exposed to the user and `DMM` just assumed the `Switch` was set up correctly)?

Exercise 10-3. Redraw the Inheritance, *uses-a*, and instantiation diagrams under the assumption made in Exercise 10-2.

Exercise 10-4. How would you implement a true power-on status state variable and method in the Instrument base class? What protected interface would you have to functionality within the Instrument derived classes?

Exercise 10-5. Describe some possible uses for the `doIdleWork` method in Instrument derived classes.

Exercise 10-6. Describe changes necessary to the `Source` class so that the class will support more functions than just sine-wave generation. Use an enum for the function choice. Modify the `Source` class declaration to indicate these changes.

Exercise 10-7. Create an implementation for the `enable` and `disable` methods in `Source`. Make any reasonable assumptions necessary.

Exercise 10-8. Implement `DMM::measCurrAc(double)`.

Exercise 10-9. Add an Instrument derived class to implement the functionality of a basic frequency counter.

11. Measurement and Test Classes

This chapter discusses the design and construction of the measurement and test classes used in the T&M system discussed in Chapter 8. In that chapter, we designed the following classes:

Topics Covered:

Measurement Class OOD

Test Class OOD

Components of all Measurements

Components of all Tests

Measurement Specific Functional Components

Test Specific Functional Components

- **`Measurement`**. Base class of all derived measurement classes. Includes basic measurement functionality.
- **`FrequencyMeasurement`**. Performs measurements of the ω_0, ω_1, and ω_2 frequencies.
- **`MaxValMeasurement`**. Performs measurements of the maximum output voltage and current. This is the output at frequency ω_0.
- **`ReadAtFreqMeasurement`**. Performs measurements of the output voltage at any given frequency.
- **`Test`**. Base class of all derived test classes. Includes basic test functionality.
- **`OutputAtFrequencyTest`**. Tests various output voltages and currents at specific frequencies of interest.
- **`FrequencyResponseTest`**. Tests the frequency response of the DUT.

Figure 8-3 contained the inheritance tree of our high-level design. The Measurement class and Test class specific sections are reproduced in Figure 11-1.

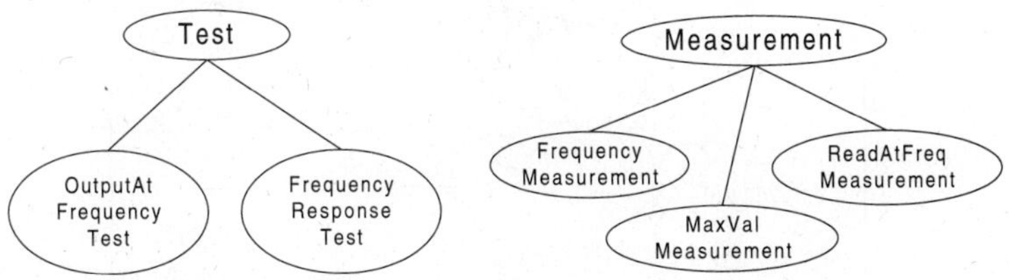

Figure 11-1: Primary Test & Measurement Inheritance Tree

Figure 8-8 contained the uses-a relationships of our high-level design. The Measurement class and Test class specific portions are reproduced in Figure 11-2. Here, the basic test inheritance tree is shown, along with the appropriate *uses-a* relationships between tests and measurements, as well as measurements and measurements.

The instantiation diagram for our high-level design was given in Figure 8-9. The Test and Measurement class specific portions are reproduced in Figure 11-2. Here, a single instance of each of the five classes are shown interconnected using the same *uses-a* connections.

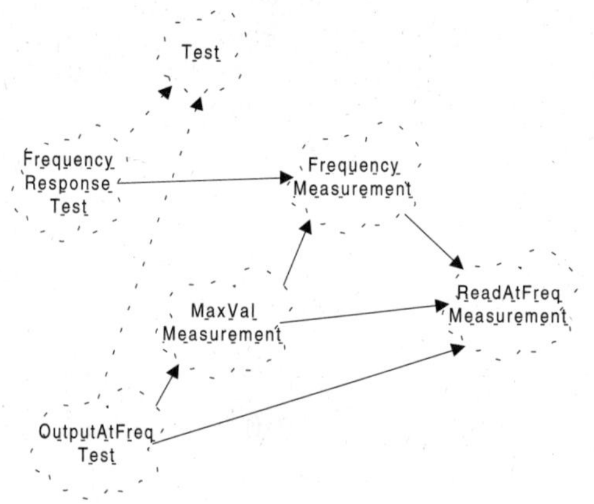

Figure 11-2: Uses-a Relationships

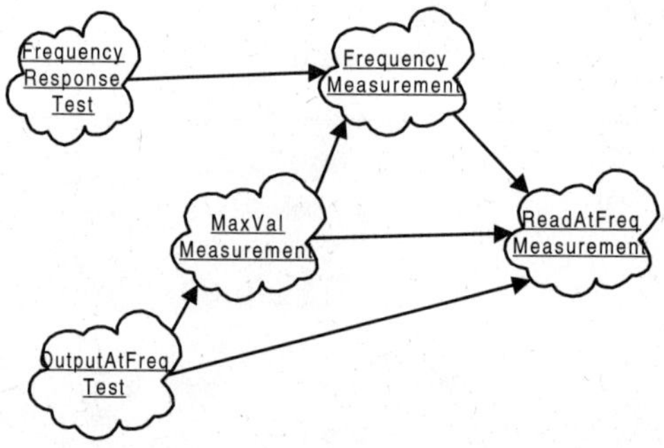

Figure 11-3: Instantiation Diagram

Designing the Base Measurement Class

First, let us discuss the design of the base Measurement class. This is the class that all specific measurements derive from. This class should contain things that are common to all measurements. This class is a very straightforward class to implement, since all the real functionality is in the derived measurement classes. In fact, this class is nothing but a place-holder for other derived Measurement classes:

```
class Measurement {
      Measurement();
};
```

Listing 11-1: Measurement Class Declaration

This class is useless without a derived class that implements measurement functionality. As such, it aids in documentation by making it clear which classes are Measurements, versus Tests, versus other class types. If we did not have the Measurement base class, then all the derived measurement classes would instead derive from Object (or nothing at all), and it would not be clear what type of objects these classes are.

Of course, we could easily implement our test system without the Measurement class. But for our design, we will leave the class in place.

Designing the Base Test Class

Next, let us discuss the design of the base Test class. This is the class that all specific tests derive from. This class should contain things that are common to all tests. During the high-level design in Chapter 8, the Test class contained the following items:

- Status of test. This indicates the status of the test on the given DUT. It can take on the values `NotRunYet`, `Passed`, or `Failed`.
- A method used to return the status of the test.
- A method used to return whether the test has run yet or not.
- A method which runs the specified test. This essentially changes the state from `NotRunYet` to either `Passed` or `Failed`.

Based on this information, we create the following declaration:

```
class Test {
    private:
        enum TestStatus {NotRunYet,Passed,Failed};
        TestStatus status;
    public:
        Test();
        int hasTestRun();
        int didTestPass();
        virtual void runTest()=0;
};
```

Listing 11-2: Test Class Declaration

In addition, we need methods that set the state of the test to either passed or failed. These methods will be called by the derived classes in the course of implementing the `runTest` method. Here is the declaration for these methods:

```
class Test {
    ...
    protected:
        void passed();
        void failed();
        void done();
    ...
};
```

Listing 11-3: Protected Members in Test Class

This class is an abstract base class. It requires a derived class to implement the `runTest` method to perform test-specific functionality. This method in the derived class must update the test status before completing. It does this by calling the protected methods `passed`, `failed`, and `done`, which update the test status to the given state.

The `passed` method simply updates the status to the Passed state. The `failed` method changes the state to the Failed state. The `done` method is the last method called by `runTest` and it simply changes the state to Passed if the state has not been previously set by a call to passed or failed.

The constructor, `passed`, `failed`, `done`, `hasTestRun`, and `didTestPass` are implemented completely within the `Test` base class. The methods for this class are very straightforward:

```
Test::Test(){
    status=NotRunYet;
};
void Test::passed(){
    status=Passed;
}
void Test::failed(){
    status=Failed;
}
void Test::done(){
    if(status==NotRunYet)
        status=Passed;
}
int Test::hasTestRun(){
    // Returns true if test was run
    return status!=NotRunYet;
}
int Test::didTestPass(){
    // Returns true if test has run and passed
    return status==Passed;
}
```

Listing 11-4: Implementation of Test Class Methods

With this declaration, a pointer to an arbitrary Test can be used to perform all the test functionality without knowledge of the Test itself. This is because the classes that derive from `Test` will not add new methods, just implement the derived methods provided in `Test`.

The following code uses only a `Test` object:

```
doWork(Test *t){
    if(!t->hasTestRun())
        t->runTest();
    if(t->didTestPass())
        printf("Passed!\n");
    else
        printf("Failed!\n");
}
```

Listing 11-5: Sample use of Test Class

Listing 11-1 does not know what specific test is being performed, nor does it need to know. This is a good example of polymorphism at work. This use-model for the `Test` class will be used in our `TestStation` class. There, we will simply have an array of Test objects, and we will run them sequentially, determining if they pass or fail. We never care what actual test is executed, just that the test ran and that it passed or failed.

Comparing the Base Classes

You will notice some differences in design choices between the base `Measurement` class and the base `Test` class. The base measurement class has very little functionality built in. It is primarily a place-holder for the derived measurement classes. There is no real polymorphism here, because there is no functionality declared in this class.

The base `Test` class, however, has virtually all of the necessary interfaces for a test defined. As such, the `Test` class has real code and makes real use of polymorphism. Why were the classes designed differently? There is one very simple answer to that question:

> All *tests* in our system have (or can have) the *same* interface.
> All *measurements* in our system have *different* interfaces.

The interface to an arbitrary test class is (or can be) the same for all tests. The result of a test is nothing more than a boolean ("did the test pass?"). The interface to an arbitrary measurement class, however, is dependent on the measurement being performed. If you are measuring a voltage, the result can be a double. If you are measuring a waveform, the result would be an array. Also, different measurements require different parameters passed to them. A "*get voltage at a certain frequency*" measurement must be passed the frequency at which to measure the voltage. A "*get frequency that maximizes voltage*" measurement either needs no parameters, or it needs a minimum and maximum frequency (two doubles) in which to perform the measurement.

Derived Measurement Classes

From Chapter 8, we have three specific measurement classes, namely:

- `ReadAtFreqMeasurement`. This class will have methods that return the voltage or current at a specified frequency.

- `FrequencyMeasurement`. This class will have methods that measure the center, low, and high frequencies (ω_0, ω_1, and ω_2, respectively).

- `MaxValMeasurement`. This class will have methods that return the maximum voltage and maximum current. This is the voltage and current at frequency ω_0.

These three measurements use the `Instrument`-derived classes to perform the actual instrument measurements needed to implement these measurements. We will explore the design and construction of each of these three classes in turn.

ReadAtFreqMeasurement

The `ReadAtFreqMeasurement` class is used to measure the DUT output voltage and current at many different DUT input frequencies. For the `ReadAtFreqMeasurement` class, we need the following data elements:

- A pointer to the `Source` instrument object. This is needed to set the DUT input frequency.

- A pointer to the `DMM` instrument object. This is needed to read the output voltage and current of the DUT.

- A variable to store the input voltage. In this design, we will make the input voltage a value passed to the constructor. As such, an instance of this class only needs to deal with a single input voltage. If a user of this class wants to calculate values for different input voltages, it can create separate instances of this class. This is an arbitrary design choice. But, as you will see later, it has some advantages.

Since each measurement request specifies a new frequency, it is difficult (or impossible) for this class to cache the measurements it has made. Therefore, each measurement request to this class will re-measure the requested voltage or current. As such, no cache-related data members are needed.

The `ReadAtFreqMeasurement` class must implement the following measurement request methods:

- `getV`. A method that returns the voltage at the frequency passed to the method as a parameter.

- `getC`. A method that returns the current at the frequency passed to the method as a parameter.

Putting this all together, the declaration of the `ReadAtFreqMeasurement` class will look like this:

```
class ReadAtFreqMeasurement:public Measurement {
    private:
        Source *src;
        DMM *dmm;
        double inVolt;
    public:
        ReadAtFreqMeasurement(double inV);
        double getV(double freq);
        double getC(double freq);
};
```

Listing 11-6: `ReadAtFreqMeasurement` Declaration

The constructor simply fills in pointers to the instruments specified, and stores the requested input voltage:

```
ReadAtFreqMeasurement::ReadAtFreqMeasurement(
    double inV
){
    // Get pointers to the instruments
    src= ...;
    dmm= ...;
    inVolt=inV;
};
```

Listing 11-7: `ReadAtFreqMeasurement` Constructor

Since there is only one Source and one DMM in our test system, and it is not acceptable to have more than one instance of each, the instances of the instruments cannot be created by the individual Measurement classes. Instead, they are created and handled by the `TestStation` class, and the Measurement classes need to ask the `TestStation` class for a pointer to them.

How does the Measurement class contact the `TestStation`? Well, we will leave this question to be answered in the next chapter, when we build the `TestStation` class, and put all of these pieces together into a working test system.

Now, let us look at the implementation of one of the two primary methods in our class: the `getV` method. This method must measure the output voltage at a given input frequency. The implementation of this method must first enable the `Source` to generate the requested frequency signal at the requested voltage, then it must read the resulting output voltage using the `DMM`. Here is a basic implementation:

```
double ReadAtFreqMeasurement::getV(double freq){
   // Disable the output while we set up the src
   src->disable();
   src->setFrequency(freq);
   src->setAmplitude(inVolt);
   src->enable();

   // Now, measure the output voltage, use a range
   // that will fit the expected voltage
   // (outV<inV).
   return dmm->measVoltAc(inVolt*2);
};
```

Listing 11-8: `getV` Implementation

The implementation of `getC` is just as straightforward.

`FrequencyMeasurement`

The `FrequencyMeasurement` class is used to calculate the DUT input frequencies ω_0, ω_1, and ω_2. For the `FrequencyMeasurement` class, we need the following data elements:

- An instance of the `ReadAtFreqMeasurement` class. This measurement object is used by the `FrequencyMeasurement` class to determine the DUT output voltage at a given input frequency.

- Variables to store ω_0, ω_1, and ω_2. Once these values have been calculated for a given DUT, they can be cached so that further requests to retrieve them can load the cached versions. Since calculating these values is time-consuming, and we may need to retrieve these values several times, and the value should not change for a given DUT once calculated, we can save a great deal of time by caching these values.

- A variable to store the input voltage. As with `ReadAtFreq-Measurement`, this value is set in the constructor and remains a constant.

The `FrequencyMeasurement` class must implement the following measurement request methods:

- `getw0`. A method that calculates the center frequency, ω_0, using a given input voltage.

- `getw1`. A method that calculates the low frequency, ω_1, using a given input voltage.

- getw2. A method that calculates the high frequency, ω_2, using a given input voltage.

A first-pass declaration for the FrequencyMeasurement class might look like this:

```
class FrequencyMeasurement:public Measurement {
    private:
        ReadAtFreqMeasurement raf;
        double w0,w1,w2;
        double inVolt;
        int gotw0,gotw1,gotw2;
    public:
        FrequencyMeasurement(double inV);
        double getw0();
        double getw1(;
        double getw2();
};
```

Listing 11-9: FrequencyMeasurement Declaration

The constructor simply marks that the three measurements have not been made yet, and fills in the input voltage:

```
FrequencyMeasurement::FrequencyMeasurement(
    double inV
)
    : raf(inV) // Needed to set input volt for raf
{
    gotw0=0;
    gotw1=0;
    gotw2=0;
    inVold=inV;
};
```

Listing 11-10: FrequencyMeasurement Constructor

The implementation of getw0, getw1, and getw2 are all similar. Here is the implementation of getw0:

```
double FrequencyMeasurement::getw0(){
    // See if we have calculated the values
    if(!gotw0){
        calculatew0();
        gotw0=1;
    }
    return w0;
};
```

Listing 11-11: getw0 Implementation

This method checks to see if we have already calculated this value or not. If we have, we simply return the cached value. If not, we call the private method `calculatew0` to do the real work of calculating that value.

The implementation of the `calcuatew0` method is very similar to the `getFreqMaxVoltage` routine implemented in Listing 4-2 in Chapter 4. You may wish to refer back to this chapter before continuing. Basically, the method does successive scans using a private `scanFreqMaxVoltage` method. Each scan uses a smaller range and a smaller step and calculates a more accurate approximation. As a result, ultimately we get an accurate answer :

```
void FrequencyMeasurement::calculatew0(){
    double tmpF;

    /*Try a step of 200Hz (entire range 200-5000Hz)*/
    tmpF=scanFreqMaxVoltage(200,5000,200);

    /* Use a step of 20Hz (range: tmpF+/-200Hz) */
    tmpF=scanFreqMaxVoltage(tmpF-200,tmpF+200,20);

    /* Use a step of 1Hz (range: tmpF+/-20Hz) */
    tmpF=scanFreqMaxVoltage(tmpF-20,tmpF+20,1);

    /* Store away w0 */
    w0=tmpF;
}
```

Listing 11-12: calculatew0 Implementation

This method makes use of the private method `scanFreqMaxVoltage`. This is similar to the routine of the same name shown in Listing 4-1. Here, we scan the requested frequency range with the requested step frequency. For each frequency we test, we measure the output voltage at that frequency. Once the maximum output voltage is measured (accurate to the given step value), we return it.

```
double FrequencyMeasurement::scanFreqMaxVoltage(
    double startF,
    double stopF,
    double stepF
){

    double currF;
    double lastVal;
    double val;

    /* Set original peak */
    lastVal=0.0;
```

```
        /* Scan thru frequency range */
        for(currF=startF;currF<stopF;currF+=stepF){

            /* Get voltage at currF */
            val=raf.getV(currF);

            /* See if last time was a peak */
            /* This is true if this value is less than */
            /* the last value (we are over the peak) */
            if(val<lastVal){

                /* We have peaked, last value was peak */
                return currF-step:
            }

            /* We have not yet peaked */
            lastVal=val;
        }

        throw "no peak voltage"; // Error
    }
```

Listing 11-13: `scanFreqMaxVoltage` Implementation

In a similar way, in order to implement `getw1` and `getw2` ,we need private methods called `calculatew1` and `calculatew2`. These methods, like their counterparts in Chapter 4, need another private method called `scanFreqSpecVoltage`.[1] The implementation of `calculatew1`, `calculatew2`, and `scanFreqSpecVoltage` are left as exercises.

After adding all these private methods, our completed class declaration for the `FrequencyMeasurement` class looks like this:

---

[1] This method is discussed in the solution to Exercise 4-4 in Chapter 4 and is included on the enclosed disk.

```
class FrequencyMeasurement:public Measurement {
   private:
      ReadAtFreqMeasurement raf;
      double w0,w1,w2;
      double inVolt;
      int gotw0,gotw1,gotw2;

      double scanFreqMaxVoltage(
         double startF,double stopF,double stepF);

      double scanFreqSpecVoltage(
         double startF,double stopF,
         double stepF,double volt);

      void calculatew0();
      void calculatew1();
      void calculatew2();

   public:
      FrequencyMeasurement(double inV);
      double getw0();
      double getw1();
      double getw2();
};
```

Listing 11-14: Complete `FrequencyMeasurement` Declaration

`MaxValMeasurement`

The `MaxValMeasurement` class is used to calculate the maximum output voltage and maximum output current. This is the output voltage and current when the input frequency is set to ω_0. For the `MaxValMeasurement` class, we need the following data elements:

- An instance of the `FrequencyMeasurement` class. This measurement is used by the `MaxValMeasurement` class to determine what ω_0 is, which is needed to determine the maximum output voltage and current.

- An instance of the `ReadAtFreqMeasurement` class. This measurement is used by the `MaxValMeasurement` class to determine the output voltage and current at a specific frequency, namely ω_0.

- Variables to store the maximum voltage and current. Once these values have been calculated for a given DUT, they can be cached so further requests return the same value.

- A variable to store the input voltage.

The `MaxValMeasurement` class must implement the following measurement request methods:

- `maxV`. A method that returns the maximum voltage of the DUT (i.e., the voltage at frequency ω_0), with a given input voltage.

- `maxC`. A method that returns the maximum current of the DUT, with a given input voltage.

Using this information, we can create our declaration for the `MaxValMeasurement::`

```
class MaxValMeasurement:public Measurement {
   private:
      FrequencyMeasurement freqMeas;
      ReadAtFreqMeasurement raf;
      double inVolt;
   public:
      MaxValMeasurement(double inV);
      double maxV();
      double maxC();
};
```

Listing 11-15: `MaxValMeasurement` Declaration

The constructor for this class must initialize the `FrequencyMeasurement` class, and the `ReadAtFreqMeasurement` class, along with storing away the input voltage:

```
MaxValMeasurement::MaxValMeasurement(double inV)
   :freqMeas(inV),
    raf(inV)
{
   inVolt=inV;
};
```

Listing 11-16: `MaxValMeasurement` Constructor

The implementation for `maxV` simply asks the `FrequencyMeasurement` class for ω_0, then asks the `ReadatFreqMeasurement` class for the voltage at ω_0:

```
double MaxValMeasurement::maxV(){
   double w0;

   w0=freqMeas.getw0();
   return raf.getV(w0);
}
```

Listing 11-17: `maxV` Implementation

The implementation of `maxC` is similarly straightforward.

Derived Test Classes

Next, we will look at the specific classes derived from the `Test` class. For our sample test system, we have two specific Test classes, namely:

- `FrequencyResponseTest`
- `OutputAtFreqTest`

These two tests use the measurement classes described above to perform the actual measurements needed to implement the tests. Each of these classes has to implement exactly one method, the `runTest` method. However, there are still design issues specific to each that must be considered.

FrequencyResponseTest

The `FrequencyResponseTest` is used to verify that ω_0, ω_1, ω_2, and β are all within the expected limits. For the `FrequencyResponseTest`, we have the following data needs:

- An instance of a `FrequencyMeasurement` class. This class is used to calculate ω_0, ω_1, and ω_2 at various voltages.

A `FrequencyResponseTest` must perform the following actions at V_i=0.5V, 1.0V, and 1.5V:

- Verify ω_0 is within expected limits.
- Verify ω_1 is within expected limits.
- Verify ω_2 is within expected limits.
- Verify β is within expected limits.

To do this, we will have internal methods that implement each of these functions, then call them all appropriately from the standard `runTest` method. Based on this, we can propose the following declaration for `FrequencyResponseTest`:

```
class FrequencyResponseTest:public Test{
    private:
        void verifyw0(FrequencyMeasurement&);
        void verifyw1(FrequencyMeasurement&);
        void verifyw2(FrequencyMeasurement&);
        void verifyB(FrequencyMeasurement&);
    public:
        virtual void runTest();
};
```

Listing 11-18: `FrequencyResponseTest` Declaration

Since we will be performing the frequency response measurements at different input voltages, and since the input voltage is a parameter to the constructor of the `FrequencyMeasurement` object, we will construct an instance of the `FrequencyMeasurement` during the `runTest` call for each voltage we use.

The `runTest` method loops through all input voltages (0.5V, 1.0V, and 1.5V). For each input voltage, it instantiates a corresponding `FrequencyMeasurement` instance. Then, using this instance, it calls the four private verify methods. Here is the implementation of `runTest`:

```
void FrequencyResponseTest::runTest(){
    int i;
    for(i=1;i<=3;++i){
        // Create a Frequency Measurement at
        // .5V, 1V, and 1.5V input voltages
        FrequencyMeasurement freqMeas(.5*i);

        verifyw0(freqMeas);
        verifyw1(freqMeas);
        verifyw2(freqMeas);
        verifyB(freqMeas);
    }
    done(); // If tests didn't fail, mark as passed
}
```

Listing 11-19: `runTest` Implementation

Now, all we have to do is implement the four internal verify methods. For example, verifyw0 might look like this:

```
void FrequencyResponseTest::verifyw0(
        FrequencyMeasurement& freqMeas
){
    // Get the DUT w0 frequency
    double freq=freqMeas.getw0();

    // Make sure it is in range
    if(freq<2025)
        failed();
    if(freq>2475)
        failed();
}
```

Listing 11-20: verifyw0 Implementation

The implementation of the other three methods is similar.

OutputAtFreqTest

The `OutputAtFreqTest` class is used to verify that the DUT output voltage and current at various DUT input frequencies are within expected limits. For the `OutputAtFreqTest`, we have the following data needs:

- An instance of a `MaxValMeasurement` class. This class is used to calculate the maximum output voltage from the DUT (output at ω_0).
- An instance of a `ReadAtFreqMeasurement` class. This class is used to calculate the output voltage at various frequencies within the test.

An `OutputAtFreqTest` must perform the following actions at V_i=0.5V, 1.0V, and 1.5V:

- Verify V_{om} is within expected limits (maximum output voltage).
- Verify I_{om} is within expected limits (maximum output current).
- Verify V_l is within expected limits (output voltage at ω_0-2000Hz).
- Verify V_h is within expected limits (output voltage at ω_0+2000Hz).

We will have internal methods to implement each of these tests, then call them all from the standard `runTest` method. These methods will all need an appropriate instance of a `FrequencyMeasurement` instance and a `ReadAtFreqMeasurement` instance. They also need the input voltage used, so they can determine if the output voltage is as expected. Here is our declaration:

```
class OutputAtFreqTest:public Test{
    private:
        void verifyVom(
            double inV,
            FrequencyMeasurement&,
            ReadAtFreqMeasurement&
        );
        void verifyIom(
            double inV,
            FrequencyMeasurement&,
            ReadAtFreqMeasurement&
        );
        void verifyVl(
            double inV,
            FrequencyMeasurement&,
            ReadAtFreqMeasurement&
        );
        void verifyVh(
            double inV,
            FrequencyMeasurement&,
            ReadAtFreqMeasurement&
        );
    public:
        virtual void runTest();
};
```

Listing 11-21: `OutputAtFreqTest` Declaration

Our `runTest` method for `OutputAtFreqTest` is similar to the `runTest` method for the `FrequencyResponseTest` class:

```
void OutputAtFreqTest::runTest(){
    int i;
    for(i=1;i<=3;++i){
        FrequencyMeasurement freqMeas(.5*i);
        ReadAtFreqMeasurement raf(.5*i);

        verifyVom(.5*i,freqMeas,raf);
        verifyIom(.5*i,freqMeas,raf);
        verifyVl(.5*i,freqMeas,raf);
        verifyVh(.5*i,freqMeas,raf);
    }
    done();
};
```

Listing 11-22: `runTest` Implementation

Looking at the private methods, here is `verifyVom`:

```
void OutputAtFreqTest::verifyVom(
    double inV,
    FrequencyMeasurement& fm,
    ReadAtFreqMeasurement& raf
){
    double w0,Vom;

    // Get w0, from that, get Vom
    w0=fm.getw0();
    Vom=raf.getV(w0);

    // Make sure Vom is within range
    if(Vom>(inV*1.05))
        failed();
    if(Vom<(inV*.95))
        failed();
};
```

Listing 11-23: `verifyVom` Implementation

Here, we use the `FrequencyMeasurement` class to calculate ω_0. Then, using the calculated ω_0, we get the output voltage at that frequency, V_{om}. We then verify to make sure that V_{om} is within expected limits.

The implementation of the other three methods is similar.

Generalized Concepts

Each T&M problem to be solved will have its own measurement and test needs. The goal of an object oriented design is to identify these needs and create specific classes to solve the appropriate portion of the problem. When creating Measurement and Test classes, it may be useful to take a step back from the immediate problem and try to create classes that solve not only the immediate needs, but are generalized enough to apply to future needs. In addition, look at previous classes you have constructed for past problems and use them when working on newer problems. It is when we do this big-picture design methodology that the object oriented promise of true code reuse can be realized.

Summary

This chapter discussed the implementation of the base and derived methods necessary to implement the measurement and test functionality of the sample test system designed in Chapter 8. Chapter 12 will put together all the pieces in the last several chapters (8-11) into a complete, working object oriented test system, similar in operation to the non-object oriented version built in Chapter 4.

It should be noted that the concepts illustrated in this chapter can be expanded for more sophisticated measurement or test needs. When implementing measurement and test classes, thought should be given to how these classes may be leveraged into future test systems and how classes from previous problems can be used for solving current design problems. Taking a step back during the design process can help greatly in taking advantage of code re-use.

Exercises

Exercise 11-1. Modify the Measurement and Test classes so that they are not a base class, but instead derive from a class called Object, such as shown in Figure 8-3.

Exercise 11-2. Implement the `getC` method in the `ReadAtFreqMeasurement` class. What value do you pass for the range to the `measCurrAc` method of the Source class?

Exercise 11-3. Define and implement a caching mechanism for the `ReadAtFreqMeasurement` class that makes it so requests to read the voltage or current at a previously requested frequency will not re-perform the measurement. What are the advantages and disadvantages of such a mechanism?

Exercise 11-4. Implement the getw1 and getw2 methods in the `FrequencyMeasurement` class. Use the getw0 implementation as a reference.

Exercise 11-5. Implement the calculatew1 and calculatew2 methods in the `FrequencyMeasurement` class. Use the result of Exercise 4-4 as a reference.

Exercise 11-6. Implement the `scanFreqSpecVoltage` method in the `FrequencyMeasurement` class. This is also discussed in the result of Exercise 4-4.

Exercise 11-7. Implement the `maxC` method of the `MaxValMeasurement` class.

Exercise 11-8. Implement the verifyw1, verifyw2, and `verifyB` methods of the `FrequencyResponseTest` class.

Exercise 11-9. Implement the `FrequencyResponseTest` private methods `verifyw1`, `verifyw2`, and `verifyB`.

Exercise 11-10. Implement the `verifyIom`, `verifyVl`, and `verifyVh` methods of the `OutputAtFreqTest`.

Exercise 11-11. Implement the `OutputAtFreqTest::runTest` method. What private methods are necessary to complete the test? Implement these private methods, too.

12. Building an Object Oriented T&M System

Topics Covered:

Creating the DUT Class.

Creating the `TestStation` Class.

Creating the `Object` Class.

Putting the Pieces Together

Using the Test System

Over the last several chapters, we have discussed various aspects of the design and construction of an object oriented T&M System. In this chapter, we will take the design we created in Chapter 8, along with the pieces we have constructed in Chapters 8-11, and put them all together into a working object oriented T&M system.

First, let's review where we are. In Chapter 8, we designed the test system. The results of that chapter were an inheritance tree, a uses-a relationship diagram, and an instantiation diagram. From this design, we created several portions of the T&M design. In Chapter 9, we built the instrument I/O interface class, which allows communication between the test computer and the instrumentation using a GPIB or VXI interface. In Chapter 10, we created the instrument classes that were necessary to communicate with the instruments used in the test system (a DMM, a Source, and a Switch). In Chapter 11, we built the Measurement and Test classes that perform the actual testing of the DUT.

Together, the code created in these chapters form the majority of what is necessary to complete the test system. However, there are a few classes remaining that we have not constructed yet. Figure 9-3 showed the completed inheritance tree for this test system. For reference, this diagram is repeated again in Figure 12-1. In this diagram, you will notice several classes that have not yet been constructed in previous chapters. Namely:

- `DUT` class
- `TestStation` Class
- `Device` and `Object` base classes

This chapter will first discuss the construction of these remaining pieces. Next, we will take all the pieces and put them together into a working system.

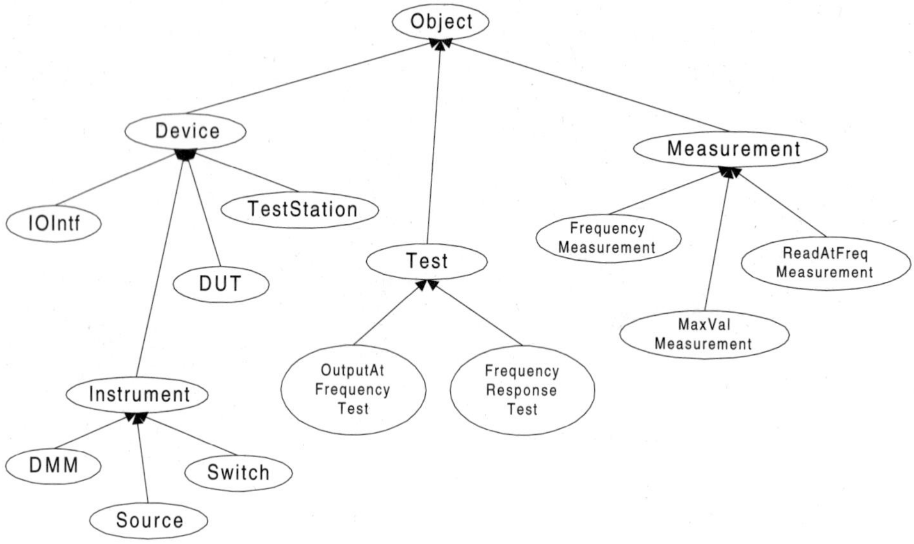

Figure 12-1: Test System Inheritance Tree

DUT Class

The DUT class is the class that represents the actual device being tested. There is one DUT object for each device to be tested. As a DUT is inserted into the test stand, an instance of a matching DUT object is connected to the `TestStation` class. When the test is complete and the device is removed from the test stand, the matching DUT object is disconnected from the `TestStation` class. The DUT class contains information that:

- Identifies the device that corresponds to the DUT object instance.
- Marks whether this DUT has been tested or not.
- Marks whether the DUT passed or failed the test (if it has been tested).
- Contains information about why the DUT failed (if it has failed a test).

Back in Chapter 8, we identified the following data needs for the DUT class:

- Flag indicating whether the DUT has been tested or not, and if so, whether it passed or failed the test.
- A value indicating why the DUT failed the test, if it has failed a test.

- A serial number that is used to physically identify the real device being tested. This serial number could correspond to a UPC barcode symbol on the device, or a simple serial number written on the device.

We also identified the following methods needed:

- Mark the DUT as passed. Specify that the DUT has been tested and passed all tests.
- Mark the DUT as failed. Specify that the DUT has been tested and failed at least one test. This method also would be passed information as to why it failed the test.
- Get the serial number. Return the serial number assigned to this device for identification purposes.
- Get an indication as to whether the DUT has been tested and whether it passed or failed the tests.
- Get the detailed information as to why the DUT failed a test.

Based on this information, we propose the following class declaration for the DUT class:

```
class DUT:public Device {
   private:
      // Type used for status
      enum Status {Passed,Failed,UnTested};

      Status stat;// has DUT been tested? Did it pass?
      Error *failedResult; // If failed, why?
      long serialNumber; // Device ID number
      DUT(); // private so we require a serNum

   public:
      // Constructor/Destructor
      DUT(long serNum); // DUT requires an ID
      ~DUT();

      // Mark as passed or failed
      void markPassed();
      void markFailed(Error& res); // Why failed

      // Get status info
      bool DUTTested(); // Was DUT tested?
      bool DUTPassed(); // Did DUT pass?
      Error *getFailedResult(); // Why failed?
      long getSerialNumber(); // Get ID number
};
```

This declaration shows the creation of an enum called `Status` that contains values indicating the test status of the DUT. We show variables that contain this status, a serial number, and a failed result if the status is `Failed`.

The implementation of this class's methods is very straightforward. The constructor simply marks the DUT as not tested, and stores the serial number:

```
DUT::DUT(long serNum){
    stat=UnTested;
    failedResult=0;
    serialNumber=serNum;
}
```

Marking a DUT as having passed or failed a test simply updates the status variable from UnTested to either Passed or Failed. If failed, it must also store the reason why:

```
DUT::markPassed(){
    stat=Passed;
}

DUT::markFailed(Error& res){
    stat=Failed;
    // Store a *copy* of the error away
    failedResult=new Error(res);
}
```

Now, getting the status as to whether it passed or not is a simple matter of looking at the status variable:

```
bool DUT::DUTTested(){
    // DUT Tested if state is not UnTested
    return stat!=Untested;
}

bool DUT::DUTPassed(){
    // DUT Passed if state is Passed
    return stat==Passed;
}
```

The DUT class will be used by the TestStation class, which is discussed next.

TestStation Class

The purpose of the TestStation class is to:

- Keep track of what tests must be executed for each DUT.
- Keep track of the instrument classes used by the tests and the measurements they use.
- Connect and disconnect a DUT to the TestStation.
- Update the DUT as appropriate after it has been tested.

As such, we will have one instance of the `TestStation` in our application. It will be in control of all activities related to the testing of a single `DUT`.

From Chapter 8, we need the following data elements in our `TestStation` class:

- A pointer to the `DUT`. The `TestStation` will record the test results in the `DUT` instance. In a full-blown test system, the `TestStation` can also decide what tests to instantiate and run based on the particular characteristics of the `DUT`. In our test system, we will assume all `DUT`s require all tests to be run.
- An array of `Test` objects, one for each test that needs to be run on this `DUT`.
- A pointer to the three instruments used in the system: a DMM, a Source, and a Switch.

In addition, Chapter 8 identified the following methods needed:

- Connect a given `DUT` to the test system. This method will store away a reference to the given `DUT` object. It will then instantiate all the tests needed for the given `DUT` and store them in the test array.
- Disconnect the `DUT` from the test system. This method will delete the tests allocated in the test array, and remove the connection to the `DUT` object.
- Test the `DUT`. This method will execute all the tests in the test array and store the results of the tests in the `DUT` object.

Based on these needs, we will create the following class declaration:

```
class TestStation:public Device {
    private:
        // Device to Test
        DUT *dut;

        // Array of tests to run on the DUT
        int numTests;
        Test **tests;

        // Instruments used with this test station
        DMM *dmm;
        Source *src;
        Switch *sw;

    public:
        TestStation();
        ~TestStation();
```

```
        // Return pointers to the instruments and DUT
        // These are used by primarly the Measurement
        // classes to get at the test instruments
        DMM *getDMM();
        Source *getSource();
        Switch *getSwitch();
        DUT *getDUT();

        // Methods to control actions of TestStation
        void connectDUT(DUT *); // Connect given DUT
        void disconnectDUT(); // Disconnect the DUT
        void testDUT(); // Test previous connected DUT
};
```

The `TestStation` constructor initializes variables and instantiates the test instruments needed. This is the only place where the instrument classes are created. All other references are created from these instances. The `TestStation` destructor deletes the test instrument objects:

```
TestStation::TestStation(){
    // Clear DUT and its tests
    dut=0;
    numTests=0;
    tests=0;

    // Instantiate the test instruments
    sw=new Switch();
    dmm=new DMM(sw);
    src=new Source();
}

TestStation::~TestStation(){
    // Delete the test instrument instances
    delete sw;
    delete dmm;
    delete src;
}
```

Now, the method to connect a `DUT` to the system must store the `DUT` pointer away, and allocate an instance of each test needed to test that `DUT`. In our simple test system, we will assume that both of our tests are needed for every `DUT`. In a more complicated system, the specific tests needed may vary depending on different characteristics of the specific `DUT`. This is why the tests themselves are not instantiated until we know what `DUT` we are testing.

```
void TestStation::connectDUT(DUT *d){
    // Store away the DUT name
    DUT=d;

    // Add the tests
    numTests=2;
    tests=new Test*[2];
    tests[0]=new FrequencyResponseTest();
    tests[1]=new OutputAtFrequencyTest();
}

void TestStation::disconnectDUT(){
    int i;

    // Remove the DUT
    DUT=0;

    // Delete the used tests
    for(i=0;i<numTests;++i)
        delete tests[i];
    delete tests;
    numTests=0;
}
```

Notice that only `connectDUT` knows which specific tests are instantiated. The `disconnectDUT` and `testDUT` (shown next) methods need not know the specific tests, only the number of tests and a reference to them.

To run the tests, we simply loop through each test. If all the tests succeed, we mark the DUT as passed. If one or more tests fail, or if an error occurs during the execution of a test, then we mark the DUT as failed. In either DUT failure case, an Error[1] instance is created and stored in the DUT for later analysis:

```
void TestStation::testDUT(){
    // Catch any errors that occur in a test
    try {
        int i;
        // Run through each individual test
        for(i=0;i<numTests;++i){
            if(!tests[i]->hasTestRun())
                tests[i]->runTest();
            if(!tests[i]->didTestPass()){
                throw *(tests[i]->results());²
            }
        }
```

[1] The `Error` class is discussed in more detail in Chapter 14.

[2] Calling `throw` with an `Error` instance here causes the catch(`Error&` err) code segment to be called. The catch clause marks the DUT as failed and stores the err instance in the DUT.

```
            // It passed all tests
            DUT->markPassed();

        }catch(Error& err){

            // Either the DUT failed a test (didTestPass
            // returned false), or the test itself
            // had an error (throw executed in a test).
            // In either case, mark the DUT as failed
            DUT->markFailed(err);
        }
    }
```

All we do in this routine is run through each test sequentially. If a test fails (i.e., `didTestPass` returns false), we throw an error which is caught by the catch clause. If we make it all the way through all the tests without throwing an error, then the DUT has passed all the test and we mark it as passed. If either the `didTestPass` returns false, or one of the tests themselves failed and throws an error, then the catch clause will mark the DUT as failed and store away the error instance in the DUT for later analysis.

> **A Note About Style:** Rather than having the tests indicate a DUT failure by returning a passed/failed status via a `didTestPass` method. The `runTest` routine in each test could "throw" Errors itself if a DUT failed. Then if the `runTest` completes without a throw, the DUT must have passed the test. This would eliminate the need for the `didTestPass` method. All errors, either the DUT failed indication, or errors in the execution of the test code itself would be thrown and caught by the catch handler specified here. We choose instead to use the `didTestPass` method and throw the DUT failures in this code. It is simply a style issue, either approach is acceptable.

Object Base Class

All classes derive ultimately from the Object base class. Therefore, the methods contained in the Object base class are available to all classes in the system.

There is only one method needed in the Object base class, but it is an important method:

- get Test Station. Return a pointer to the `TestStation` class associated with this system.

This method simply returns a pointer to the `TestStation` class. This is important because the `TestStation` class contains methods to access the test instruments and the

DUT. The methods to access the instruments are used by the Measurement classes to get access to the test instruments themselves to perform the measurements needed. The method to access the DUT could be used by the Test classes to decide what functions to test based on characteristics of the DUT.

We start with the following declaration for our Object base class:

```
class Object {
    protected:
        Object();
        virtual ~Object();

        // Return pointer to TestStation
        TestStation *getTestStation();
};
```

Question: How does the `getTestStation` method get a pointer to the `TestStation` to return? There are two ways this could be implemented.

Solution #1: The `TestStation` constructor, when it is instantiated, could store a pointer to itself in a global variable (or static public method variable). Then the `getTestStation` method in Object could access this variable and return the result. The implementation of `getTestStation` would look like this:

```
TestStation *Object::getTestStation(){
    // return pointer to TestStation
    return TestStation::tsInstance;
}
```

The `TestStation` constructor would have to be modified to store away a pointer to itself:

```
TestStation::TestStation(){
    // Store away pointer to self
    tsInstance=this;

    ... rest of TestStation constructor ...
}
```

Finally, a static variable would have to be put into the `TestStation` class:

```
class TestStation:public Object {
    ...
    public:
        static TestStation *ts;
    ...
};
```

Solution #2: The `Object` constructor could require a pointer to the `TestStation` be passed to it (the default constructor to `Object` would be disallowed). The `Object` class would store a copy of the `TestStation` instance within the `Object` class itself.

The declaration for Object would be changed to the following:

```
class Object {
    private:
        const TestStation *ts;
        Object(); // Disallow
    protected:
        Object(TestStation *tst);
        virtual ~Object();

        // Return pointer to TestStation
        TestStation *getTestStation();
};
```

The above declaration disallows the `Object()` constructor from being used by making it private. A private constructor is not usable, since no one outside of `Object` may use it to create instances of `Objects`.

The default constructor to Object would then be disallowed, and the new constructor would look like this:

```
Object::Object(TestStation *tst)
    : ts(tst)
{
}
```

This approach requires no global variables to store the `TestStation` instance. However, all classes that derive from `Object` (which is all classes) would have to be updated to use the new constructor. This means that all constructors in all classes would have to pass `Object` a pointer to the `TestStation`. This means that all constructors in all classes would have to be passed the `TestStation` pointer. For example, here is the old constructor for Measurement:

```
Measurement::Measurement(){
}
```

Here is the new constructor for measurement:

```
Measurement::Measurement(TestStation *ts)
    :Object(ts)
{}
```

This change to the Measurement constructor requires a change to the `FrequencyMeasurement` constructor as well:

```
FrequencyMeasurement::FrequencyMeasurement(
        double inV,
        TestStation *ts
)
    :Measurement(ts)
{
    ... rest of constructor ...
}
```

All constructors in all classes would have to changed. Ultimately, the creation of the classes in `TestStation` would need to pass a pointer to itself as it creates the instances. For instance, creating the instrument objects in the constructor would have to change from this:

```
sw=new Switch;
dmm=new DMM(sw);
src=new Source;
```

to this:

```
sw=new Switch(this);
dmm=new DMM(sw,this);
src=new Source(this);
```

And the test creation would have to change from:

```
    tests[0]=new FrequencyResponseTest();
    tests[1]=new OutputAtFrequencyTest();
```

to this:

```
    tests[0]=new FrequencyResponseTest(this);
    tests[1]=new OutputAtFrequencyTest(this);
```

After all of these changes, each class that derives from `Object` will have a pointer to the `TestStation` object. The `getTestStation` method in `Object` now simply returns the `ts` variable:

```
TestStation *Object::getTestStation(){
    return ts;
}
```

We choose to use Solution #2. It is clear that Solution #2 requires more changes to more classes, so...

Why are we using this mechanism?

The answer is simple. If at some point in the future we decide we want to support multiple `TestStations` within a single application (so we can simultaneously test multiple DUTs), then the approach of using a global variable as is used in Solution #1 in TestStation fails. Solution #1 limits us to exactly one instance of the TestStation class in our system. While we only need one instance in our example system, it is not unreasonable to assume we will need more than one instance in the future. Solution #2 allows us to have multiple TestStation classes, since each Object contains its own local pointer to the correct TestStation instance. Solution #2 is a little bit more work now for a potentially large advantage in the future.

> ***A Good Rule of Thumb*:** If your design requires a global variable to provide easy access to an object, you are potentially limiting the future usability of your design. Rethink the use of that variable. Does it really make sense? Is it really needed? Is it appropriate? Does another, potentially more complicated design make more sense? It is usually easier to make such changes earlier in the design, than later.

Calling the Test System

Before we can use this test system, we must create a main program that instantiates our TestStation and calls it appropriately. We will make a simple main program that creates the TestStation and five DUTs. It will then connect each of the five DUTs to the test system sequentially and test the DUTs. When it is done, it will examine the DUTs and print the results of the tests.

First, we must declare the appropriate variables:

```
main(){
    int i;
    TestStation ts; // Create the TestStation object
    DUT *DUT[5]; // Create room for the DUTs
```

Then we must create the DUTs themselves:

```
    for(i=0;i<5;++i)
        DUT[i]=new DUT(10+i); // Serial num are 10..14
```

Now, let us connect each DUT in turn to the test system and test it:

```
for(i=0;i<5;++i){
    printf("Connect DUT#%ld to test station,"
            " press <return>\n",
            DUT[i]->getSerialNumber());
    getchar();
    printf("Testing DUT#%ld...",
            DUT[i]->getSerialNumber());
    ts.connectDUT(DUT[i]);
    ts.testDUT();
    printf("done.\n");
    ts.disconnectDUT();
}
```

Now that all DUTs have been tested, let us see which ones have passed and which ones have failed:

```
printf("The following DUTs passed all tests:\n");
for(i=0;i<5;++i){
    if(DUT[i]->DUTPassed()){
        printf("    DUT#%ld\n",
                DUT[i]->getSerialNumber());
    }
}
printf("The following DUTs failed a test:\n");
for(i=0;i<5;++i){
    if(!DUT[i]->DUTPassed()){
        printf("    DUT#%ld\n",
                DUT[i]->getSerialNumber());
    }
}
```

If the DUT fails, we also want to print out why it failed. So in the second *if* clause above, let us get the DUT results (the Error class instance) and print it out as well:

```
    if(!DUT[i]->DUTPassed()){
        Error *res;
        printf("    DUT#ld:\n",
                    DUT[i]->getSerialNumber()
                );
        // Get the results from this DUT and print
        res=DUT[i]->getFailedResult();
        res->displayError();
    }
```

The output of this main program may look like this:

```
Connect DUT#10 to test station, press <return>
Connect DUT#11 to test station, press <return>
Connect DUT#12 to test station, press <return>
Connect DUT#13 to test station, press <return>
Connect DUT#14 to test station, press <return>
The following DUTs passed all tests:
    DUT#10
    DUT#11
    DUT#12
    DUT#14
The following DUTs failed a test:
    DUT#13:
Error(5): DUT Failed: Thu Jul 27 14:01:44 1995:
   Failed to calculate w0, w1, or w2 correctly
   Details: scanFreqMaxVoltage: no peak

FileName=C:\OOTM\Measurement\Frequency\Frequency.cxx
   Line=130
```

In our test system, we require the user of this application to manually attach the device to the test fixturing, then press the <return> key before we test it. In a real test system, this would probably be an assembly-line robot that would attach the device before the test would run.

Putting It All Together

The disk provided with this book contains a working example of the test system we have created over the last several chapters. It is contained in several directories that are organized similar to the inheritance tree for this system. For example, there is a directory for the `FrequencyMeasurement`, `MaxValMeasurement`, and `ReadAtFreqMeasurement` classes. Each of these directories is contained within the `Measurement` directory, which also contains the code for the `Measurement` base class.

In the base directory is a makefile designed for use with Microsoft's Visual C++ 2.0. The project should be able to be built and executed as is.

Pseudo-Instruments

There is an implementation of pseudo-instrumentation classes included on the disk. This is an implementation of the `DMM` and `Source` classes that do not talk to any hardware and do not make use of the `IOIntf` class. Instead, the `DMM` and `Source` pseudo-instruments communicate to make it look like the test system is connected to real instruments. In particular, when you attempt to measure the voltage or current from the `DMM`, it asks the `Source` what the input voltage and current is. Using these two values, the pseudo-`DMM` figures out what the output voltage of an ideal `DUT` would be and returns the correct result. Using these pseudo-classes, you can get the test system up and working without any instruments or other hardware other than the computer to run the program. This is a good environment for debugging the test system. The pseudo-`DMM` also does a special check to the `DUT` connected. If the `DUT` has a serial number of 13, then the pseudo-`DMM` generates an invalid voltage (it acts like the output voltage is always 0). This should cause the testing of `DUT` #13 to fail. You may update this pseudo-`DMM` to perform other invalid calculations to simulate other `DUT` failures, if you desire.

Appendix B contains more information about the contents of the disk and how to install the code on your system.

Summary

This chapter brings together all the pieces for the object oriented test system that we have been building since Chapter 8. We discuss the creation of the `DUT` class, the `TestStation` class, and the `Object` class. Finally, we show a sample main program that calls the `TestStation` class to test a series of `DUT`s. A complete working example of the test system discussed in these chapters is included on the disk provided with this book. This example can be compiled and executed without using any real test hardware by making use of the pseudo-instruments also contained on the disk. These pseudo-instruments simulate the actions of the instruments and the `DUT` connected to them.

Exercises

Exercise 12-1. Think of three possible extensions to the `DUT` class that would make it more useful in a real test system design.

Exercise 12-2. In order to save time testing `DUT`s, you have decided to only spot check the `DUT`s. Modify the `TestStation` class as follows: Execute the `FrequencyResponseTest` only on every other `DUT`. Execute the `OutputAtFrequencyTest` only on three out of every four `DUT`s. However, make sure that at least one of the tests is executed on every `DUT`. What method(s) in `TestStation` need to change? Do any other classes need to change?

Exercise 12-3. Modify the `TestStation` class to take every fourth `DUT` and run all tests five times on the `DUT`, in order to determine if there is any intermittent faults. Do any classes other than `TestStation` have to be modified?

Exercise 12-4. Modify the `DUT` class to return information about whether the `DUT` should be tested simply, completely, or completely repetitively. Allow specifying of how the `DUT` is to be tested in the constructor of the `DUT`. Modify the `TestStation` class to check the `DUT` to see how it should be tested. If it should be tested simply, then only spot test it as discussed in Exercise 12-2. If it should be completely tested, run all tests on this `DUT`. If it should be tested completely repetitively, test it as discussed in Exercise 12-3.

Exercise 12-5. Modify the `DUT` and `TestStation` classes to record in the `DUT` the number of tests that have been executed on the `DUT`. Use this number in the sample main program to determine how completely the `DUT` has been tested and print out the result along with the passed/failed indication.

Exercise 12-6. What are some of the ramifications of using throw instead of the `didTestPass` method in the `TestStation` base class?

Exercise 12-7. Why does using Solution #1 for the creation of the Object class cause create problems for testing multiple `DUT`s simultaneously?

Exercise 12-8. Modify the pseudo-DMM class to cause four other `DUT`s with serial numbers 6, 9, 10, and 14 to fail in different ways. Modify the main program to test `DUT`s with serial numbers 0-19.

Exercise 12-9. Compare and contrast the test system constructed in Chapter 4 with the test system constructed in this chapter. What are the advantages and disadvantages of this design over the design in Chapter 4?

Exercise 12-10. Using Exercise 12-9, what do you see are the advantages to an object oriented design vs. a non-object oriented design? Consider not only the process of creating the system, but also the long-term support and upkeep of the system, and the ability to add future extensions to the system as needed.

Exercise 12-11. How hard would it be to make this test system test multiple `DUT`s simultaneously compared to the test system in Chapter 4? What changes would be needed to each? How would using multiple operating system threads to test different `DUT`s make each design change?

Part IV

Advanced Topics

13. Creating OO Data Types

Topics Covered:

Using C++ Classes

New C++ Data Types

Type Conversion

Math Operators

Reference Counts

Assignment Operator

Copy Constructor

Complex Number Type

`UnitData` Type

Signal Type

What happens if the data your application uses contains both real and imaginary components? What support for complex numbers is provided in C? The answer is quite simple...none.

Typically, programmers who want to deal with complex numbers have to deal with complex numbers as a pair of numbers (usually in a structure). Then, when math operations are necessary on these numbers (such as multiplying two complex numbers together), you must perform the math operations yourself manually.

Now, what was that equation again.....

Wouldn't it be nice to be able to write complex number arithmetic code that looks just like real number arithmetic code? Code like the following:

```
Complex num1 = 3+2i;
Complex num2 = 4;
Complex num3 = 3i;
Complex answer;

answer = ( num1 + num2 ) *
num3;
```

While C++ does not directly support complex numbers as shown above, it does allow creation of new, user-defined data types that behave similar to the above. This capability allows a user (or library supplier) to create a user-defined data type called "Complex" that performs complex number arithmetic.

This is a very powerful feature of C++. It allows an application that handles specialized data to handle that data in a natural, non-convoluted way, while isolating the convoluted math and other operations necessary to manipulate the specialized data into easy to understand and identify sections.

This chapter discusses how to create new user-defined data types in C++. It does this by showing three example user-defined data types:

- **Complex Number**: This is a user-defined data type that allows handling complex numbers (numbers with real and imaginary components). It allows performing basic math operations (such as addition, subtraction, multiplication, and division) on these numbers and conversion of complex numbers to and from the standard C++ **`double`** data type.

- **`UnitData`**: This is a user-defined data type that allows handling a floating point number (`double`) with basic units applied (mass, length, and time). So, for example, an element of type `UnitData` can store the value "3.5 met/sec," or "9.2 kg-met/sec^2." It allows performing basic math operations (such as addition, subtraction, multiplication, and division) on these numbers and conversion between standard C++ data types and the `UnitData` data type.

- **`Signal`**: This is a user-defined data type that allows handling an arbitrary "signal". In this context, a "signal" is a sequence of Y-values along an X-axis that describe some event. The classic example of a signal that could be stored in this data type is an oscilloscope sweep. This data type allows basic math operations (addition, subtraction) of multiple signals (one signal added to another signal), as well as adding, subtracting, multiplying, and dividing real numbers to signals (such as multiplying a signal by a constant value of 10.0). In addition, you can pull individual values out of the signal and store individual values into the signal. The class allows efficient handling of the signal, including passing a signal by value to procedures, and assigning a signal to new variables efficiently (without necessarily copying all of the data).

We will first discuss how to use C++ classes for creating new data types. Then, each of these three data types will be discussed in turn, each bringing up new issues associated with creating data types.

Using C++ Classes for New Data Types

The basic building block for new data types in C++ is the C++ class. We have already learned how the class worked for creating objects in a traditional object oriented programming environment. We even alluded to the fact that the relationship between a C++ Class and a C++ Object is very similar to the relationship between a data type (such as `integer`) and a variable (such as x).

In fact, the relationships are so close that C++ treats them exactly the same. Creating a new C++ Class creates a new data type within C++. Creating an instance of a C++ Class (an Object) creates a new variable of that type. All operations (+, -, *, /, =, etc.) that can be performed on variables from built-in data types can be performed on C++ class instances. This allows us to make C++ classes that look and act just like built-in C++ data types.

Creating a New C++ Type

Creating a new C++ data type involves the following steps:

- Design the data your new type will contain
- Create constructors/destructors for creating and destroying instances of your new data type.
- Create assignment operator and copy constructor to copy data from one instance to another.
- Create type conversion operations to convert data back and forth from standard C++ data types to your new data type.
- Create the math operations that you want to perform on your data type.
- Create the remaining operations, such as +=, *=, [], etc.
- Create methods to display instances of your type in human-readable form.

Data Contained in the New Type

A new user-defined data type needs some way of representing the data the type is trying to define. Often, there can be many ways the data can be represented. For example, a complex number can be represented as two floating point numbers, one containing the real portion of the complex number and another containing the imaginary portion. An alternate way to represent the same complex number is to use two floating point numbers with the first containing the polar magnitude of the complex number, and the other containing the polar angle of the complex number. Both are acceptable representations for the same number.

The creator of the new user-defined data type must choose how to represent the number. This decision may be arbitrary, or it may be based on how the new data type will be used. It is possible that during the creation of a new data type, it will become clearer what representation is better or easier, and the data representation can be adjusted to match.

Constructors/Destructor

The constructors are used to initialize data within the class and perform any other setup that is necessary for the data within the class. The destructor is used to perform any cleanup the data needs before it is destroyed.

Assignment/Copy Constructor

The assignment operator (operator =) and the copy constructor are used to create duplicates of an instance of a data type.

The assignment operator (operator =) copies the variable on the right-hand side of the equal sign into the variable on the left-hand side, destroying any previous contents of the left-hand side variable. The assignment operator implements the functionality necessary to perform actions such as the following:

```
Newtype a,b,c;

a=b;
a=c;
b=c;
...
```

The copy constructor is used to create a new instance of the data type by duplicating the value of another instance of the data type. The copy constructor is used when an instance of the data type is passed by value to a procedure (which temporarily creates a new variable of the given type), when creating temporary instances of variables for performing complex math operations, and when initializing a new variable with a given variable. The following are some examples:

```
procedure(Newtype x){
    // x is created using the copy constructor
    // changes to x do not affect a or b below
}

main(){
    Newtype a;

    // Copy constructor is used during call:
    procedure(a);

    // Copy constructor is used to create new variable
b:
    Newtype b=a;

    // Copy constructor is used again during call
    procedure(b);
}
```

Both the assignment operator and the copy constructor are needed for a complete user-defined data type.

Type Conversion

Type conversions are necessary to convert data from built-in data types to the new user-defined type, and to convert from the user-defined type to built-in data types. Each of these is performed with different types of methods.

Converting from Built-In to User-Defined

Let us say you want to be able to convert a floating-point `double` into the new user-defined type. This would allow code such as the following to work:

```
Newtype a;
double x;

x = 3.5;

a = (Newtype)x;
a = (Newtype)4.2;
```

This is accomplished by creating specialized constructors within the new user-defined data type. For example, to convert a `double` to a `Newtype`, you must have a constructor in `Newtype` that accepts one parameter, which is a `double`. The following code segment shows the declaration of such a constructor:

```
class Newtype{
   public:
      // Used to convert double's to Newtype's
      Newtype(double);
};
```

As many one-parameter constructors as is desired may be included in the new user-defined type. Each of these one-parameter constructors allows conversion from the parameter's data type to the user-defined type.

Converting from User-defined to Built-in

Let us say you want to be able to convert a variable of the user-defined type into a double. This would allow code such as the following to work:

```
Newtype a;
double x;

x = (double)a;
```

This is accomplished by special operators in the class called type-conversion operators. In order for the above code to work, you would need a type-conversion operator for a double. The following code segment shows the declaration of such an operator:

```
class Newtype{
   public:
      double operator double();
};
```

The implementation of this operator would convert the given `Newtype` into a double and return it. This method would allow automatic conversion from variables of type `Newtype`, to variables of type double.

Operators

Math operators need to be implemented to perform whatever math the user-defined type wants to support. The declaration for these operators was discussed in Chapter 6, but essentially looks something like this:

```
class Newtype{
    ...
    public:
        Newtype operator +(Newtype& rhs);
        Newtype operator -(Newtype& rhs);
        Newtype operator ++();
    ...
};
```

These declarations allow operations such as:

```
Newtype a,b,c;

a = b + c;
b++;
a = b - c;
```

Math Assignment Operators

Math assignment operators perform a combination of assignment, like the `operator=` operator described above, with the math operators. Examples of these operators are:

```
class Newtype {
    public:
        NewType& operator +=(Newtype& rhs);
        NewType& operator -=(Newtype& rhs);
        ...
};
```

These declarations allow operations such as:

```
Newtype a, b, c;

a += b;
a -= c;
```

Complex Number Type

This section discusses the implementation of an example user-defined data type for handling complex numbers. A complex number, for purposes of this example, is defined as a number that contains a real component and an imaginary component. An arbitrary complex number can be represented as follows:

$$x + iy$$

Where:

x = real portion of the number.
y = imaginary portion of the number.
$i = \sqrt{-1}$

Complex numbers can be stored, converted to/from pairs-of-doubles, and have math operations (+, -, *, /) performed on them. Other operations may be performed on complex numbers, but these are outside the scope of this example.

Data Contents

There are two potential representations for the complex number that we can choose. The first is the *rectangular coordinate* version of the number, that is:

$$x + iy$$

This was discussed briefly above in the definition of a complex number. The other representation is the *polar coordinate* version of the number, that is:

$$|r| + \alpha\angle$$

Where:

r = polar-magnitude of the number.
α = polar-angle of the number.

The relationship between these two representations is shown in Figure 13-1. Here, the real portion of the complex number is shown along the X axis, while the imaginary portion of the complex number is shown along the Y axis. The dot is the value of a given complex number – it has both a real component and an imaginary component. The rectangular representation of the number can be expressed with the real values x and y, where x is the length of the real portion and y is the length of the imaginary portion. The number can also be expressed as a radius and angle. The radius, r, and the angle, α.

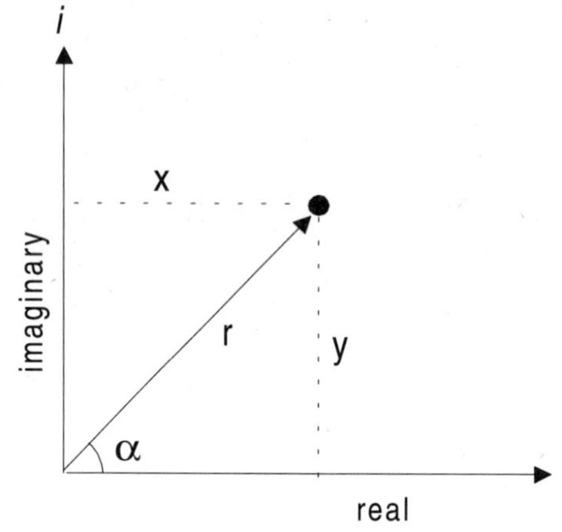

Figure 13-1: Polar and Rectangular Coordinates

The conversion from rectangular to polar can be expressed easily using simple trigonometry:

$$r = \sqrt{x^2 + y^2}$$

$$\alpha = \tan^{-1} \frac{y}{x}$$

Equation 13-1: Converting from rectangular to polar

The conversion from polar to rectangular can also be expressed easily:

$$x = r * \cos \alpha$$

$$y = r * \sin \alpha$$

Equation 13-2: Converting from polar to rectangular

Either representation is acceptable. For this example, we will choose the rectangular coordinates. So, the data contained in the Complex class will look like this:

```
class Complex{
   private:
      // real + i * imag
      double real;
      double imag;
   ...
};
```

Constructors/Destructor

There are three styles of creation that we desire with the Complex class. The first is to create a variable without caring what its initial value is, the second is to create a variable and initialize it to a value given in rectangular coordinates, the third is to create a variable and initialize it to a value given in polar coordinates.

This can be achieved with three constructors. The first constructor is the default constructor that accepts no parameters:

```
Complex();
```

The second constructor requires two doubles, the first for the X coordinate of the number and the second for the Y coordinate of the number:

```
Complex(double x,double y);
```

Now, the third is a little tricky. We also need two doubles for the polar coordinate version. However, we can only have one constructor that accepts just two doubles, so we will add an artificial third parameter, an int, that identifies this constructor as the polar constructor. The parameter's value is ignored:

```
Complex(double r,double a,int);
```

This constructor has the polar-magnitude, r, and the polar angle, a. The polar-angle is represented in radians, not degrees.

The following code segment shows a sample of how these three constructors can be used:

```
// Create 'a' with any initial value
Complex a;

// Create 'b' with the initial value 5.1+7.3i:
Complex b(5, 7);

// Create 'c' with the initial value |2.1|+1.414∠:
Complex c(2.1, 1.414, 1);
```

The declaration of these constructors looks like the following:

```
class Complex{
    ...
    public:
        Complex();
        Complex(double x,double y);
        Complex(double r,double a,int);
    ...
};
```

The implementation of the default constructor will simply store the value 0 into the complex number:

```
Complex::Complex(){
    // Store 0 into variables
    real = 0.0;
    imag = 0.0;
}
```

The implementation of the rectangular coordinate constructor is also trivial, we simply store the values passed to the constructor into the member variables:

```
Complex::Complex(double x,double y){
    real = x;
    imag = y;
}
```

The implementation of the polar coordinate constructor is a little bit more involved. This constructor involves converting the polar coordinate values to rectangular coordinate values and storing them into the member variables. Take a look at Equation 13-2 again. Here is the implementation:

```
Complex::Complex(double r,double a,int){
    real = r * sin(a);
    imag = r * cos(a);
}
```

The destructor for the Complex type does not have to perform any operations. It may be omitted, or may be implemented as a null procedure:

```
class Complex{
    ...
    public:
        ~Complex();
    ...
};

Complex::~Complex(){
}
```

Assignment/Copy Constructor

All standard assignment operators and copy constructors have similar declarations:

```
Complex {
    ...
    public:
        Complex(Complex& c);
        Complex& operator=(Complex& rhs);
    ...
};
```

The copy constructor simply creates a new Complex variable given another, its implementation is simple:

```
Complex::Complex(Complex& c){
    real=c.real;
    imag=c.imag;
}
```

All we are doing is copying all of the data elements from the source variable, named c, to the destination which is the variable we are creating.

The assignment operator does basically the same thing, with one added step:

```
Complex& Complex::operator =(Complex& rhs){
    real=rhs.real;
    imag=rhs.imag;

    return *this;
}
```

This operator is used to execute code segments similar to the following:

```
Complex a, b;
a = b;
```

In this example, the `operator=` method is executed within the complex number a, and it passes the complex number b to the `operator=` method as the `rhs` parameter. The `rhs` parameter name is short for "right-hand-side" which is used to signify it is the complex number on the right-hand side of the = assignment.

The extra step that is added to this operator is the return code. It returns a reference to a complex number, with the return value being `*this`. What this means is that the `operator=`, after assigning the value of `rhs` to the `lhs` (a, the number whose instance is used to execute the `operator=` method), returns the result of the assignment. In the case of the `operator=`, the result of the assignment is the new value of the `left-`

`hand side` (which is `*this`). This is used to implement multiple assignments, such as:

```
Complex a, b, c;

a = b = c;
```

This code segment is equivalent to:

```
Complex a,b,c;

a=(b=c);
```

So, b is assigned the value of c. Then a is assigned the value returned from the assignment of `b=c`. Normally, the return from `operator=` is ignored, but in this case the return from the `operator=` executed to assign b to c is used as the `rhs` parameter to the `operator=` call on a. This nesting can continue any number of levels.

Type Conversion

There are two conversions that are desired, the first is converting a `double` to a `Complex`, and the other is converting a `Complex` to a `double`.

Converting a double to a Complex

What does it mean to convert a double into a Complex? Since a complex number is actually two doubles, what could we possibly do with a single double? How about using the double as the real portion of the number, and set the imaginary portion of the number to 0.

```
Complex a;
double b;

b=5.0;
a=(Complex)b;

// What is value of 'a' and 'b' here?
```

At the end of this code, the double b will contain 5.0 and a will contain:

$$5.0 + i\,0.0$$

which is the same value as b. This is the expected behavior. So the definition we will use will be to use the double number as the real portion of the Complex, and set the imaginary portion of the Complex to 0.

The following is the declaration of this conversion constructor:

```
Complex(double x);
```

The following is the implementation of this constructor:

```
Complex::Complex(double x){
    real=x;
    imag=0;
};
```

Converting a Complex to a Double

How about converting a complex number to a double? Well, we could use the reverse of the above, that is the conversion of a complex number to a double means to use the real portion of the number and ignore the imaginary portion. Another implementation is to return the polar radius of the complex number and ignore the angle.

We will choose the latter, since in the special case where the imaginary portion of the number is zero, the two implementations are the same. This ends up being very consistent with the double to Complex conversion, above. But in the case where there is an imaginary portion, the polar radius may be a more useful number to use. This argument is, of course, subjective but this definition allows code similar to the following to work correctly:

```
Complex a;
double x,y;

x=2.5;

a=(Complex)x;
y=(double)a;

if(x==y)
    ... // They are the same
```

The conversion of a Complex to a double involves the following declaration within the Complex data class:

```
Complex{
    ...
    public:
        double operator double();
    ...
};
```

The following is the implementation of this operator:

```
double Complex::operator double(){
    return sqrt(real*real+imag*imag);
}
```

Math Operators

The Complex class will implement the four basic math operators, addition (+), subtraction (-), multiplication (*), and division(/).

operator +

The math involved in adding two complex numbers in rectangular coordinates is fairly simple:

$$R = A + B$$
$$R_r + i R_i = (A_r + i A_i) + (B_r + i B_i)$$
$$R_r + i R_i = (A_r + B_r) + i * (A_i + B_i)$$

so:

$$R_r = A_r + B_r$$
$$R_i = A_i + B_i$$

Equation 13-3: Adding Complex Numbers

The declaration for the addition operator is as follows:

```
class Complex{
    ...
    public:
        Complex operator+(Complex& rhs);
    ...
};
```

And the implementation is as follows:

```
Complex Complex::operator+(Complex& rhs){
    Complex res;

    res.real = real + rhs.real;
    res.imag = imag + rhs.imag;

    return res;
}
```

This routine will add the left-hand side of the addition command (the `lhs` is the instance that the method is executed with, so *this* is `lhs`) to the right-hand side. It stores the result in a temporary complex number called `res`, then returns the result.

It should be noted that when we execute the line `return res`, the *contents* of `res` are returned to the caller (by value), not `res` itself. This is because `res` is a local variable to this method and goes away when the routine returns. The contents of `res` are copied into a temporary complex number, which is used to complete the operation in the caller routine. This temporary complex number is created using the copy constructor we described above. The `res` variable itself has its default constructor called when this routine is executed and the variable is declared, and its destructor called when the return statement is executed.

operator –

The math involved in subtracting two complex numbers in rectangular coordinates is just as straightforward:

$$R = A - B$$
$$R_r + i R_i = (A_r + i A_i) - (B_r + i B_i)$$
$$R_r + i R_i = (A_r - B_r) + i * (A_i - B_i)$$

so:

$$R_r = A_r - B_r$$
$$R_i = A_i - B_i$$

Equation 13-4: Subtracting Complex Numbers

The declaration for the subtraction operator is as follows:

```
class Complex{
    ...
    public:
        Complex operator-(Complex& rhs);
    ...
};
```

And the implementation is as follows:

```
Complex Complex::operator-(Complex& rhs){
    Complex res;

    res.real = real - rhs.real;
    res.imag = imag - rhs.imag;

    return res;
}
```

operator *

The math for complex number multiplication is a bit more complicated:

$$R = A * B$$
$$R_r + i R_i = (A_r + i A_i) * (B_r + i B_i)$$
$$R_r + i R_i = (A_r B_r) + i A_r B_i + i A_i B_r + i^2 A_i B_i$$
$$R_r + i R_i = A_r B_r + i(A_r B_i + A_i B_r) - A_i B_i$$
$$R_r + i R_i = (A_r B_r - A_i B_i) + i(A_r B_i + A_i B_r)$$

so:

$$R_r = A_r B_r - A_i B_i$$
$$R_i = A_r B_i + A_i B_r$$

Equation 13-5: Multiplying Complex Numbers

The implementation of this method is as follows:

```
Complex Complex::operator*(Complex& rhs){
    Complex res;

    res.real = real * rhs.real
                - imag * rhs.imag;
    res.imag = real * rhs.imag
                + imag * rhs.real;

    return res;
}
```

operator /

The math for division is fairly complex:

$$R = \frac{A}{B}$$

$$R_r + i\,R_i = \frac{(A_r + i\,A_i)}{(B_r + i\,B_i)}$$

$$R_r + i\,R_i = \frac{(A_r + i\,A_i)}{(B_r + i\,B_i)} \bullet \frac{(B_r - i\,B_i)}{(B_r - i\,B_i)}$$

$$R_r + i\,R_i = \frac{(A_r + i\,A_i) \bullet (B_r - i\,B_i)}{(B_r + i\,B_i) \bullet (B_r - i\,B_i)}$$

$$R_r + i\,R_i = \frac{A_r B_r - i\,A_r B_i + i\,A_i B_r - i^2 A_i B_i}{B_r^2 + B_i^2}$$

$$R_r + i\,R_i = \frac{(A_r B_r + A_i B_i) + i(A_i B_r - A_r B_i)}{B_r^2 + B_i^2}$$

$$R_r + i\,R_i = \left(\frac{A_r B_r + A_i B_i}{B_r^2 + B_i^2}\right) + i\left(\frac{A_i B_r - A_r B_i}{B_r^2 + B_i^2}\right)$$

so:

$$R_r = \frac{A_r B_r + A_i B_i}{B_r^2 + B_i^2}$$

$$R_i = \frac{A_i B_r - A_r B_i}{B_r^2 + B_i^2}$$

Equation 13-6: Dividing Complex Numbers

The implementation of these equations is equally complex:

```
Complex Complex::operator/(Complex& rhs){
    // R = res
    // A = *this
    // B = rhs
    Complex res;

    double divisor;

    divisor = rhs.real * rhs.real
                + rhs.imag * rhs.imag;

    res.real = ((real * rhs.real)
                + (imag * rhs.imag))
             / divisor;
    res.imag = ((imag * rhs.real)
                + (real * rhs.imag))
                / divisor;

    return res;
}
```

This method should, if nothing else does, show the power of user-defined types. The math to implement complex division is not simple or intuitive at all. However, once you have implemented it within the user-defined Complex type class, it can be used anywhere as simply as dividing two integers, or doubles, and so forth:

```
Complex a,b,c;

a = b / c;
```

This is the power of user-defined data types.

Math Assignment Operators

Now that we have "=" implemented, and "+" implemented, what about "+="? This operator is very straightforward as well:

```
Complex& Complex::operator+=(Complex& rhs){
    *this = *this + rhs;

    return *this;
}
```

This routine uses the `operator+` method to add `*this` to `rhs`. It then uses the `operator=` method to store the result back into `*this`. Then, just like `operator=`, this routine returns `*this`, which is the result of this addition.

A similar sort of implementation can be used for:

```
operator -=
operator *=
operator /=
```

Other Methods

We need other methods to complete our class, namely:

```
class Complex{
    ...
    // Return the real portion of a complex number
    double getReal();
    // Return the imaginary portion of number
    double getImag();
    // Return the polar radius of a complex number
    double getRadius();
    // Return the polar angle of a complex number
    double getAngle();
    ...
};
```

The implementation of these simply return the relevant portion of the complex number, or calculate it as necessary:

```
double Complex::getReal(){
    return real;
}
double Complex::getImag(){
    return imag;
}
double Complex::getRadius(){
    return sqrt(real*real + imag*imag);
}
double Complex::getAngle(){
    return atan2(imag,real);
}
```

Finally, we need methods that return human-readable versions of the complex number:

```
class Complex{
    ...
    public:
        char *getRectString(char *buf);
        char *getPolarString(char *buf);
    ...
};
```

These functions are implemented as:

```
char *Complex::getRectString(char *buf){
    sprintf(buf,"%g + %g i",real,imag);
    return buf;
}
char *Complex::getPolarString(char *buf){
    sprintf(buf,"|%g| + %g
rad",getRadius(),getAngle());
    return buf;
}
```

These methods can be used as follows:

```
Complex a(2,2);
char buf[80];

printf("The value of a is: %s\n",
                              getRectString(buf));
printf("The polar value of a is: %s\n",
                              getPolarString(buf));
```

We now have a fairly complete and usable implementation of a `Complex` number type.

`UnitData` Type

This section discusses the implementation of a user-defined data type for handling *unitful* data. This is data that has not only a value associated with it, but also units. Some examples of values that instances of type `UnitData` can contain are:

$$3.5\frac{meters}{sec}$$

$$5.4\frac{kgram \bullet meters}{sec}$$

$$2.1\frac{kmeters}{sec}$$

`UnitData` values can be stored, assigned, converted to/from doubles, and have basic math operations performed on them. With the basic math operations, correct unit updating is performed as well.

Unlike the Complex example, above, only a partial description of the class will be given. Only the portions of `UnitData` that are unique to it and not discussed in the `Complex` example will be given. The rest of the `UnitData` definition will be left as an exercise. However, a complete working example of `UnitData` is included on the enclosed disk.

Data Contents

The data elements for `UnitData` consist of two main parts:

- The value portion of the `UnitData`.
- The units portion of the `UnitData`.

The value portion of the `UnitData` will be treated as a simple floating-point double value:

```
double value; // Base value of UnitData
```

The units portion requires a little more thought. While there are many different types of units that can be represented, this simple example will limit itself to three base unit types:

- meters -- A unit of length.
- seconds -- A unit of time.
- grams -- A unit of mass.

Other potential units of value to the test and measurement engineer that are not contained in the base implementation but can be easily added later include:

- volts -- A unit of electrical potential.
- amps -- A unit of electrical current flow.
- ohms -- A unit of electrical resistance.
- farads -- A unit of electrical capacitance.
- henries -- A unit of electrical inductance.

These will not be considered in this example. Now, for each unit type, we can have powers of the base unit, such as:

- meters
- kilometers (1000 meters)
- centimeters (.01 meters)
- millimeter (.001 meters)

Also, we may have multiples of each unit:

- sec
- sec^2
- sec^{-1}

So, in general, a unit can have the following characteristics associated with it:

- **Exponent**. The power-of-10 that the unit has (km vs. meters, etc.).
- **Power**. The number of units that apply (sec vs. sec^2 vs. sec^{-1})

This can be expressed mathematically as:

$$10^{\exp} * unit^{power}$$

We need an exponent and power for each of the three base units.

The entire data contents of the `UnitData` class can be expressed as:

```
class UnitData {
   private:
      struct Unit{
         int exp;
         int power;
      };

      double value;
      Unit time;
      Unit length;
      Unit mass;
};
```

Mathematically, the entire data element can be expressed as:

$$UnitData = \left\{ \begin{array}{l} value * \\ (10^{time.\exp} * \sec^{time.power}) * \\ (10^{length.\exp} * meters^{length.power}) * \\ (10^{mass.\exp} * grams^{mass.power}) \end{array} \right\}$$

Constructors

We will create three different constructors for our class. The default constructor creates a base value of 0, with no units applied. The second constructor takes a single parameter that is a double. This is also used to convert doubles to `Data`'s. This constructor creates a `Data` variable with data value of the double, but with no units. The third constructor is a little different. It takes six integers:

```
UnitData(int massExponent,
         int massPower,
         int lengthExponent,
         int lengthPower,
         int timeExponent,
         int timePower);
```

This constructor creates a `UnitData` variable with a value of 1.0, with the given units. In addition, the following constant data variables are created with the `UnitData` class:

```
const Data grams=Data(0,1,0,0,0,0); // 1.0 grams
const Data kgrams=Data(3,1,0,0,0,0); // 1.0 kgrams
const Data meters=Data(0,0,0,1,0,0); // 1.0 meters
const Data kmeters=Data(0,0,3,1,0,0); // 1.0 kmeters
const Data seconds=Data(0,0,0,0,0,1); // 1.0 seconds
```

All together, along with the `operator=`, copy constructor, and multiplication and division operators (discussed later), the following code segments are allowed for creating variables with various values:

```
UnitData val, val2;

val = 3.5*kgrams*meters/seconds;
val2 = 2.1*meters/seconds;
```

The above code creates `val` and `val2` with the following values:

$$val = 3.5\frac{kgram \bullet meters}{seconds}$$

$$val2 = 2.1\frac{meters}{\sec onds}$$

Type Conversion

We discussed above the conversion of a double to a `UnitData`. What about converting a `UnitData` to a double?

The following operator converts a `UnitData` to a double by simply stripping off the units and returning the base value.

```
double UnitData::operator double(){
    normalize();
    return value;
}
```

The normalize() method simply changes all the units to base units by adjusting the units and the value. For example, the value 3.0 `kg` is converted to 3000 grams. This is necessary before the `value` can be returned, since the real value expressed in base units is not necessarily the same as the `value` parameter. This method is discussed later.

Math Operators

This section will discuss each of the four base math operations in turn.

operator *

Multiplication is the most interesting operator, because of the unit conversion that has to go on. As an example, take the following operation:

$$2.0\frac{meters}{seconds} \times 1.5kgrams$$

You would expect the result of this multiplication to be:

$$3.0\frac{kgrams \cdot meters}{seconds}$$

To multiply two `UnitData`'s together, you must multiply the values, then multiply each value's individual unit. To multiply two units together, you must perform the following arithmetic:

$$\left(10^{e_r} \cdot unit^{p_r}\right) = \left(10^{e_1} \cdot unit^{p_1}\right) \cdot \left(10^{e_2} \cdot unit^{p_2}\right)$$
$$\left(10^{e_r} \cdot unit^{p_r}\right) = 10^{e_1+e_2} \cdot unit^{p_1+p_2}$$
$$e_r = e_1 + e_2$$
$$p_r = p_1 + p_2$$

So, to multiply two `UnitDatas` together, you must:

1. Multiply the base values together.
2. For each unit, add the powers together.
3. For each unit, add the exponents together.

The following is the implementation of the multiplication operator:

```
UnitData UnitData::operator*(UnitData& rhs){
    UnitData prod;

    prod.value = value * rhs.value;
    prod.time.exponent = time.exponent
                           + rhs.time.exp;
    prod.time.power = time.power
                           + rhs.time.power;
    prod.length.exponent = length.exponent
                           + rhs.length.exp;
    prod.length.power = length.power
                           + rhs.length.power;
    prod.mass.exponent = mass.exponent
                           + rhs.mass.exp;
    prod.mass.power = mass.power
                           + rhs.mass.power;

    return prod;
}
```

operator /

Division is the same as multiplication, except the exponents and powers must be subtracted instead of added:

```
UnitData UnitData::operator/(UnitData& rhs){
    UnitData prod;

    prod.value = value / rhs.value;
    prod.time.exponent = time.exponent
                           - rhs.time.exp;
    prod.time.power = time.power
                           - rhs.time.power;
    prod.length.exponent = length.exponent
                           - rhs.length.exp;
    prod.length.power = length.power
                           - rhs.length.power;
    prod.mass.exponent = mass.exponent
                           - rhs.mass.exp;
    prod.mass.power = mass.power
                           - rhs.mass.power;

    return prod;
}
```

operator + and operator –

Addition and subtraction are a little trickier, since the units must match. It is an error, for example, to add 2 kg to 7 meters. As such, the operator + and operator - must verify unit correctness before performing the operation. Once the units are verified, then the operators may simply add or subtract the base value.

The following is the implementation of operator +:

```
UnitData& UnitData::operator+(UnitData& rhs){
    UnitData res;

    normalize(); // Normalize the lhs
    rhs.normalize(); // Normalize the rhs

    // Check units
    if(time.power != rhs.time.power)
        throw unitsMismatch;
    if(length.power != rhs.length.power)
        throw unitsMismatch;
    if(mass.power != rhs.mass.power)
        throw unitsMismatch;

    // Do the addition
    // First copy the units over
    res = rhs;
    // Next, store the correct value
    res.value = value + rhs.value;

    return res;
}
```

Subtraction is the same, except for the second to the last line, which should read:

```
    res.value = value - rhs.value;
```

If the units do not match when adding or subtracting two `UnitData` numbers, this routine throws a `unitMismatch` error. The `unitsMismatch` may be an integer, a string, an enum, or some other value that represents a `unitsMismatch` error.[1]

The Normalize Method

The normalize method takes a variable with non-base units (such as kg instead of grams) and converts it to a variable with only base units. It does this by taking the exponent parameters for each unit and changing them to 0. At the same time, it updates `value` so that it contains the same value as it did before the normalization.

For example, the following value:

$$2.1\,\frac{kgrams^2}{meters^2}$$

will convert to:

---

[1] This is discussed in more detail in Chapter 14.

$$2{,}100{,}000\ \frac{grams^2}{meters^2}$$

It did this by changing the exponent of grams from 3 to 0. This means that the base value must be updated by 1000^2 (it is squared because the original unit was squared).

The implementation of normalize() is left as an exercise.

Signal Type

This section discusses the implementation of a user-defined data type for handling signals. A "signal" is a sequence of Y-values along an X-axis that describes some event. A simple example of a signal is an oscilloscope sweep.

A signal is a series of floating-point numbers (Y-values) that each can be identified by a unique index. The indexes are also floating point numbers (X-values). The indexes are all equally spaced (so that Y-values are all equally spaced along the X-axis), but the spacing can be changed based on the signal type.

A Signal consists of the following elements:

1. An array of Y-values.

2. The starting X-axis value (the X-value for the first Y element in the array).

3. The delta X-axis value (the value that is added to each X-value to get the X-value of the next element in the array).

Figure 13-2 shows a sample signal. This signal shown contains the following values:

1. An array of 14 elements. Each element (Y-axis values) range from 2.0-8.0.

2. A starting X-axis value of 12.0.

3. A delta X-axis value of 1.5.

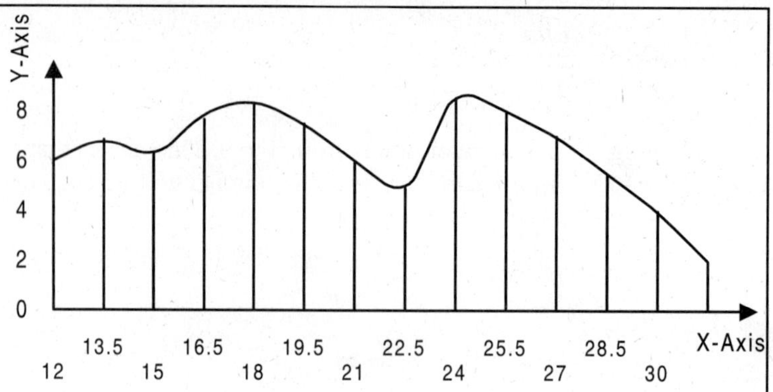

Figure 13-2: Example Signal

This signal type allows the following operations:

1. Add two signals to each other.

2. Subtract one signal from another.

3. Add, subtract, multiply, and divide a constant number from each element in the signal.

4. Access individual elements of the signal, and store values into individual elements of the signal.

5. Efficient handling of copying the signal from one variable to another. This is used for assignment operations, pass-by-value parameters, etc.

Data Contents

The signal class will contain the following data elements:

- An array of doubles, which corresponds to the elements of the signal.

- An integer specifying the number of elements in the array.

- The starting X-axis value for the signal.

- The delta X-axis value for individual elements of the signal.

There are some other interesting values of the array that can be calculated from the above values. One of them is the ending X-axis value. The ending X-axis value can be calculated by:

$$end = start + delta * (numElements - 1)$$

The next is an index into the array, given a specific X-axis value. This can be calculated by:

$$index = \left\lfloor \frac{xAxis - start}{delta} \right\rfloor$$

Where $\lfloor\ \rfloor$ means to round the value down to the nearest whole number.

The data for this class looks like the following:

```
class Signal {
   private:
   // Pointer to the array of double's
   //       -- This is the data
   double *data;
   // Number of elements in data
   long dataLen;

   // Delta-X, number of X-units per array element
   double xUnits;

   // The value of the first array element
   //       (X-axis):
   double xOffset;

   // Pointer to the refCnt -- the variable
   // *refCnt will contain the number of
   // Signal classes that refer to the array
   // 'data'. This is discussed later.
   int *refCnt;
   ...
};
```

Special Concerns

The biggest concern with the signal class is the data storage needed for the array. Since the size of the array varies based on individual instances of the signal class, the array must be dynamically allocated. It is dynamically allocated in the constructor, and the array is destroyed in the destructor. This is the first example of a user-defined data type that allocates memory, and has other than a default destructor.

This creates a special concern for the copy constructor and the `operator=`. These special methods must also allocate and free memory as appropriate. The copy constructor must allocate an array of the same size as the to-be-copied signal, then copy element by element into the new array. The `operator=` method must first delete the old array in the left-hand side of the assignment, then create a new one the same size as the right-hand size, then each element must be copied into the array.

Needless to say, this is a tedious task. It is also very inefficient, especially since the copy constructor can be called often (every time you pass a signal by value to a procedure).

So, rather than copying the array every time, we simply copy a pointer to the array. Then, we update a reference count that tells us how many signals point to the same array. The copy constructor simply copies the array pointer and increments the reference count. The primary constructor sets the reference count to 1, and the destructor decrements the reference count and only deletes the array if the reference count drops to 0.

In this model, the assignment operator (`operator=`) will do the functionality of a destructor first (removing its reference to the old array, possibly deleting it in the process), then perform the functionality of the copy constructor to increment the references to the right-hand side array.

Figure 13-3 shows the example of a copy constructor. In this case, we are creating the signal B from the signal A. To create B, we simply store a pointer to the array for A into B and update the reference count. Figure 13-4 shows the `operator=` method. In this case, we first delete the array allocated for A, then store a pointer to the array that B points to into A.

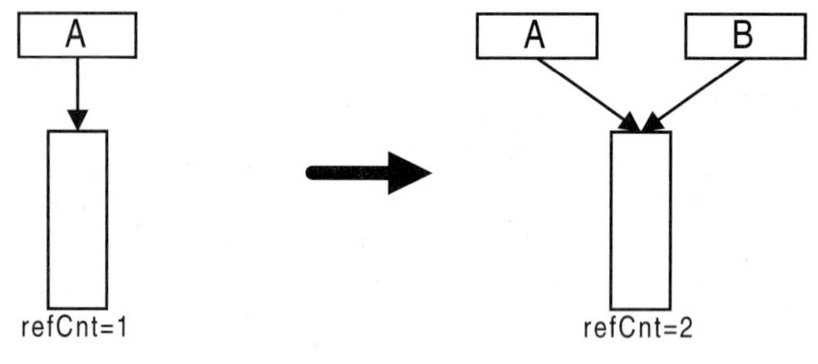

Figure 13-3: Copy Constructor (Creating B from A)

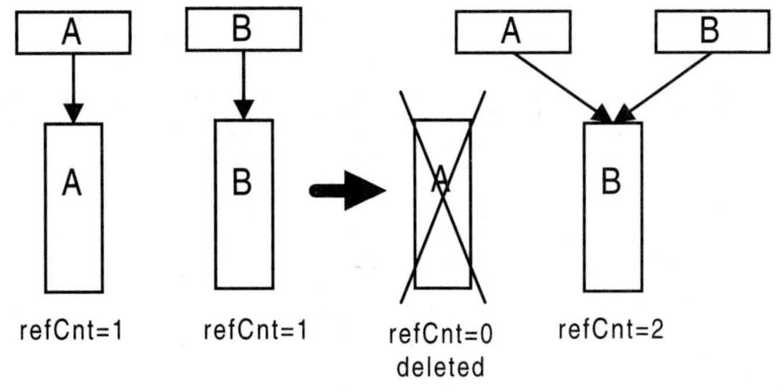

Figure 13-4: Assignment Operator (A=B)

The remaining issue is, what happens when it is necessary to change the array, such as to implement the `operator*=` method. The answer is simple. Before a signal is changed, it checks to see if its reference count is anything other than 1. If it is greater than 1, then we must unlink ourselves from the remaining copies, to prevent those other copies from also being changed. Figure 13-5 shows an example of this. Here, A is about to be updated. Since we do not want B to be updated as well, we create a new array of the same size, then copy the data element by element. Even though we are still doing data copies, we now only have to do data copies when we want to update a linked array, not during the original copy operation itself.

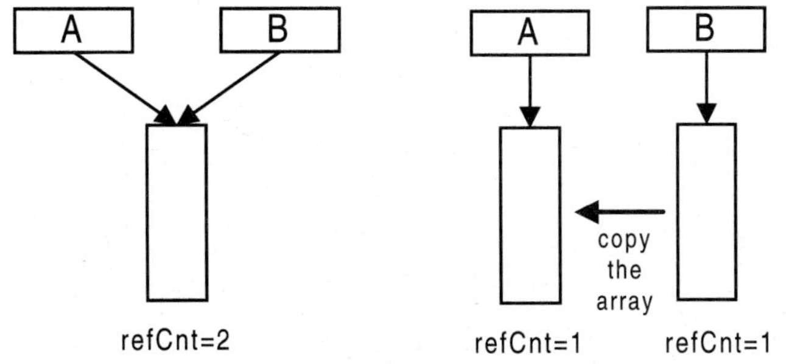

Figure 13-5: Unlinking 'A' from all others

Constructors/Destructor/Assignment Operator

There are several constructors that are included with the Signal class:

1. Default constructor. This creates a Signal with no data store in it. It has no starting X-value, delta X-value, or array size. It has no default ability to store data. The only operation that is valid with a Signal created this way is to be the left-hand side of an assignment, to copy another Signal into this Signal.

2. A constructor that specifies a starting X-value, delta X-value, and number of data points. This constructor creates the Signal of the specified size, but assigns all the points of the Signal (Y-values) the value 0.0.

3. A variant of the previous constructor, this constructor specifies a starting X-value, an ending X-value, and a delta X-value. It calculates the correct number of data points. Like the previous constructor, it stores the value 0.0 into all the points of the Signal.

4. A constructor that specifies a starting X-value, delta X-value, and the number of data points. Unlike constructor #2 above, this constructor also is given an array of doubles of the appropriate size. This array becomes the default value of the Signal, rather than 0.0. Each element in the array becomes a point in the Signal.

5. A copy-constructor. This constructor, as discussed above, actually does not copy the data, but makes a link to the data and increments a reference count. Only when the data is going to be modified is the link destroyed and the data copied.

There is also one destructor that performs the following activities:

1. Decrement the reference count to the data.

2. If the reference count is non-zero, simply return. The destructor does not actually do anything to the data.

3. If the reference count is 0, then the data, and the reference count variable itself, are deleted and the memory is freed.

We will describe the operation of one of the constructors, the destructor, and the copy constructor here. The code for the assignment operator is very similar to the copy constructor and the destructor. Its implementation is left as one of the exercises.

Constructor

We will show only one of the primary constructors to this class. Constructor #2 (above) has the following prototype:

```
Signal(long numElem, double deltaX, double startX);
```

It creates a `Signal` with `numElem` number of elements to it, with a starting X position of `startX`, and an increment in X-axis value for each element of `deltaX`. The implementation of this constructor looks like this:

```
Signal::Signal(
   long numElem,
   double deltaX,
   double startX
){
   int i;

   // Store away the offset and units (delta-X)
   xOffset = startX;
   xUnits = deltaX;

   // Create the refCnt variable, set it to 1
   //(this is a new data array)
   refCnt = new int;
   if(!refCnt)
      throw OUTOFMEMORY;[2]
   (*refCnt)=1;

   // Create the array
   dataLen = numElem;
   data = new double[dataLen];
   if(!refCnt)
      throw OUTOFMEMORY;

   // Store 0.0 into the array
   for(i=0 ; i<dataLen ; ++i)
      data[i]=0.0;
}
```

This constructor simply stores away the `startX` and `deltaX` values. Then it must create a new `refCnt` variable and set its value to 1, to show that this is the first `Signal` instance that will point to the newly created array. Finally, it creates the data array itself and stores 0.0 into each element of the array.

---

[2] Error handling is discussed in more detail in Chapter 14.

Copy Constructor

The copy constructor is very simple:

```
Signal::Signal(const Signal& copySignal){
    // Copy all the variables of the Signal
    xOffset=copySignal.xOffset;
    xUnits=copySignal.xUnits;
    dataLen=copySignal.dataLen;

    // Create a link to the data and refCnt
    data=copySignal.data;
    refCnt=copySignal.refCnt;

    // Since we now have another link to data, we
    // must increment the reference count
    (*refCnt)++;
};
```

The copy constructor simply copies all the primary variables one by one, then it creates a link to the data. Finally, it increments the reference count to show the new link to the data.

Destructor

The destructor is also quite simple:

```
Signal::~Signal(){
    (*refCnt)--;

    if((*refCnt)==0){
        delete refCnt;
        delete data;
    }
}
```

The destructor decrements the reference count. If the count is not 0, that means another Signal class is referring to the data. In that case, the destructor simply terminates. If, however, this Signal instance is the last Signal instance to refer to this data (i.e., `refCnt` is now 0), then the data and the `refCnt` variable itself are deleted.

Unlinking for Change

The last remaining activity related to the linking of data is how to manage unlinking a `Signal` from other `Signals` in order to make a change. This is needed because you do not want a change to one `Signal` instance to appear in other copies of the `Signal`. If the data was just updated directly, the change would appear in all `Signal` instances that have a link to this data.

To avoid this problem, before a `Signal` is modified, it must *unlink* itself from other copies of the data. To do this, all methods of the `Signal` class that modify data must first call the private method `unlink`, which makes sure this `Signal` instance has its own copy of the data.

The `unlink` method looks like this:

```
void Signal::unLink(){
    double *copyData;
    int i;

    // See if we need to do anything
    if((*refCnt)==1)
        return; // Already a private copy

    // Ok, so we need to create a copy of data
    // and refCnt

    // Create a new refCnt variable
    (*refCnt)--;
    refCnt = new int;
    if(!refCnt)
        throw OUTOFMEMORY;
    (*refCnt)=1;

    // Store our old data for copy, then allocate
    // new memory
    copyData = data;
    data = new double[dataLen];
    if(!data)
        throw OUTOFMEMORY;

    // Copy the old data into the new data
    for(i=0 ; i<dataLen ; ++i)
        data[i]=copyData[i];
};
```

This routine first must see if the data we have is private to this `Signal` instance, or is shared by other instances. If `*refCnt` is 1, then this is a private copy and we can use it directly, so we simply return. No other action is required.

If `*refCnt` is >1, then we must unlink ourselves from the shared copy. This means first decrementing the shared `*refCnt` by 1, then creating a new copy of `refCnt` for our private copy and setting the value of it to 1, just like the primary constructors do.

Next, we must create a new array to store the data into and copy the data, element by element, into the new copy.

What we end up with is an identical copy of the Signal class, but with its own private copy of the data (i.e., the `*refCnt` to this data is 1). We can now make changes to this data without having any affect on other Signal instances.

An example use of this function is to set the value of a point within the data to a new value. Before we can change the value of a data point, we must unlink ourselves from other copies of the data. Here is an example usage:

```
Signal::setPoint(double x,double y){
    // Make sure this is our own copy
    unLink();

    // Now, set the point
    data[getIndex(x)]=y;
}
```

Math Operators

Only two operators will be discussed here. The `operator+=` that adds a constant double to each element of the Signal, and the `operator+=` that adds one Signal to another.

operator+=(Double)

The `operator+=(double)` is a fairly straightforward operator, but is indicative of what is needed for most of the other math operators:

```
Signal& Signal::operator+=(double rhs){
    int i;

    // Make a clean copy, since we are changing data
    unLink();

    // Add rhs to each element in data array
    for(i=0 ; i<dataLen ; ++i)
        data[i]+=rhs;

    return *this;
}
```

This operator first must unlink itself from other copies, to make sure that changes made by this operator do not affect other copies. Next, for each element in the array it adds the right-hand side value to the old value. It then returns a copy of itself, for other operators to use.

operator+=(Signal&)

This operator is more complicated, and more limited in its functionality:

```
Signal& Signal::operator+=(Signal& rhs){
    int i;

    // Make sure signals are of the same size/shape
    if(dataLen!=rhs.dataLen)
        throw MISMATCH;
    if(xUnits!=rhs.xUnits)
        throw MISMATCH;
    if(xOffset!=rhs.xOffset)
        throw MISMATCH;

    // Make a clean copy
    unLink();

    // Add the two data's element by element
    for(i=0 ; i<dataLen ; ++i)
        data[i]+=rhs.data[i];
};
```

This operator performs the unlink, verifies the `Signals` are of the same size and structure, then adds the two `datas` element by element.

This implementation of this operator has a major shortcoming. It only allows adding two Signals that are of the same size and shape. If one Signal is a different size, or starts at a different X position, or has a different `deltaX`, this operator throws an error and fails.

You can imagine an `operator+=` that does not have this restriction. If we assume that a `Signal` is only defined in the given range (`startX` to `endX`), and contains the value 0 elsewhere, then we can add Signals that are of different sizes and different start positions.

We would have to create a new Signal that is the size to contain the overlap of the two Signals, and store the results in that Signal. Then, we could add the two Signals, being aware of the different offsets, and store the results in the third Signal. We would then simply delete the `lhs` Signal and replace it with the new, larger Signal.

The above describes an implementation of `operator+=` that is somewhat more complicated than the given implementation, but not overly so. The implementation of this improved `operator+=` is left as an exercise at the end of this chapter.

While the improved definition allows adding two signals with different array sizes, `startX`, and `endX` values, it does not allow different `deltaX` values. How could you implement an `operator+=` that allows two Signals with different `deltaX` values? The answer would depend on the use of such an operator, and is beyond the scope of this chapter. However, as a starting point, imagine creating a third Signal with a `deltaX` that is evenly divisible into the `deltaX` values for each of the two source `Signals`. Then each source `Signal` element would be equivalent to multiple elements in the new `Signal`.

Summary

This chapter discussed the creation of new C++ data types using object oriented concepts. This chapter discussed user-defined vs. built-in types, type conversion, operators, assignment operators, copy constructors, and data normalization.

An example math type, the `Complex` number type, was described. A type was shown that adds data units to arbitrary numbers, such as seconds, grams, meters, and so forth (`UnitData`). Finally, a class showing an array of data handled as a single element (`Signal` type) was described.

The concept of linking instances of a particular type to each other in a transparent way was introduced using reference counts. This is a very useful concept for efficiently passing around instances of large data elements, such as Signal instances, without having to copy the data itself.

The disk included with this book contains complete implementations of all three classes discussed in this book, Complex, `UnitData`, and `Signal`.

Exercises

Exercise 13-1. What other methods could be added to the `Complex` class to make it even more useful?

Exercise 13-2. Create an implementation of the `Complex` class where the data is stored in polar coordinates instead of rectangular coordinates. What methods become trivial and what methods become more complicated?

Exercise 13-3. Implement the normalize method for the `UnitData` class.

Exercise 13-4. What other units would be useful to add to the `UnitData` class? How could concepts such as volts, amps, and watts be added? How would you deal with units that overlap, such as watts and volts×amps?

Exercise 13-5. How would the normalize method change when other units are added? How can the normalize method be enhanced to deal with overlapped units?

Exercise 13-6. Create the `operator=` for the `Signal` class. How do you deal with an assignment such as the following:

```
a = a;
```

Exercise 13-7. Create a version of `operator+=` and `operator+` that expects two `Signals` (`lhs` and `rhs`), but the `Signals` may be of different sizes. In the case of `operator+=`, it should change the `lhs` `Signal` to be the size necessary to store both signals. In the case of `operator+`, it should return a Signal large enough to store both signals.

14. Error Handling

Error handling is always an issue in a good application design. What do I do when I get an error? Can I recover from this error? How do I check to see if an error occurred? Often, a test application contains more error handling code than regular code. This can make a program difficult to read and understand.

Topics Covered:

C++ Exception Handling Mechanism

Error Handling Classes

Error Logging

Error Archiving

Indicating Success

Test vs. DUT Errors

Debugging Applications

Complete Error Handling Mechanism

Take, for example, the following simple application without error handling:

```
main(){
    setupTest1();
    doTest1();
    setupTest2();
    doTest2();
}
```

Listing 14-1: Application Without Error Handling

Using basic error handling techniques usually employed in an application, this simple application becomes the following:

```
main(){
    int err;
    err = setupTest1();
    if(err != 0){
       printf("Setup of Test#1 failed\n");
       exit(1);
    }

    err = doTest1();
    if(err != 0){
       printf("Run of Test#1 failed\n");
       exit(1);
    }
```

```
        err = setupTest2();
        if(err != 0){
            printf("Setup of Test#2 failed\n");
            exit(1);
        }

        err = doTest2();
        if(err != 0){
            printf("Run of Test#2 failed\n");
            exit(1);
        }
    }
```

Listing 14-2: Application with Basic Error Handling

Look at the code in Listing 14-2. There are 17 lines dedicated to error handling and 4 lines dedicated to the real code within this listing. Therefore, 81% of the code is used for error handling! Needless to say, for large applications this can become unwieldy.

Alternatively, an error handling function can be used to clean up the code a little bit:

```
void checkError(int err,char *str){
    if(err != 0){
        printf("%s\n",str);
        exit(1);
    }
}

main(){
    int err;
    err = setupTest1();
    checkError(err,"Setup of Test#1 failed");
    err = doTest1();
    checkError(err,"Run of Test#1 failed");
    err = setupTest2();
    checkError(err,"Setup of Test#2 failed");
    err = doTest2();
    checkError(err,"Run of Test#2 failed");
}
```

Listing 14-3: Application with Error Procedure

This is much better, but still requires code in the main execution path to handle errors. Another option is to have the routines you are calling (such as setupTest1, doTest1, and so forth) call an error method directly if they fail. For example:

```
void doError(char *str){
    printf("%s\n", str);
    exit(1);
}

main(){
    // These routines call "doError" if an
    // error occurs
    setupTest1();
    doTest1();
    setupTest2();
    doTest2();
}
```

Listing 14-4: Application with Routine Error Handling

This is much better, but still has disadvantages:

1. The routines `setupTest1`, and `doTest1` must know about the procedure `doError` and call it when a failure occurs.

2. The application cannot decide how to handle errors differently for each call. It must have one and only one error handling procedure to use each time you call a given procedure.

An alternative, which solves some of these problems, is shown in the following example:

```
// Declare an error routine variable
typedef void (*errorRoutineT)(char *str);
errorRoutineT errRoutine;

// Error handler functions
void doError1(char *str){
    processErrorThisWay();
}
void doError2(char *str){
    processErrorThatWay();
}

main(){
    // All routines call the procedure stored in
    // 'errRoutine' if an error occurs
    errRoutine = doError1;
    setupTest1();
    doTest1();
    errRoutine = doError2;
    setupTest2();
    doTest2();
}
```

Listing 14-5: Error Handling Variable

While more complicated, this mechanism allows more flexibility in error handling. All the routines `setupTest1`, `doTest1`, and so forth need to know about is to call the routine that is stored in the function variable `errRoutine`. The main application program can then set this variable to whatever error procedure it desires, thus giving the main application the flexibility again to handle errors. However, this mechanism still requires special support within the test routines `setupTest1`, and so forth. In addition, this mechanism requires the use of a global variable that both the caller and callee must agree on. Using a global variable also means this code is not-reentrant, nor thread-safe. A better way is needed.

Exception Handling in C++

C++ has a built in exception handling mechanisms that solve most of the problems of the existing error handling mechanisms. C++ allows creation of `try` blocks which contain code that may generate an exception (error). If some code within the `try` block (or in a routine called by the `try` block) tries to *throw* an exception, then execution transfers to a `catch` block immediately following the `try` block. The following code illustrates how this works:

```
void proc2(){
    ... do work ...
    if(... error detected ...)
        throw "Error Occurred"; // Generate an error
}

main(){
    try{
        proc1();
        proc2();
        proc3();
    }
    catch(const char *str){
        printf("Error Occurred: %s\n", str);
        exit(1);
    }
}
```

Listing 14-6: C++ Exception Handling

Here, `proc2` is shown *throwing* an exception. *Throwing* an exception occurs whenever a section of code needs to generate an error or other exception condition. The `try` block contains the calls to the code for which error detection is desired. If any piece of code within the `try` block `throws` an exception, then execution immediately follows after the `try` block to the appropriate `catch` block. When the `catch` block has finished, execution continues after the `catch` block to the end of the program (in this case, however, the `exit` statement will terminate the application first). If all the code within the `try` block completes without throwing an exception, then the `catch` block is ignored and not executed.

Multiple Catch Handlers

We said the *appropriate* `catch` block. Multiple `catch` blocks are allowed after a `try` block. Each `catch` block can specify a parameter of a different type. When an exception is thrown, the type of the parameter passed to the `throw` procedure is compared against the `catch` blocks specified until a `catch` block is found such that the `throw` *variable* is of the same type as the `catch` block, or can be easily converted to the same type (using standard type conversions). For example:

```
proc(){
    try{
        if(...)
            throw 5; // Throw an int
        if(...)
            throw "Error"; // Throw a const char *
        if(...)
            throw proc; //Throw a pointer to procedure
    }
    catch(const char *str){
        // Catch throws of strings
        // Such as: throw "Error";
        printf("Error: %s\n",str);
    }
    catch(int n){
        // Catch throws of integers
        // Such as: throw 5;
        printf("Error: %d\n",n);
    }
    catch(void *d){
        // Catch anything else (not a char* or int)
        // Such as: throw proc;
        printf("Error: Ptr = %p\n",d);
    }

    // After the try completes, or the processing
    // of athrow completes, execution continues here
    printf("Done\n");
}
```

Listing 14-7: Example of Multiple Catch Handlers

Nested Try Blocks

In C++, `try` blocks can be nested to any level. When an exception is thrown, C++ keeps unwinding the stack until an appropriate `catch` block is found, even if this means unwinding out of one `try` block and into an encompassing `try` block. For example:

```
proc1(){
    if(...)
        throw 5;
    if(...)
        throw "Error #3";
    if(...)
        throw 2.5; // See below
}

proc2(){
    try{
        proc1();
    }
    catch(const char *str){
        // Catches throw "Error #3";
        printf("Error: %s\n",str);
        throw 3; // See below
    }
}

main(){
    try{
        proc2();
        proc1();
    }
    catch(int n){
        // Catches throw 5; from either calling
        // proc1 via proc2, or from calling proc1
        // directly
        printf("Error: %d\n",n);
    }
    catch(const char *str){
        // Catches throw "Error #3" from calling
        // proc1 directly, when we call proc1
        // via proc2, then the catch handler
        // in proc2 is executed instead
        printf("main Error: %s\n",str);
    }
}
```

Listing 14-8: Nested Try Blocks

Listing 14-8 shows us three things:

1. **Nested `try` blocks.** If we generate a `throw` "Error #3" from calling `proc1` directly from main, then the `catch(const char *)` handler in `main` is executed. However, if we generate a `throw` "Error #3" from calling `proc1` via calling `proc2`, then the `catch(const char*)` handler in `proc2` is executed instead.

2. **Throwing exceptions from a `catch` handler.** Notice the `catch(const char*)` handler in `proc2`. Right at the end of the `catch` handler we

throw another exception by calling "`throw` 3;". This generates a new exception that tries to find a `catch` handler. In this case, it will find the `catch(int)` handler within `main` and execute there. This can be useful if a `catch` handler generates an error, or if a `catch` handler can only partially process an error and still wants to pass an error condition on to the caller program. We will see examples of this later in this chapter.

3. **Throwing uncaught exceptions.** Look in `proc1`, you will see the line "`throw 2.5;`", this generates an exception containing a **`double`** floating point number. As we unwind the stack, we find there is no `catch` handler for a `double`. Once the stack is completely unwound (out of "`main`"), and a *thrown* exception is still not *caught*, the application generates a run-time error and terminates. Therefore, the "`throw 2.5;`" statement generates a fatal run-time error. You will probably remember earlier in this book a discussion of using `throw` to generate run-time errors. This was just a special case of the C++ exception handling mechanism. These run-time errors could have been caught just like any other `throw`.

Error Return Types

We have shown you four types of error parameter types used in `throw` and `catch` handlers:

1. `int` -- `throw` 5;
2. `const char *` -- `throw` "Error #5";
3. `double` -- `throw` 2.5;
4. arbitrary pointer -- `throw` proc1;

Any type of variable can be thrown. So, what should you throw? The choice is up to the application, but must be agreed upon by both the caller and the callee. Any mechanism may be used to come upon the agreement (user documentation, application standard, etc.), but C++ allows the function prototype to specify what types of throws it generates. For example, the function prototype:

```
void proc1(int,double) throw(int);
```

guarantees that `proc1` will only throw exceptions of type `int`; it will not generate `throw`s of any other type. In addition, the function prototype:

```
void proc1(int,double) throw (int,const char *);
```

guarantees that `proc1` will only throw exceptions of type `int` or `const char *`; no other `throw` types will be generated.

When writing procedures that use functions with such prototypes, you can have some level of assurance that only the specified types will be generated. When writing the implementations of procedures with such prototypes, trying to throw an exception with a type other than that specified will generate a run-time error.

Throwing User-Defined Types

Besides throwing built in types such as `int`, `double`, and `const char *`, any user-defined type may be thrown as well. This allows you to throw errors using code such as the following:

```
class Error {
    // Error Class Definition
    ...
};

proc1(){
    if(...)
        throw Error(3,"Error String for #3");
    if(...)
        throw Error(5,"Error String for #5");
}

main(){
    try{
        proc1();
    }
    catch(Error& err){
        printf("Error #%d occurred: %s\n",
                    err.getNum(),err.GetStr());
    }
}
```

Listing 14-9: User-Defined Error Types

The advantage of this mechanism is that it allows you to generate an error class that is customized to your application and contains all the information needed for your application to process the error. In this example, the error contains both an error number and an error string. In addition, the error class could contain special methods for handling errors of various types.

Much of the rest of this chapter is dedicated to creating Error classes and advanced functionality of these error handlers.

Error Class

First, let us start with a basic error class. Let us assume all we want is an error class that contains the following information:

- A number that corresponds to a particular error condition. This number could have any meaning.
- A string giving more complete information as to why the error occurred and where.

We will now go through the design and construction of this class. We have several design decisions that we need to make:

1. **What type is the error code and what values can it have?** We will assume the error number is an integer. We will reserve the value 0 to be success. All other values are considered to be various error codes. We will not go into any more detail as to what the numbers mean. Instead we will leave it up to the user of this class to put meaning on various error numbers.

2. **What should the string contain and how should we store it?** We want the string to contain more detailed information about why the error occurred. This can be a string that contains the name of the procedure that generated the error, what the condition was that generated the error, and any other relevant information.

3. **What other variables do we need?** Let us create a second string that contains information about a suggested cure. It could give information about potential remedies for how to fix the problem so the error does not re-occur. Since not all errors will have easy cures, this string will be optional.

4. **How do we handle passing of strings around?** We will assume the strings are all literal text constants, and we will simply pass a `const char *` pointer to this string around. This means we do not have to deal with memory allocation, and we do not have to worry about freeing of string memory. This also simplifies the implementation of the class, since we do not have to worry about a copy constructor, or other such issues. We will remove this restriction later in this chapter.

5. **What private variables do we need?** We need a variable for each value the Error will store. In this example, it will be an `int` for the error number, and two `const char *`'s for the two strings.

6. **What constructors/destructors do we need?** We do not want the default constructor to work (after all, what would it mean to generate an error with no values?). We also can live with the default copy-constructor (we are not performing any memory allocation and we are storing just values -- the string pointers do not need to be created or freed). We also do not need a destructor. As far as other constructors, we need a constructor that accepts an error number, error string, and a cure string. We also need a constructor that does not provide the cure string. It might also be useful to have a constructor with an error number, but no specific information for an error string or a cure string.

7. **What methods do we need?** We need methods that return each of the values contained in the Error class. We probably do not need any other methods.

The class declaration looks like this:

```
class Error {
   private:
      int errNum;
      const char *detailsStr;
      const char *cureStr;
      Error(); // Disallow this constructor

   public:
      // Constructor for just an error number
      Error(int eNum);
      // Constructor including error string
      Error(int eNum,const char *eStr);
      // Constructor including cure string
      Error(int eNum,const char *eStr,
                  const char *cStr);

      // Methods that return appropriate values
      int getErrNum(); // return errNum
      const char *error(); // return errStr
      const char *cure(); // return cureStr
};
```

Listing 14-10: Declaration of Basic Error Class

The implementation of this class is very straightforward, we only have six methods to implement, and they can all be inline functions:

```
inline Error::Error(int eNum)
    :  errNum(eNum),
       detailsStr(0),
       cureStr(0)
{}

inline Error::Error(int eNum, const char *dStr)
    :  errNum(eNum),
       detailsStr(dStr),
       cureStr(0)
{}

inline Error::Error(int eNum,
                    const char *dStr,
                    const char *cStr)
    :  errNum(eNum),
       detailsStr(dStr),
       cureStr(cStr)
{}

inline int getErrNum(){
    return errNum;
}

inline const char *details(){
    return detailsStr;
}

inline const char *cure(){
    return cureStr;
}
```

Listing 14-11: Implementation of Basic Error Class

Once this class is created, we can use it very easily. We will use the example program we showed in Listings 14-1 through 14-5, but make use of our Error class:

```
void setupTest1(){
    if(...)
        throw Error(5);
}
void doTest1(){
    if(...)
        throw Error(7,"doTest1: ... failure");
    if(...)
        throw Error( 9,
                        "doTest1: xyzzy failure",
                        "Try using yzzyx instead");
}
main(){
    try{
        setupTest1();
        doTest1();
        setupTest2();
        doTest2();
    }
    catch(Error& err){
        printf("Error #%d Occurred:\n",
                        err.getErrNum());
        if(err.error())
            printf("    Reason: %s\n",err.error());
        if(err.cure())
            printf("    Cure: %s\n",err.cure());
    }
}
```

Notice that all the test calling code is isolated within the `try` block. This makes it just as readable as it does in Listing 14-1. However, we do process errors and process them more completely than any other example. All the error handling code is localized to the `catch` handler. The `throw` calls themselves are also easy to read and understand.

Handling Error Instances

Now that we have a way to catch errors, and way to communicate the errors, what can we do with the errors when we get them? There are many potential answers to this question:

1. *Ignore the error.* There are cases where we *expect* an error and getting an error is not a problem. In this case, we can simply ignore the error or even generate a different error if we didn't get the error we were expecting.

2. *Handle the error.* There are cases where we get an error that is easy to recover from automatically. Such errors are things like "Network temporarily unavailable." In this case, we may simply wait and try again, hoping the network becomes available again.

3. *Pass the error on.* Sometimes an error can only be partially handled at a given layer, in these cases, the error needs to be passed on to the next higher calling layer for it to be processed.

4. *Terminate.* Sometimes an error is so severe that all we can do is display a message and terminate. Sometimes simple applications use this approach to ease their error handling code.

5. *Display a message in a time-critical way.* Sometimes we want to pop-up a dialog box and display the error directly to the user of the application or the operator of the test system. These are errors that need to be handled immediately.

6. *Store the error instance away in a log file.* Usually, storing an error in an off-line archival system (like a disk file) allows us to do postmortem analysis of the errors. In this case, the more detailed the error, the better.

All of these answers are things that the `catch` handler has to perform. However, in some of these cases, the Error class itself can assist in performing these actions. We will look into adding support for many of these actions directly to our Error class.

Time-Critical Error Displays

Sometimes it is desired to simply print information about the error either to a log console or into a dialog box. This could be done within the catch handler, but it would be useful if the catch handler had a single entry point within the error instance to call that printed all the information about the error. Let us add the following method to our basic Error class:

```
class Error{
    ...
    public:
        void displayError();
    ...
};
```

This routine could display a dialog box or log to the console, depending on what is appropriate. Here is a simple implementation of this method:

```
#include <stdio.h>

void Error::displayError(){
    fprintf(stderr, "Error Occurred:\n");
    fprintf(stderr, "      Code = %d (0x%x)\n",
                             errNum,errNum);
    if(errStr)
        fprintf(stderr, "       %s\n",errStr);
    if(cureStr)
        fprintf(stderr, "       Cure: %s\n",cureStr);
}
```

Automatic Application Termination

For simple applications, and for "throw-away" sample applications, sometimes doing nothing more than terminating the application when an error occurs is the appropriate action to take. There are three ways this can be accomplished:

1. **Do not install any catch handlers.** When an Error instance is created and thrown, there will be no catch handlers to catch it. The result will be a run-time error and your application will exit.

   This is by far the easiest way to handle the problem, but not necessarily the most desirable. The run-time error you get only says that an unhandled exception occurred, it doesn't give you any information as to why.

2. **Install a catch handler that prints out the error and terminates.** In this case you install a catch handler in `main` that simply prints out the information contained in the error and terminates the application.

   This is better than the above mechanism in that information about the error can be printed before termination. However, you still must handle the error in a normal catch handler way.

3. **Support application termination in the Error class**. In this case you add a static boolean variable to the Error class that specifies what to do when an error is created. If the variable is false, the error is created normally. If the variable is true, the error is created, printed to an error console, and the application terminates automatically.

   This is essentially the same as the last mechanism, except that no catch handler is needed. Once this static variable within the Error class is set, any error that is generated simply terminates the application before the throw even occurs.

The third approach has the least impact on the calling application. Since the goal of application termination on error is to allow simple applications and throw-away applications to work, this seems to be the best approach.

In order to support automatic application termination, all we need is a static variable within the Error class and a static method to update it:

```
class Error{
    ...
    private:
        static int terminateOnError;
    public:
        static void terminateMode(int m){
            termianteOnError=m;
        }
    ...
};
```

Then, when an error is created, we need to check this variable. We must make a minor change to all of our constructors to include code such as the following:

```
Error::Error(...){
    ... do Error construction here ...

    // Check to see if we should terminate
    if(terminateOnError){
        displayError();
        exit(1);            // Terminate
    }
}
```

The default value of this static variable should be 0 (do not terminate).

The following program enables this error mode, then calls procedures that may generate errors:

```
main(){
    Error::terminateMode(1);
    setupTest1();
    doTest1();
    setupTest2();
    doTest2();
};
```

Storing Error Instances (Archival)

Usually, you want to save away the fact that an error occurred to a log file of some sorts. Even if the errors are recovered, having a record of all the information contained within all the errors that occurred can be useful for postmortem analysis.

The information can be stored in the log file in one of two different ways:

1. **Stored in a human-readable format.** This is essentially the same format as the output of the `displayError` method, above. A method could be created that performs the same operation as `displayError`, but instead stores the information into a log file. This log file can be examined later using a simple word processor or printed as a text file.

   This is the easiest and best way if all you want to do is look at the errors later.

2. **Stored in a machine-readable format.** This essentially stores the data contained in the error instance in a binary format, so that the error instances can be re-created later and processed postmortem.

   This has the advantage that, in a postmortem environment, all information is available within the original error instances as it was during the test run. Therefore, the information may be processed, sorted, and filtered before it is presented to the user.

We will use two methods to implement these logging mechanisms:

```
#include <stdio.h>

class Error {
    public:
        log(FILE *);
        save(FILE *);
};
```

The log method will save the error in a human readable format; the save method in a machine-readable format. The implementation of log is easy:

```
void Error::log(FILE *fp){
    fprintf(fp,"Error Occurred:\n");
    fprintf(fp,"      Code = %d (0x%x)\n",
                           errNum,errNum);
    if(errStr)
        fprintf(fp,"        %s\n",errStr);
    if(cureStr)
        fprintf(fp,"        Cure: %s\n",cureStr);
}
```

The save method is a bit more complicated, since it needs to store information in a format that is retrievable. This is easy for the `errNum` variable, but a bit more complicated for the strings:

```
void Error::save(FILE *fp){
   int sz;

   // Store the error number
   fwrite(&errNum,sizeof(errNum),1,fp);

   // Store the errStr
   // First, store the size of the errStr
   sz=strlen(errStr);
   fwrite(&sz,sizeof(sz),1,fp);
   // Next, store the string itself (if sz!=0)
   if(sz>0)
      fwrite(errStr,sizeof(char),sz,fp);

   // Do the same for cureStr
   sz=strlen(cureStr);
   fwrite(&sz,sizeof(sz),1,fp);
   if(sz>0)
      fwrite(cureStr,sizeof(char),sz,fp);
}
```

Listing 14-12: Saving Error State

Now, all we need to do is figure out how to load these errors back into the system postmortem. Since we are taking data in a file and using it to create a **new** instance of an Error, we will implement loading as a new constructor within Error:

```
class Error{
   public:
      Error(FILE *fp);
};
```

The implementation of this constructor is simply the opposite of the save method:

```
Error::Error(FILE *fp){
    int sz;
    // Get the error number
    fread(&errNum, sizeof(errNum), 1, fp);

    // Get the errStr size
    fread(&sz, sizeof(sz), 1, fp);
    if(sz>0){
        // Allocate memory for the string
        errStr = new char[sz+1];
        // Read the string and null-terminate it
        fread(errStr, sizeof(char), sz, fp);
        errStr[sz] = 0;
    }else{
        // No string
        errStr = 0;
    }

    // Same for cureStr
    fread(&sz, sizeof(sz), 1, fp);
    if(sz > 0){
        // Allocate memory for the string
        cureStr = new char[sz+1];
        // Read the string and null-terminate it
        fread(currStr, sizeof(char), sz, fp);
        currStr[sz] = 0;
    }else{
        // No string
        currStr = 0;
    }
};
```

Listing 14-13: Loading Saved Error State

Huh? The use of a constructor to implement load may not have been obvious at first. However, since what we are doing is creating a new variable of type Error, we need a constructor to create that variable. This special constructor can be thought of as a constructor that accepts the data to initialize the Error instance from a file pointed to by the FILE * parameter, rather than from individual parameters itself.

There is one bug in this implementation. Can you spot it? It has to do with our assumption about how strings work within our original design of the basic Error class. The problem is that, unlike the other constructors, this constructor allocates memory. No one frees this memory. Later in this chapter we will have all the constructors allocate string memory, then implement a destructor to free the memory correctly. In addition, a correct assignment operator and copy constructor will be presented that will deal with the memory requirements.

Now that we have a machine readable save/load mechanism, it would be useful if the errors were automatically saved to a log file as they were generated. Let us create the following static methods to implement automatic saving of Error instances as they are created:

```
class Error {
    ...
    private:
        static FILE *log;
    ...
    public:
        static void openLog(const char *fileName);
        static void setLog(FILE *logFile);
        static FILE *getLog();
        static void closeLog();
    ...
};
```

With the following implementation:

```
FILE *Error::log=NULL;
void Error::openLog(const char *fileName){
    log = fopen(fileName, "wb");
}

void Error::setLog(FILE *logFile){
    log = logFile;
}

FILE *Error::getLog(){
    return log;
}

void Error::closeLog(){
    fclose(log);
    log = NULL;
}
```

This code allows opening and closing log files, as well as using existing log files. Notice with this implementation, either `openLog`/`closeLog` pairs should be used, or `setLog(fp)`/`setLog(NULL)` pairs should be used. The two sets should not be intermixed.

With these methods, the following code needs to be added to each constructor within the Error class:

```
Error::Error(...){
    ... do Error construction here ...

    // Check to see if we should save to a log file
    if(log != NULL)
        save(log);
}
```

Now, by making appropriate calls to `openLog` or `setLog`, all errors that are generated can be saved to a log file.

Postmortem Error Displays

Suppose we wanted to write a simple application that printed a list of all errors that occurred during a test run. Let us assume that all errors that were generated were logged to a file using the save methods discussed above. The following code would then read all errors from the log file and print them to the screen:

```
main(){
    FILE *fp;
    char ch;

    if((fp = fopen("logfile","rb")) == NULL){
        printf("Can't open logfile\n");
        exit(1);
    }
    printf("Output of all error events"
             " in logfile:\n");

    ch=fgetc(fp); // Force feof() to be valid
    while( !feof(fp) ){
        ungetc(ch, fp); // Return the fgetc character

        // Create an error variable from the logfile
        Error err(fp);

        // Print in human-readable form to stdout
        err.log(stdout);

        ch = fgetc(fp); // Force feof() to be valid
    }
    fclose(fp);
}
```

Listing 14-14: Postmortem Error Display Application

The `fgetc` and `ungetc` calls are simply to force the `feof` check to return true if we are at the end of file. Until that point, all we do is create an error variable using the load constructor, then print the result in a human-readable format. This continues until we have reached the end of the file and the last error is printed.

This program can be a general purpose application that prints error instances from any application that uses the Error class.

Error Types

Sometimes, in order to determine what to do with an error, the severity of the error is needed. Often, the severity can be obtained from the error number, in other words you can tell by the type of error how severe it is. However, often this is difficult or impossible to do, without checking each and every possible error code.

Instead, we add a new variable to the error class:

```
class Error {
    ...
    private:
        severType severity;
    ...
};
```

Various values for severity can be assigned. We recommend the use of an enum for the type of severity. Here is a possible declaration:

```
enum severType {
    sevWarn, // This is just a warning
    sevDutFail, // This means the DUT failed a test
    sevTestFail, // This means the test code failed
    sevAbort // This is a severe error, no recovery
};
```

We can then update our constructors to accept a severity number. This can even be an optional parameter with a default severity:

```
class Error {
    ...
    public:
        Error( int eNum,
               severType sev = sevTestFail);
    ...
};
```

We then need a method to return the severity:

```
class Error {
    ...
    public:
        severType getSeverity() {return severity; };
    ...
};
```

Of course, now that we have added a variable, lots of other methods need to be updated, namely:

- void `displayError()`
- void `log(FILE *)`
- void `save(FILE *)`
- `Error(FILE *)`
- all the constructors (either default the variable, or assign it a value)

We will not show the details of these implementations here, since the changes are minimal and fairly obvious.

Error Labeling

There are other values that are sometimes useful to store in an error instance.

Time and Date Stamping

When multiple errors occur, and the errors are stored in a log file, it is often useful (or necessary) during postmortem analysis to have a time and date stamp on the error. A time and date stamp is an indication of when the error was created.

Creating a time and date stamp involves another variable in the class, and methods to access it:

```
#include <time.h>
class Error {
    private:
        time_t timeStamp;
    public:
        time_t getTime();
        char *getTimeStr();
};
```

The methods are easy to implement:

```
time_t Error::getTime(){
    return timeStamp;
}
char *getTimeStr(){
    return ctime(&timeStamp);
}
```

The variable type `time_t` is a structure that stores a time and date in a machine-readable format. There are several standard C routines that manipulate `time_t` structures, including `ctime`, which returns the specified time as a string, adjusting for time zone.

We use the ctime routine to implement our getTimeStr method. This time returns a string in a format similar to the following:

```
Thu May 26 16:05:26 1994
```

All that remains is setting the timeStamp variable when the error occurs. This requires a change to all of our constructors to add the following code:

```
Error::Error(...){
    ... do Error construction here ...

    // Get current time for timeStamp
    time(&timeStamp);
}
```

The time procedure is a standard C procedure that sets the time_t variable passed into it to the current time.

Error Description

While having an error number (errNum) is useful for processing errors automatically, it is not as useful for humans to read. It would be useful if we could return a human-readable string that is equivalent to the errNum variable.

Notice, this is different than errStr variable. The errStr variable is a human-readable string that *enhances* the meaning of the errNum variable (giving reasons why and how an error occurred, etc.). The string we are talking about is a string describing *what* the errNum variable means.

Since all we are doing is describing what an existing variable means, we do not need to add a new string variable to our class. We can create the strings as we need them from the errNum variable. This has the advantages of not increasing the size of our class, and not increasing the complexity of error creating, saving, and loading. We add the following method to our class:

```
class Error {
    ...
    public:
        const char *getDescript();
    ...
};
```

The implementation of this method would depend on the meaning assigned to the errNum values, but the following is a good start:

```
const char *getDescript(){
    switch(errNum){
        case 0:
            return "Success";
        case 1:
            return "Description for Error #1";
        case 2:
            return "Description for Error #2";
        ...
        default:
            return "<No Descrition Available>";
    }
}
```

A user of this class could call this method directly, but we would probably also want to update our methods that print human-readable information about errors to use this string. These include:

- `void displayError();`
- `void log();`

File Name / Line Number

Finally, it is occasionally useful to know where an error was created. Specifically, what line of code within what file created the error. We can add the following variables and access methods to our class:

```
class Error {
    ...
    private:
        long lineNum;
        const char *fileName;
    public:
        long getLineNum();
        const char *getFileName();
    ...
};
```

The implementation of these methods is straightforward and will not be shown. However, how do we fill in the `lineNum` and `fileName` variables? A simple answer could be to add them to every constructor. We would then have a constructor with a syntax similar to the following:

```
Error::Error(int eNum,long line,const char* file){
    ... do construction here ...
    lineNum = line;
    fileName = file;
}
```

How do we get the values to pass to the constructor? ANSI C and C++ have standard macros that can help us with this. They are the __FILE__ and __LINE__ macros. All C and C++ compilers supply these macros, which correspond to the current filename and line number, respectively. Therefore, when we throw an error instance, we can do the following:

```
throw Error(5, __LINE__, __FILE__);
```

While this works just fine, it isn't as easy to use as simply saying "throw Error(5);". However, we have to provide these macros as parameters, as these macros are evaluated and return the file name and line number of where they appear. Alternatively, we can create a macro similar to the following:

```
#define ERROR(a) Error((a), __LINE__, __FILE__)
```

and write the following code to use it:

```
throw ERROR(5);
```

Here, since `ERROR` is a macro, the `__LINE__` and `__FILE__` macros are evaluated on the line where `ERROR` exists, which is the correct line. However, what do we do for constructors with variable number of parameters and alternate constructors? Unfortunately, the #define mechanism does not support variable parameters. We could do something like the following:

```
#define ERROR1(a)    Error((a),__LINE__,__FILE__)
#define ERROR2(a,b) Error((a),(b),__LINE__,__FILE__)
#define ERROR3(a,b,c) \
            Error((a),(b),(c),__LINE__,__FILE__)
...
```

We can then use them like this:

```
throw ERROR1(5);
throw ERROR2(5,"Error String");
throw ERROR3(5,"Error String","Cure String");
...
```

This works just fine, but there is another solution that is more general. We will define the following macro:

```
#define MARK      __LINE__, __FILE__
```

Now, we can throw any Error instance we want, just insert a `MARK` at the end:

```
throw Error(5, MARK);
throw Error(5,"Error String", MARK);
throw Error(5,"Error String", "Cure String", MARK);
...
```

This still is not perfect, but it is about as close as we can get.

Inheritance and Errors

Now that we have a fairly complete Error class, what happens if we have a specific type of error that has unique needs that are independent of other errors? For example, remember the I/O class we implemented in Chapter 9? We used the C++ exception handling mechanism to generate errors. We could use the Error class described here as the error instance to be thrown. The problem is that we probably want more information in our error class for errors generated from our I/O class than our Error class contains, but the information is I/O class specific. For example:

- `ViStatus`. The VISA error code was returned by the VISA function that generated this error instance.
- `ViSession`. The VISA session that was used when the error code was returned.
- `VISAFunction`. What VISA function was called that generated the error instance.

Let us create a new class called `IOError` that derives from Error:

```
class IOError: public Error {
   private:
      ViStatus visaErr;
      ViSession visaSess;
      const char *visaFunc;
   public:
      IOError(ViStatus,ViSession,const char *);
      ViStatus getVisaErr();
      ViSession getVisaSess();
      const char *getVisaFunc();
};
```

This has several advantages over either using Error directly, or creating a new class that does not derive from Error.

First, this class contains I/O specific error mechanisms, *plus* all the features of Error. The features of Error were inherited for free.

Second, a catch handler can be written either to specifically catch all `IOError` instances, or to catch all Error instances, whether they are `IOErrors` or not. This is a really powerful mechanism. Imagine the following code:

```
main(){
    try{
        proc1();
        proc2();
    }
    catch(Error &err){
        // This will catch either Error instances
        // or IOError instances!!!
    }
}
```

We have all the advantages of creating the more detailed error (such as logging the error, etc.), but also have the ability to catch them and handle them generically.

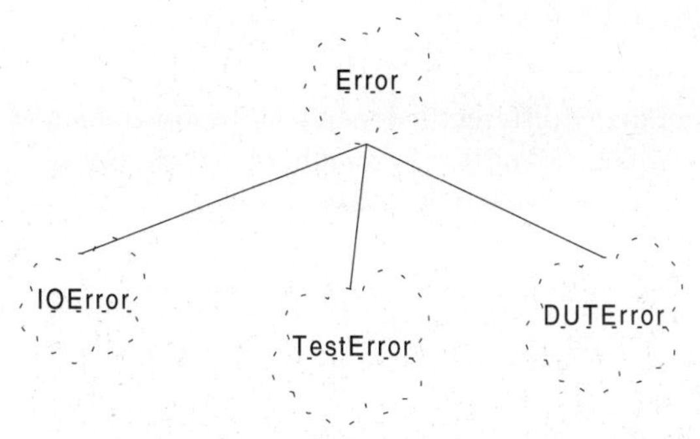

Figure 14-1: Error Inheritance Tree

Imagine we have the inheritance tree of `Error` classes shown in Figure 14-1. We now have the ability to throw errors of four different types: `IOError`, `TestError`, `DUTError`, or the generic `Error`.

Now, imagine the following code:

```
main(){
    try{
        ...
    }
    catch(IOError& err){
        // Catch all IOError's
    }
    catch(DUTError& err){
        // Catch all DUTError's
    }
    catch(Error& err){
        // Catch all TestError's and base Error's
    }
}
```

This code shows how we can selectively process errors of different types if we care about the details of that error, such as `IOError` and `DUTError` in this example. However, if we do not care, we can have a generic Error catch handler that will catch any of them, such as `TestError` and `Error` in this example.

Putting It All Together

We have talked about many different independent improvements we can make to the `Error` class. So, how does all of this fit together into a complete working `Error` class? First, let us look at the data needs in our class:

```
class Error {
   private:
      int errNum;
      int lineNum;
      time_t timeStamp;
      sevLev severity;
      char *detailsStr;
      char *cureStr;
      char *fileName;
      // Reference Count for copy construction
      int *refCnt;
   ...
}
```

These are all variables that were discussed earlier in this chapter, except for `refCnt`, which will be discussed later.

Next, let's look at the constructors. With all the changes that were talked about, we now have the following parameters that can potentially be passed to a constructor:

- `errNum`. This is the only required parameter. This is the error number that occurred.
- `detailsStr`. This is the string that describes the details of why or how the error occurred. This is optional.
- `cureStr`. This is the string that describes how to fix the error. This is optional.
- `severity`. This is the severity of the error. This is optional (a default severity is assumed).
- `lineNum`. This is the line number of the source file where the error occurred. This is optional.
- `fileName`. This is the file name of the source file where the error occurred. This is optional.

With so many parameters optional, you can easily imagine different combinations of parameters that would make sense, thus creating a need for several constructors. We can imagine constructors with the following combination of parameters:

- `errNum`
- `errNum`, `severity`
- `errNum`, `details`
- `errNum`, `details`, `severity`
- `errNum`, `details`, `cure`
- `errNum`, `details`, `cure`, `severity`
- `errNum`, `lineNum`, `fileName`
- `errNum,details,lineNum,fileName`
- `errNum,details,cure,lineNum,fileName`
- `errNum,severity,lineNum,fileName`
- `errNum,details,severity,lineNum,fileName`
- `errNum,details,cure,severity,lineNum,fileName`

Although using optional parameters can reduce this complexity, it cannot be reduced to a single constructor. We are going to need several constructors. In fact, we will have nine:

```
Error(int num, sevLev sev=sevTestFail);
Error(int num, char *det, sevLev sev=sevTestFail);
Error (int num, char *det, char *cure,
          sevLev sev=sevTestFail);
Error(int num, int line, char *file);
Error(int num, char *det, int line, char *file);
Error(int num, char *det, char *cure,
          int line, char *file);
Error(int num, sevLev sev, int line, char *file);
Error(int num, char *det, sevLev sev,
          int line, char *file);
Error(int num, char *det, char *cure, sevLev sev,
          int line, char *file);
```

All of the constructors do basically the same work. The only difference is that most of the constructors default some of the parameters. Therefore, we will create a helper method that performs all of the work of the constructors:

```
class Error {
    private:
        void create(int num, char *det, char *cure,
                    sevLev sev, int line, char *file);
};
```

Then, each of the constructors can be implemented as an inline method that simply calls this support method with the appropriate parameters passed through, and the others defaulted:

```
class Error {
    private:
        void create(int num, char *det, char *cure,
                    sevLev sev, int line, char *file);
    public:
        Error(int num, sevLev sev=sevTestFail){
                create(num, 0, 0, sev, 0, 0);
        }
        Error(int num, char *det,
                sevLev sev=sevTestFail){
            create(num, det, 0, sev, 0, 0);
        }
        ...
        Error(int num, char *det, char *cure,
                sevLev sev, int line,char *file){
            create(num,det,cure,sev,line,file);
        }
};
```

The create method is what does all the work for the constructors. Here is the implementation of that method:

```
void Error::create(int num, char *details,
                    char *cure, sevLev sev,
                    int line, char *file){
   // Create refCnt
   refCnt = new int;
   if(!refCnt)
      throw "Out of Memory";
   *refCnt = 1;

   // Set the error strings
   detailsStr = dupStr(details);
   cureStr = dupStr(cure);
   fileName =dupStr(file);

   errNum = num;
   lineNum = line;
   severity = sev;
   time(&timeStamp);

   if(terminateOnError){
      displayError();
      exit(1);
   }

   if(logFile != NULL){
      save(logFile);
   }
}
```

Notice that this constructor makes use of another private method called `dupStr` which allocates memory for the strings and copies them. Here is the implementation of this method:

```
char *Error::dupStr(char *str){
   char *tmpStr;
   tmpStr = new char[strlen(str)+1];
   if(!tmpStr)
      return "Out of Memory";
   strcpy(tmpStr,str);
   return tmpStr;
}
```

The destructor, then, has to free the memory allocated by this method:

```
Error::~Error(){
   // Decrement the refCnt
   (*refCnt)--;
   // If 0, then clean up
   if((*refCnt) == 0){
      delete refCnt;
      delete detailsStr;
      delete cureStr;
      delete fileName;
   }
}
```

You will also notice that this class makes use of reference counts, just like some of the other classes discussed (remember the `Signal` class in Chapter 13?). This is to make the copy constructor efficient, so it does not have to copy strings:

```
Error::Error(const Error& err){
   refCnt = err.refCnt;
   (*refCnt)++;
   detailsStr = err.detailsStr;
   fileName = err.fileName;
   cureStr = err.cureStr;
   errNum = err.errNum;
   lineNum = err.lineNum;
   timeStamp = err.timeStamp;
   severity = err.severity;
}
```

Next, let us talk about saving and loading machine-readable versions of our errors. This involves implementing the save() method and a special constructor to implement loading. First, let us look at save:

```
void Error::save(FILE *fp){
   int sz;

   fwrite(&errNum, sizeof(errNum), 1, fp);
   fwrite(&lineNum, sizeof(lineNum), 1, fp);
   fwrite(&timeStamp, sizeof(timeStamp), 1, fp);
   fwrite(&severity, sizeof(severity), 1, fp);
   sz=min(strlen(detailsStr), MAXSTRLEN);
   fwrite(&sz, sizeof(sz), 1, fp);
   fwrite(detailsStr, sizeof(char), sz, fp);
   sz=min(strlen(cureStr), MAXSTRLEN);
   fwrite(&sz, sizeof(sz), 1, fp);
   fwrite(cureStr, sizeof(char), sz, fp);
   sz=min(strlen(fileName), MAXSTRLEN);
   fwrite(&sz, sizeof(sz), 1, fp);
   fwrite(fileName, sizeof(char), sz, fp);
}
```

This method simply saves all the variables out to the file specified by `fp`. For strings, it first saves the length of the string, then the string itself.

Now, to load the data back into a new instance of an error, we use this special constructor:

```
Error::Error(FILE *fp){
   int sz;

   refCnt = new int;
   if(!refCnt)
      throw "Out of Memory";
   *refCnt = 1;
   fread(&errNum, sizeof(errNum), 1, fp);
   fread(&lineNum, sizeof(lineNum), 1, fp);
   fread(&timeStamp, sizeof(timeStamp), 1, fp);
   fread(&severity, sizeof(severity), 1, fp);
   fread(&sz, sizeof(sz), 1, fp);
   sz=min(sz, MAXSTRLEN);
   if(sz >0){
      detailsStr = new char[sz+1];
      if(!detailsStr)
         throw "Out of Memory";
   }
   fread(detailsStr, sizeof(char), sz, fp);
   detailsStr[sz] = 0;
   fread(&sz, sizeof(sz), 1, fp);
   sz=min(sz, MAXSTRLEN);
   if(sz > 0){
      cureStr = new char[sz+1];
      if(!cureStr)
         throw "Out of Memory";
   }
   fread(cureStr, sizeof(char), sz, fp);
   cureStr[sz] = 0;
   fread(&sz, sizeof(sz), 1, fp);
   sz=min(sz, MAXSTRLEN);
   if(sz > 0){
      fileName = new char[sz+1];
      if(!fileName)
         throw "Out of Memory";
   }
   fread(fileName, sizeof(char), sz, fp);
   fileName[sz] = 0;
}
```

This simply reads all the data for creating an instance of an Error class from the file `fp`, rather than from parameters. This is easy for integer variables. For strings, we first read this size, allocate memory of the correct size, then load the string into the newly allocated memory. Since our destructor now deals with freeing allocated memory, the bug we discussed previously has disappeared.

This is, obviously, only a portion of the complete Error class. A complete implementation of this class is included on the enclosed disk. The only aspect of this class that is not complete in the enclosed disk is the `descript()` method, which takes the `errNum` and converts it to a human-readable string. Since the implementation of this method will vary depending on the user of the Error class (what error codes match to what error strings), this routine must be implemented by the user of the class. Some of the exercises below discuss implementation of various aspects of this class. The enclosed disk also does not show any derived classes from `Error`.

Also included on the disk is the simple `dumperror` application that reads errors from the machine readable file and prints them in human-readable format.

Summary

This chapter discussed the issues and problems associated with error handling within large applications. We first discussed the C++ throw/catch handler mechanism and described how that worked. We then created a simple Error class that makes use of the throw/catch exception handling mechanism. Next, we discussed several improvements we could make to the Error class to make it more useful in solving more sophisticated error handling problems. Finally, we described a complete Error class that included all of the subjects we discussed in this chapter.

Exercises

Exercise 14-1. Implement a `try/catch` handler mechanism that will catch anything that is thrown, no matter what type it is.

Exercise 14-2. Why do you want to throw instances of Error, instead of pointers to Error? Wouldn't using pointers to Error eliminate the need for a copy constructor? How else can you remove the need for a copy constructor?

Exercise 14-3. Suppose your application uses throwing of Error instances exclusively. However, you are using a commercial C++ library that throws "`const char *`" strings that represent the error that occurred. Describe a `try/catch/throw` mechanism that converts throws of type "`const char *`" to throws of `Error` instances.

Exercise 14-4. What other improvements could you make to the `Error` class to make it more useful? Make the appropriate changes to the `Error` class to include these improvements.

Exercise 14-5. What changes are needed to `Error` to make it easy to inherit from it?

Exercise 14-6. What are the disadvantages of inheriting from `Error`? How can you work around them?

Exercise 14-7. How would you implement `save` with classes that inherit from `Error`? What changes would you make to `Error` to facilitate this?

Exercise 14-8. How would you implement loading of machine-readable Errors from a file when you have classes that inherit from `Error`? Are there any changes necessary to the inherited save() mechanism to make this easy or even possible? What changes would you make to the base class `save` and `Error(FILE *)` methods to make this easy or possible? Is it possible at all to implement this without changes to the existing `Error` class?

Exercise 14-9. How much of the base `Error` class can be implemented inline in the header file? How much of it has to be implemented as non-inline methods in the source file? What are the advantages and disadvantages of making more of the Error class inline?

Exercise 14-10. How would you support longer cure strings? What things, other than strings, may be useful in describing the cure?

Exercise 14-11. What other details about the error, other than the details string, line number, and file name, might be useful to add to the `Error` class in order to make finding and diagnosing the errors easier?

Exercise 14-12. How would you add error filtering to the `dumperror` application? What kinds of filters would you add?

Exercise 14-13. Make improvements to the automatic terminate and automatic log mechanisms to perform their actions only with given severity values that are chosen by the user.

Exercise 14-14. What improvements would you make to the `displayError` method? This is the method that displays Time-Critical Error messages. Currently, it simply calls the log() method and sends the results to `stderr`. What else could this method do?

Exercise 14-15. Add changes to the `create` method that allow automatic time-critical display of errors with a severity of `sevAbort`.

Exercise 14-16. How would you change the Error class to support automatic time-critical display of errors with a given severity, where the severity that generates the display is assigned by the user in advance, in a way similar to the automatic terminate and automatic log mechanisms.

15. Advanced Instrument Classes

Topics Covered:

Polymorphism

Function Groupings

Multiple Inheritance

Options to Multiple Inheritance

Virtual Instruments

In Chapter 10 we discussed the construction of an Instrument class for our example T&M system. Now that we have completed this system, there are a number of topics related to the construction of `Instrument` and `Instrument`-derived classes that can take advantage of object oriented programming principles. These topics will be discussed in this chapter.

Polymorphism

Back in Chapter 5 we discussed the topic of dynamic binding. We used the example of a "get speed" method of a Vehicle class that has different implementations for each derived class, namely a Boat class and a Plane class. In Figure 5-10, we showed a variable called "Active" that pointed to either a Boat or a Plane. In this example, the user of the "get speed" method on Active did not have to know whether the vehicle it pointed to was a Boat or a Plane, it only needed to know it was a vehicle. The dynamic binding of the "get speed" method figured out which implementation of "get speed" to call. The concept of having one method having multiple implementations that are hidden from the user of the method is called *polymorphism*.

Polymorphism can be applied quite naturally to the concept of instrumentation classes. Consider the following example. Let us say we have two different voltmeters (an HPE1410 and an HPE1411, for example). Both have basically the same set of functionality:

- Ability to measure AC voltage.
- Ability to measure AC current.
- Ability to measure DC voltage.
- Ability to measure DC current.
- Ability to measure resistance.

We used two of these capabilities in our example test system, namely measure AC voltage and measure AC current. Now, let us create instrument classes similar to those used in our test system. We will have our instrument classes derive from the base class instrument, as shown in Figure 15-1.

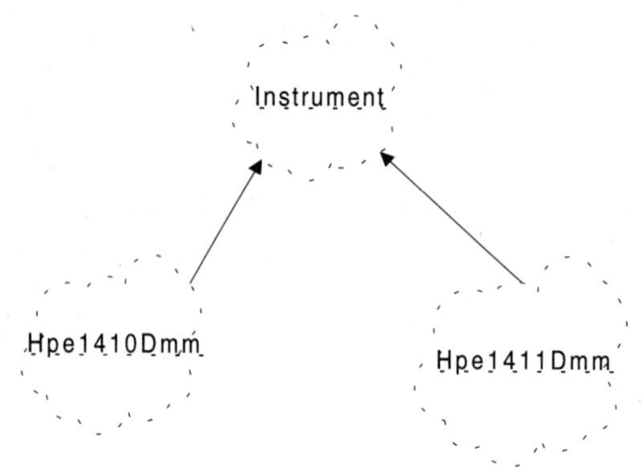

Figure 15-1: Basic DMM Inheritance

In this design, we simply treat the two instruments as independent instruments with different APIs. Using the class declaration for our sample DMM class in Figure 11-4 as a guide, we can create the following class declarations:

```
enum DMMSetting {dcV,acV,dcC,acC};

class HPe1410Dmm:public Instrument {
   private:
       ...
   public:
       HPe1410Dmm();
       ~HPe1410Dmm();
       double measVoltAc(double range);
       double measCurrAc(double range);
       double measVoltDc(double range);
       double measCurrDc(double range);
       double measResistance(double range);
};

class HPe1411Dmm:public Instrument {
   private:
       ...
   public:
       HPe1411Dmm();
       ~HPe1411Dmm();
       double measVoltAc(double range);
       double measCurrAc(double range);
       double measVoltDc(double range);
       double measCurrDc(double range);
       double measResistance(double range);
};
```

Listing 15-1: Declaration of Basic DMM Classes

The private declaration of each of these two classes would be different, as would the specific implementation of each of the methods.[1] However, notice that the public declarations are the same. Each supports the same basic APIs. So, what happens if we put polymorphism to work? Well, let us try building an abstract base class named `Dmm`, and have each of our two specific DMMs inherit from it. We end up with an inheritance diagram that looks like Figure 15-2.

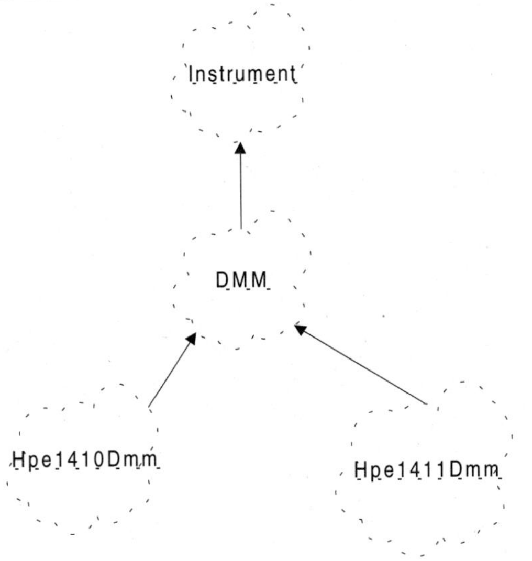

Figure 15-2: Inheritance with DMM Abstract Base Class

Now, let us put the common APIs for the two specific DMM classes into the base DMM class as pure virtual methods, and provide implementations for them in the specific derived classes. We would end up with a declaration similar to the following:

---

[1] It is safe to assume that, in general, the code to talk to two different instruments will be different, even with the advent of the SCPI instrumentation standard. In this specific example, one of these two VXI-based `DMMs` is message based, while one is register based. So, even the mechanisms for talking to them (sending strings vs. peek/poke) is different.

```
enum DMMSetting {dcV,acV,dcC,acC};

class DMM:public Instrument {
    private:
        ...
    public:
        DMM();
        ~DMM();
        virtual double measVoltAc(double range)=0;
        virtual double measCurrAc(double range)=0;
        virtual double measVoltDc(double range)=0;
        virtual double measCurrDc(double range)=0;
        virtual double measResistance(double range)=0;
};

class HPe1410Dmm:public DMM {
    private:
        ...
    public:
        HPe1410Dmm();
        ~HPe1410Dmm();
        virtual double measVoltAc(double range);
        virtual double measCurrAc(double range);
        virtual double measVoltDc(double range);
        virtual double measCurrDc(double range);
        virtual double measResistance(double range);
};

class HPe1411Dmm:public DMM {
    private:
        ...
    public:
        HPe1411Dmm();
        ~HPe1411Dmm();
        virtual double measVoltAc(double range);
        virtual double measCurrAc(double range);
        virtual double measVoltDc(double range);
        virtual double measCurrDc(double range);
        virtual double measResistance(double range);
};
```

Listing 15-2: Declaration of Polymorphic DMM Classes

This declaration shows the five basic DMM methods occurring in the abstract base class DMM, but the implementations do not occur until the derived classes HPe1410Dmm or HPe1411Dmm.

What does this implementation buy us? It allows us to use our DMM class without knowing which specific DMM is being used. For example, we can write code like this:

```
void useDmm(DMM *dmm){
    double val;

    val = dmm->measVoltDc(10.0);
    val = dmm->measCurrAc(1.0);
    val = dmm->measResistance(1.0e6);
    ...
}
```

Listing 15-3: Using Polymorphism

This code knows nothing about the specific DMM available to us. We can call this method by passing it instances of either DMM type:

```
HPe1410Dmm e1410;
HPe1411Dmm e1411;

useDmm(&e1410);
useDmm(&e1411);
useDmm(&e1410);
...
```

Listing 15-4: Specifying Which DMM Class to Use

We can even add another DMM to our tree, for instance, an HPE1311 DMM, and the `useDMM` method discussed above would not have to change. We can use our DMMs without knowing which DMM we are using.

Taking this process one step further, we can create many abstract base classes for different types of instrumentation we want to generate. For example:

- `class DMM;`
- `class Source;`
- `class Switch;`
- `class Oscilloscope;`
- `class LogicAnalyzer;`

Then, we can generate standard APIs for each of these base classes. As we add a new instrument to our system, we simply have to derive it from the appropriate base class and implement the pure virtual methods necessary to implement our class. Figure 15-3 shows an example inheritance tree for this system.

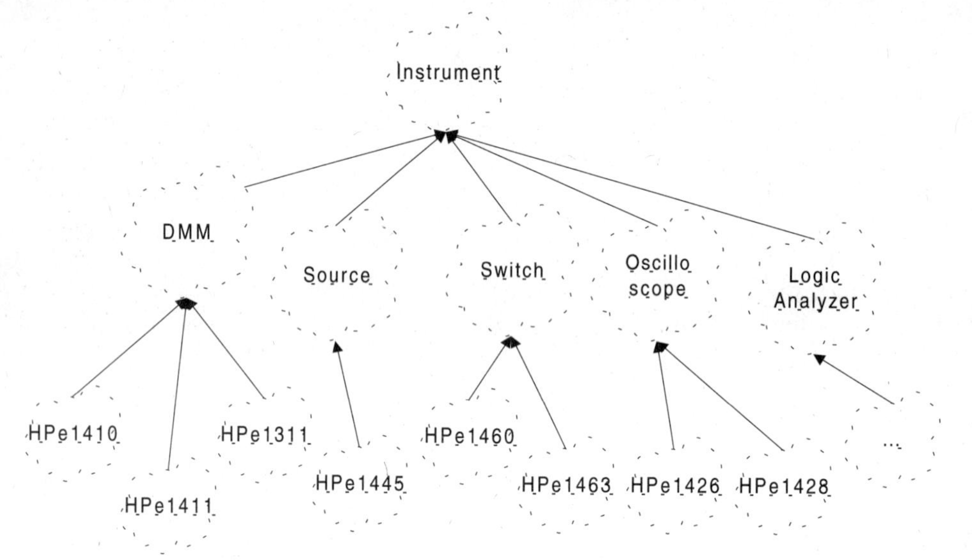

Figure 15-3: Example Instrument Inheritance

Function Groupings

There is a problem with the functional groupings discussed above. What is a DMM? What is a Source? In an idealized, example world as we have been talking about, it is easy to imagine what a DMM is. However, in the real world, things are not quite as clean. What we have are things like Oscilloscopes that can read voltage, and DMMs that can read frequencies. In the real world, what we want is not necessarily a DMM base class, but base classes such as the following:

- `class ReadVolt`
- `class ReadCurrent`
- `class ReadResistance`
- `class ReadFrequency`
- `class ReadPower`
- `class ReadDigital`
- `class ReadArb`
- `class SourceVolt`
- `class SourceCurrent`
- `class SourceResistance`
- `class SourceFrequency`

- `class SourcePower`
- `class SourceDigital`
- `class SourceArb`
- and potentially many, many more

We then can construct our instruments by inheriting from the functionality we desire in our instrument. For example, a DMM may inherit from the following classes:

- `ReadVolt`
- `ReadCurrent`
- `ReadResistance`

while a Source may inherit from the following classes:

- `SourceVolt`
- `SourceCurrent`
- `SourceFrequency`
- `SourceArb`

and an oscilloscope may inherit from the following classes:

- `ReadVolt`
- `ReadArb`

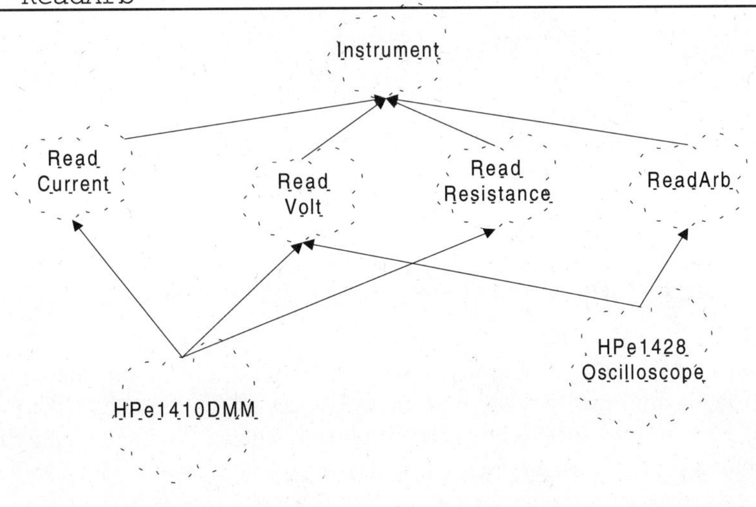

Figure 15-4: Multiple Inheritance with DMM and Oscilloscope

Figure 15-4 shows two example instruments (a DMM and an Oscilloscope) inheriting from these base classes. A simple declaration for these classes can be expressed as:

```
class ReadCurrent:public virtual Instrument{
    public:
        double measCurrAc(double range)=0;
        double measCurrDc(double range)=0;
};
class ReadVolt:public virtual Instrument {
    public:
        double measVoltAc(double range)=0;
        double measVoltDc(double range)=0;
};
class ReadResistance:public virtual Instrument {
    public:
        double measResistance(double range)=0;
};
class ReadArb:public virtual Instrument {
    public:
        Signal measSignal()=0;
};

class Hpe1410DMM
    : public ReadCurrent,
      public ReadVolt,
      public ReadResistance
{
    public:
        double measCurrAc(double range);
        double measCurrDc(double range);
        double measVoltAc(double range);
        double measVoltDc(double range);
        double measResistance(double range);
};

class HPe1428Oscilloscope
    : public ReadVolt,
      public ReadArb
{
    public:
        double measVoltAc(double range);
        double measVoltDc(double range);
        Signal measSignal();
};
```

Listing 15-5: Declaration Using Multiple Inheritance

The advantage of this approach is that you can now write applications that only need to know that the instruments they use perform the requested functionality (like, `ReadVolt`), and it becomes pretty much irrelevant whether the functionality is implemented by a DMM or an Oscilloscope:

```
void useMeasVolt(MeasVolt *volt){
    ... = volt->measVoltAc(10.0);
    ... = volt->measVoltDc(20.0);
}

void useMeasCurr(MeasCurr *curr){
    ... = curr->measCurrAc(1.0);
    ... = curr->measCurrDc(2.0);
}

proc(){
    HPe1410Dmm dmm;
    HPe1411Dmm dmm2;
    HPe1428Oscilloscope scope;

    useMeasVolt(&dmm);
    useMeasVolt(&dmm2);
    useMeasVolt(&scope);
    useMeasCurr(&dmm);
    useMeasCurr(&dmm2);
    useMeasCurr(&scope); // Error Scope != MeasCurr
}
```

Listing 15-6: Example Usage of Multiple Inheritance

The biggest disadvantage of this approach is that we need to create a list of all possible functionality groups we desire. This can be a large, complex task that is potentially error prone.[2]

Multiple Inheritance

In this approach, we have introduced an example of multiple inheritance. Multiple inheritance was first introduced in Chapter 5, where we had the Plane class inherit from both the Vehicle and the Asset base classes (refer back to Figure 5-8). However, this is the first time we have put the concept to a practical use. This lack of an example of multiple inheritance is intentional. It is often desirable to avoid multiple inheritance because of the complexity it builds into a system.[3] Plus, often a system that uses multiple inheritance can be redesigned slightly to use only single inheritance.

---

[2] There is some help here. The SCPI standard creates instrument grouping similar to the groupings we are discussing here. By leveraging the work that the existing SCPI standard has performed, we can create our instrument groupings. We will discuss this in more detail in Appendix A.

[3] The use of multiple inheritance is a controversial subject. Many people believe it is a powerful object oriented tool that should be used to its fullest. Others believe it should

Alternatives to Multiple Inheritance

When facing a decision as to whether to use multiple inheritance or not, consider the following question:

> Can we change some or all of the *is-a* relationships to *has-a* relationships?

Almost always, the answer is yes. Consider the following simple multiple inheritance example:

```
class X{
    public:
        virtual method1();
        virtual method2();
};

class Y{
    public:
        virtual method3();
        virtual method4();
};

class MIX:public X,public Y{
    public:
        method5();
};
```

Listing 15-7: Example Multiple Inheritance

We may use this class with the following code:

```
void useX(X *x){
    x->method1();
    x->method2();
}
void useY(Y *y){
    y->method1();
    y->method2();
}
```

---

never, ever be used. Some people believe it is a necessary evil. The author believes it should **always** be avoided. Using multiple inheritance correctly in C++ often has a run-time performance penalty associated with it (notice the new use of the keyword virtual in the inheritance declarations in Listing 15-5). There are many other reasons, but the complete rational is beyond the scope of this book.

```
void proc(){
    X xx;
    Y yy;
    MIX mix;

    useX(&xx);
    useX(&mix);
    useY(&yy);
    useY(&mix);

    mix.method1();
    mix.method3();
    mix.method5();
}
```

Listing 15-8: Example Usage of Multiple Inheritance

This example is a classic use for multiple inheritance. However, what happens if we change our code to use no inheritance, but two *has-a* relationships:

```
class X{
    public:
        virtual method1();
        virtual method2();
};

class Y{
    public:
        virtual method3();
        virtual method4();
};

class MIX{
    X xxx;
    Y yyy;
    public:
        X& getX(){return xxx;};
        Y& getY(){return yyy;};
        method5();
};
```

Listing 15-9: Changed Declaration to Uses-A Relationships

This declaration is very similar to the declaration in Figure 15-7, but employs no multiple inheritance. To use this class, we need a slightly modified example:

```
void useX(X *x){
    x->method1();
    x->method2();
}
void useY(Y *y){
    y->method1();
    y->method2();
}

void proc(){
    X xx;
    Y yy;
    MIX mix;

    useX(&xx);
    useX(&mix.getX());
    useY(&yy);
    useY(&mix.getY());

    mix.getX().method1();
    mix.getY().method3();
    mix.method5();
}
```

Listing 15-10: Example Usage of Uses-A Relationships

This example usage is very similar to Listing 15-8, but rather than using the inheritance mechanism to provide the conversion from a MIX class to an X or a Y class, we use the inline methods `getX` and `getY`. No, this is not as elegant as the previous example, but avoids the complexities of multiple inheritance.

What happens, though, if we want the class MIX to override some of the virtual methods in either X or Y? Using multiple inheritance, this would be nothing more than providing a declaration for the appropriate methods in our derived class:

```
class MIX:public X, public Y{
    public:
        virtual method1(); // From X
        virtual method3(); // From Y
        method5();
};
```

Listing 15-11: Overriding and Multiple Inheritance

This can also be accomplished with our *uses-a* example, with just a little bit more work:

```
class MixX:public X{
   public:
      virtual method1(); // From X
};
class MixY:public Y{
   public:
      virtual method3(); // From Y
};
class MIX{
   private:
      MixX xxx; // Use MixX instead of X
      MixY yyy; // Use MixY instead of Y
   public:
      X& getX(){return xxx;};
      Y& getY(){return yyy;};
      method5();
};
```

Listing 15-12: Overriding Without Multiple Inheritance

This declaration is exactly the same declaration as that from Listing 15-9. In fact, our example code from Listing 15-10 will work just fine with this declaration, since the public portion of the declaration has not changed one bit. The only difference is that when we call `method1` and `method3` from the code in Listing 15-10, we will execute the `MixX::method1` and `MixY::method3` instead of the `X::method1` and `Y::method3`. We have accomplished the same thing as we did with multiple inheritance in Listing 15-11, but without using any multiple inheritance.

Applying to the Instrument Classes

How does this apply to our instrument classes? It works in much the same way. We can change our HPe1410Dmm class from Listing 15-5 as follows:

```
class HPe1410ReadCurrent:public ReadCurrent{
   public:
      double measCurrAc(double range);
      double measCurrDc(double range);
};
class HPe1410ReadVolt:public ReadVolt{
   public:
      double measVoltAc(double range);
      double measVoltDc(double range);
};
```

```
class HPe1410ReadResistance:public ReadResistance{
    public:
        double measResistance(double range);
};
class HPe1410DMM{
    private:
        HPe1410ReadCurrent curr;
        HPe1410ReadVolt volt;
        HPe1410ReadResistance res;
    public:
        ReadCurrent& getCurr(){return curr;};
        ReadVolt& getVolt(){return volt;};
        ReadResistance& getRes(){return res;};
};
```

Listing 15-13: HPe1410DMM Without Multiple Inheritance

Our usage for this class is very similar to Listing 15-6. The only change is to the `proc` function, which looks like the following:

```
proc(){
    HPe1410Dmm dmm;
    HPe1411Dmm dmm2;
    HPe1428Oscilloscope scope;

    useMeasVolt(&dmm.getVolt());
    useMeasVolt(&dmm2.getVolt());
    useMeasVolt(&scope.getVolt());
    useMeasCurr(&dmm.getCurr());
    useMeasCurr(&dmm2.getCurr());
    useMeasCurr(&scope.getCurr()); // Error
}
```

Listing 15-14: Using HPe1410DMM Without Multiple Inheritance

This method allows us all the versatility of the instrument-functionality groups, without the disadvantages associated with multiple inheritance.

Nested Classes

There is one more change we can make to Listing 15-13. You will notice that we had to create several smaller classes in order to use single inheritance from the appropriate functional groups. Namely, we created the HPe1410ReadCurrent, HPe1410ReadVolt, and HPe1410ReadResistance classes. Each of these three classes share common characteristics:

- All three of these classes appear in the global name space. This means that the class name must be unique. That is why we had to append the "HPe1410" prefix to the class names.
- All three of these classes are only used within the HPe1410 class, and nowhere else.

This is a good indication that we can use *nested classes* for our declaration. *Class nesting* involves declaring one class within the scope of another class. By doing this, the names of the nested classes are only relevant within the scope of the outermost class. So, we can rewrite Listing 15-13 as follows:

```
class HPe1410DMM{
   public:
      class ReadCurrent:public ::ReadCurrent{
         public:
            double measCurrAc(double range);
            double measCurrDc(double range);
      };
      class ReadVolt:public ::ReadVolt{
         public:
            double measVoltAc(double range);
            double measVoltDc(double range);
      };
      class ReadResistance:public ::ReadResistance{
         public:
            double measResistance(double range);
      };
   private:
      ReadCurrent curr;
      ReadVolt volt;
      ReadResistance res;
   public:
      ::ReadCurrent& getCurr(){return curr;};
      ::ReadVolt& getVolt(){return volt;};
      ::ReadResistance& getRes(){return res;};
};
```

Listing 15-15: HPe1410DMM Without Multiple Inheritance

This example shows the `HPe1410ReadCurrent` renamed to `ReadCurrent` nested within the HPe1410DMM class. Since this class is only used within the `HPe1410DMM` class, we can get away with this. Notice several things about this declaration:

- Only one class, namely HPe1410DMM, appears as a global class name.
- The three HPe1410DMM specific classes are only accessible within the class HPe1410DMM, as we desire.
- The class name `ReadCurrent` now refers to the `HPe1410DMM` specific version, while within the declaration or implementation of the class itself.

- If, within the scope of the `HPe1410DMM` class, you wish to refer to the global class `ReadCurrent` (the base class), rather than the `HPe1410DMM` specific version, you must prefix the name with the global scope operator "`::`". So, the global class `ReadCurrent` becomes `::ReadCurrent`. This scoping is only necessary from within the `HPe1410DMM` class.

How would the implementation of the `HPe1410DMM` specific version of `measVoltDc` be written? Using the declaration of Listing 15-13, the answer is simple:

```
double HPe1410MeasVolt::measVoltDc(double range){
    ...
};
```

However, using the declaration of Listing 15-15, we need to provide a little bit more scoping:

```
double HPe1410DMM::MeasVolt::measVoltDc(
                double range
){
    ...
};
```

This says "the `measVoltDc` method of the `MeasVolt` class nested within the `HPe1410DMM` class." This would be as opposed to any potential implementation of this method that would exist in the base class:

```
double MeasVolt::measVoltDc(double range){
    ...
};
```

This would be the implementation (if one existed) for the base class `MeasVolt` implementation of the `measVoltDc` method. We will call classes such as the HPe1410DMM that simply provide access to nested sub-class functionality *class organizer* classes.

Standardized Instrument Interfaces

Now that we have a model in place for how to create instrument functional groupings and instrument implementations, what remains is a standard set of functional groupings and a standard API for calling instrument functionality. This is a very dicey subject, as different people have different ideas on what a standardized instrument API really means.

The most successful group to work on standardized instrument interfaces is the SCPI Consortium. SCPI, which stands for *Standard Commands for Programming Instruments*, is a standard that describes standardized instrument functional groupings, and an API that matches. Unfortunately, the API the SCPI standard described is an ASCII interface to the instrumentation. However, the SCPI interface is a good starting point for creating our standard instrument functionality classes. Appendix A describes a proposed standard extension to the SCPI ASCII interface that provides an object oriented interface to SCPI using the concepts of functional groupings discussed in this chapter.

Summary

This chapter discussed several advanced concepts related to creating Instrument classes. First, the concept of polymorphism was described and applied to Instrument classes. Polymorphism allows us to create interfaces to instruments that were independent of the specific instrument or the specific instrument class that implemented the functionality. We then extended the concept of polymorphism to describe functional groups, which were nothing more than groupings of instrument functionality that can be applied to different instrument implementations.

The functional groups lead naturally, unfortunately, to a discussion about multiple inheritance. While multiple inheritance helps immensely with the ability to use functional groups, and allows creating complex instruments with a variety of functionality, there are other ways that use simple single inheritance to accomplish the same tasks. A generalized way of avoiding multiple inheritance was discussed, then applied to the instrumentation classes. Finally, class scoping and nesting provided a nice, clean, easy to understand model for providing instrument functionality and functionality groupings that are independent of the actual implementation of the functionality itself.

Finally, Appendix A describes a standardized mechanism for converting the SCPI instrument standard into an object oriented interface based on the concepts discussed in this chapter.

Exercises

Exercise 15-1. Using the same interface described in Chapter 10, create a version of the DMM, Source, and Switch class that uses abstract base classes and implement the real functionality in a derived class.

Exercise 15-2. Create a set of functional groups that would be needed to implement the example test system described in Part III of this book. In other words, do not use a `DMM` base class, use `MeasVolt`-style base classes. Create the class declarations needed.

Exercise 15-3. Create declarations for a `DMM`, `Source`, and `Switch` class that uses multiple inheritance from the classes declared in Exercise 15-2.

Exercise 15-4. Implement the declarations created for Exercise 15-3.

Exercise 15-5. Create declarations for a `DMM`, `Source`, and `Switch` class that does not use multiple inheritance from the classes declared in Exercise 15-2. Use nested classes as appropriate.

Exercise 15-6. Implement the declarations created for Exercise 15-5.

Exercise 15-7. Compare and contrast the declarations and implementations for the two systems described in Exercise 15-3 through Exercise 15-6.

Appendices

A. OO-SCPI and Instrument Standards

Chapter 15 discussed the concept of instrument functional groupings, instrument implementations, and class organizers. It provided a framework for putting polymorphism to work with instrumentation classes. This chapter by itself allows a test engineer to create the interfaces to the functional groupings that are needed for solving specific problems.

However, wouldn't it be useful to have a ***standardized*** interface to the functional groupings that are shared among all engineers?

A standardized object oriented instrument interface would allow the instrument providers themselves to provide an object oriented API to their instrument drivers that is standard among all vendors. Using the framework discussed in Chapter 15, the instrument providers would provide a class organizer for their instrument along with an implementation of the derived functional grouping classes appropriate for their instruments. Once this is in place, test engineers would be able to simply use these instrument classes, and not have to develop them for themselves.

Object Oriented Standard using SCPI

This appendix discusses creating such a standard interface to instrument classes. We will use the existing SCPI[1] standard for the basis for our work. SCPI provides a standardized mechanism for grouping instrument functionality, and an ASCII interface to match.

In this appendix, we will:

1. Use the instrument functionality groupings of Chapter 15 as the basis for our class functional groupings.

2. Convert the SCPI ASCII interface specified in the SCPI standard to methods and class names appropriate for our standard.

3. Create a set of rules for describing our object oriented standard in terms of the SCPI standard.

---

[1] SCPI. *Standard Commands for Programmable Instruments.* A standard created by the SCPI Consortium to provide standardized interfaces to instruments.

Essentially, what we will be creating will be an object oriented interface to the SCPI standard. It is **not** our intent to improve on the SCPI standard, or remove any of the shortcomings of the SCPI standard. Rather, we will leverage the effort already put into the SCPI standard to making our object oriented C++ instrument interface. The advantage of this approach is that we can avoid all the political work associated with creating a new interface standard by leveraging the work of an existing standardization group (the SCPI Consortium). In addition, as the SCPI Consortium adds new elements to the SCPI standard, we can quickly and easily expand our OO-SCPI standard to match.

It is obvious that the advantages of such an OO instrument interface standard are only relevant when a significant number of instrument users and instrument manufacturers adopt this standard and keep with it. Ultimately, a standardization body such as the SCPI Consortium or the VXI*plug&play* Systems Alliance will have to take on the task of creating this standard. It is hoped that the ideas discussed in this appendix can be used as a starting point for this standardization work.

If you are not yet familiar with the SCPI standard, you may want to acquaint yourself with it before continuing with this appendix. The front of this book contains bibliographic information for obtaining a copy of the standard.

SCPI Design

SCPI commands utilize a tree hierarchy to categorize the commands and guarantee they are unique and are not ambiguous with respect to the instrument functionality they support. SCPI describes how to build the command hierarchy for an instrument and how to map the hierarchy to instrument functionality. SCPI rules provide mechanisms to add new commands and functions to the hierarchy, as well as how multiple instances of the same command can exist within a single instrument to provide access to separate segments of the instrument (e.g., provide for measurements from multiple inputs on an oscilloscope).

SCPI specifies two types of program headers, commands and queries. Commands are essentially requests to the instrument to perform some function or to enter some state. Queries are essentially requests for the state of the instrument to be returned, or measurement results to be returned. Commands generally affect the state of the instrument. Queries generally do not affect the state of the instrument, but rather return information about the instrument or its state. This is a broad generalization, and there are notable exceptions to this statement.

SCPI commands and queries may have parameters that affect the actions of the command or query. The exact meaning of the parameters, of course, depends on the specific command or query. However, SCPI provides a well-defined structure for what these parameters should look like, and is generally a restrictive subset of those allowed by the IEEE 488.2 specification.

Making an Object Oriented SCPI

Before we look at the rules needed to create an object oriented SCPI, let us define some terms related to the ASCII version of SCPI. First, let us assume an arbitrary ASCII SCPI command looks something like this:

```
AAA:BBB:CCC:DDD:EEE PARM1 PARM2 PARM3
```

and an arbitrary ASCII SCPI query looks something like this:

```
AAA:BBB:CCC:DDD:EEE? PARM1 PARM2 PARM3
```

The following terms will be used to describe the components of ASCII SCPI:

- *node*. A single ASCII phrase within the ASCII SCPI, in this example, the *nodes* are AAA, BBB, CCC, DDD, and EEE.
- *base node*. The first *node* in an ASCII SCPI command or query. In this example, the *base node* is AAA.
- *terminal node*. The last *node* in an ASCII SCPI command or query. In this example, the *terminal node* is EEE. The *terminal node* is the only node that is not followed by a colon.
- *non-terminal nodes*. All *nodes* but the last *node*. In this example, the *non-terminal nodes* are AAA, BBB, CCC and DDD.
- *final non-terminal node*. The last (right-most) *non-terminal node*. In this example, the *final non-terminal node* is DDD.

It is possible for a node in ASCII SCPI to be, for example, both a *terminal node* and a *non-terminal node*, depending on how it is used. For example, both of the following commands are valid in SCPI:

```
SOURCE:POWER:RANGE 3.0
SOURCE:POWER:RANGE:AUTO TRUE
```

In the first example, RANGE is a *terminal node*, in the second, RANGE is a *non-terminal node*. In the following set of rules, if a SCPI *node* can be applied to multiple node types depending on its use, then **all** of the relevant rules will apply.

The following terms will be used to describe the object oriented components created:

- *organizer class*. A class that contains other classes, instances of these classes, and methods to return instances of the contained classes (*get class methods*). It may have methods to perform command or query operations as well (*functional methods*). In Chapter 15, the MIX class is an example of an *organizer class*.

- *base organizer class*. An *organizer class* that is the root of all other *organizer classes*.

- *non-organizer class*. A class that does not contain any other classes and has no *get class methods*. It will contain methods that perform command or query operations (*functional methods*).

- *get class methods*. A method that simply returns a reference to an instance contained class. *Get class methods* only exist within *class organizers*.

- *functional methods*. Methods that perform actual command or query operations within a class. *Functional methods* can exist in either *organizer classes*, or *non-organizer classes*.

Now, let us present a set of rules to convert from ASCII SCPI to C++ object oriented classes. We will use the principles of instrument functionality groups discussed in Chapter 15 for our core design:

1. We will have one *base organizer class*, called `SCPI`. All other classes will be contained within this class.

2. The *base organizer class* will contain an *organizer class* for each possible *base node* within the ASCII SCPI language. In addition, it will contain a *get class method* for each *organizer class*. In the previous example, SOURCE is a *base node* that will become an *organizer class* and a *get class method* within the SCPI *base organizer class*.

3. Each *organizer class* will contain an *organizer class* for each possible *non-terminal node*, except the *final non-terminal node* within the ASCII SCPI language. In addition, it will contain a *get class method* for each *organizer class*. In the last example, POWER is a non-final *non-terminal node* that will become an *organizer class* and a *get class method* within the SOURCE *organizer class*.

4. Each *organizer class* will contain a *non-organizer class* for each possible *final non-terminal node* within the ASCII SCPI language. In addition, it will

contain a *get class method* for each *non-organizer class*. In the last example, RANGE is a *final non-terminal node* that will become a *non-organizer class* within the POWER *organizer class*.

5. Each *organizer class* and *non-organizer class* will contain a *functional method* for each possible *terminal node* within the ASCII SCPI language. In the last example, AUTO will be a *functional method* within the RANGE non-*organizer class*. In addition, RANGE will be a *functional method* within the POWER *organizer class*.

6. The class names and method names will be the full name of the ASCII SCPI *node*, but will be in all lower case. An alias will also be made available that matches the shortcut ASCII SCPI name. For class names, the alias will be a typedef, for methods, it will be an inline method that simply calls the full name method.

7. All methods will be implemented as virtual methods, so that they may be inherited by specific implementations. The base implementation of the methods will simply *throw* an error. It will be up to the derived class to implement the appropriate functionality. All classes and methods will be made public.

8. Query *functional-methods* will end with a capital Q.

9. The return value from query *functional-methods* shall be the real return value of the ASCII SCPI query. The return value from command *functional-methods* shall be void.

Class Declaration

Let's specify a subset of SCPI and create the base class declarations needed for the C++ interface:

```
MEASure:VOLTage?
MEASure:VOLTage:DC?
MEASure:VOLTage:AC?
MEASure:VOLTage:FREQuency?
MEASure:CURRent?
MEASure:CURRent:DC?
MEASure:CURRent:AC?
MEASure:CURRent:FREQuency?
SOURce:VOLTage   value
SOURce:VOLTage:OFFSet   value
SOURce:VOLTage:HIGH value
SOURce:VOLTage:LOW  value
SOURce:FREQuency value
```

```
SOURce:FREQuency:START  value
SOURce:FREQuency:STOP   value
SOURce:FREQuency:CENTer value
SOURce:FREQuency:SPAN   value
SYSTem:BEEPer frequency [,time [,value]]
SYSTem:BEEPer:FREQuency val
SYSTem:BEEPer:TIME val
SYSTem:BEEPer:VOLume val
SYSTem:ERRor?
```

Using this subset, let us create the base class declarations. First, let us start with the base `SCPI` class:

```
class SCPI {
    public:
    // Organizer classes
    class measure{
        ...
    };
    class source{
        ...
    };
    class system{
        ...
    };
    // get-class methods
    virtual measure& measure();
    virtual source& source();
    virtual system& system();
    // Aliases
    typedef measure meas;
    typedef source sour;
    typedef system syst;
    inline meas& meas(){return measure();}
    inline sour& sour(){return source();}
    inline syst& syst(){return system();}
};
```

In this class declaration, we show several aspects of our design:

1. An embedded class for each *base node* in our SCPI subset.

2. A virtual method that returns a pointer to an instance of the corresponding type for each *base node* in our SCPI subset.

3. Typedef aliases for each *base node* allowed abbreviation. In general, SCPI only allows one abbreviation for each *node*.

4. Inline methods for each virtual method that corresponds to the abbreviations.

Now, we must create the embedded class `measure`. Looking back at our SCPI subset, we have the *nodes* `voltage` and `current`. Our class declaration looks like this:

```
class measure{
   public:
   // Organizer classes
   class voltage{
      ...
   };
   class current{
      ...
   };
   // get-class methods
   virtual voltage& voltage();
   virtual current& current();
   // functional methods
   virtual double voltageQ();
   virtual double currentQ();
   // Aliases
   typedef voltage volt;
   typedef current curr;
   inline volt& volt(){return voltage();}
   inline curr& curr(){return current();}
   inline double voltQ(){return voltageQ();}
   inline double currQ(){return currQ();}
};
```

In this listing, we show the embedded classes, methods, and aliases for the *nodes* `voltage` and `current`. In addition, we show:

1. A *functional-method* for the two possible *terminal-nodes* `voltage` and `current`. These two *terminal-nodes* are both queries, so we end the method names with a `Q`.

2. Aliases for the *functional-methods*.

Now, we must design the `voltage` and `current` classes embedded within `measure`. Since they are both basically the same, we will show only the `voltage` class:

```
class voltage{
   public:
   // functional methods
   virtual double dcQ();
   virtual double acQ();
   virtual double frequencyQ(double exp,
                             double res);
   // Aliases
   inline double freqQ(double exp,double res){
      return frequencyQ(exp,res);
   }
};
```

This class is a *non-organizer class* corresponding to the *final non-terminal node* voltage. In this class, we show:

1. A *functional-method* for each *terminal node*. These methods are all queries, so all end in a `Q`.

2. An alias for the `frequencyQ` *terminal node*. The other two *terminal-nodes*, `dcQ` and `acQ` do not require aliases.

We apply the same principles to filling in the other classes until we have the complete base class structure filled in. We will not show these other classes here.

Resolving Conflicts

The `system` *organizer class* is interesting. Here is its declaration:

```
class system{
    public:
    // Organizer classes
    class beeper{
        public:
        void frequency(double val);
        void time(double val);
        void volume(double val);
        // Aliases
        inline void freq(double val){
            frequency(val);
        }
        inline void vol(double val){
            volume(val);
        }
    }
    // get-class methods
    virtual beeper& beeper();
    // functional methods
    virtual void beeper(double freq,
                         double time=0,
                         double vol=0);
    virtual int error();
    // Aliases
    typedef beeper beep;
    inline beep& beep(){return beeper();}
    inline void beep(double freq,
                     double time=0,
                     double vol=0){
        return beeper(freq,time,vol);
    }
    inline int err(){return error();}
};
```

This shows a few new twists to our design:

1. Within the `system` class, we have two methods named `beeper`. The first returns an instance of the `beeper` class, the second is a *functional-method* that performs the `beeper` function.

2. The `beeper` *functional-method* has optional parameters that are defaulted in both the virtual method and the inline alias.

We never had the problem with multiple methods of the same name in any of our previous classes because all cases where *nodes* were both *non-terminal* and *terminal* in the same class occurred with queries. In the case of queries, the *terminal* method (the *functional-method*) ended with a Q, so there was no method name ambiguity. However, when a *node* is both a *terminal* and a *non-terminal*, where the *terminal, functional-method* is a command and not a query, we have a potential ambiguity. However, it is the author's belief that in all such cases in SCPI, the *functional-method* command will always expect at least one parameter, and the C++ name resolution mechanisms can resolve the ambiguity. If there ever is a case where the *functional-method* does not have a parameter, then another mechanism must be utilized to resolve the name conflict. One or the other of the methods would have to be renamed, or an unused parameter would have to be required to resolve the ambiguity.

Putting It All Together

Let us put all of the pieces of our class declaration together. Here is what we get:

```
class SCPI {
    public:
    // Organizer classes
    class measure{
        public:
        // Organizer classes
        class voltage{
            public:
            // functional methods
            virtual double dcQ();
            virtual double acQ();
            virtual double frequencyQ(double exp,
                                      double res);
            // Aliases
            inline double freqQ(double exp,
                                double res){
                return frequencyQ(exp,res);
            }
        };
```

```
        class current{
            // functional methods
            virtual double dcQ();
            virtual double acQ();
            virtual double frequencyQ(double exp,
                                      double res);
            // Aliases
            inline double freqQ(double exp,
                                double res){
                return frequencyQ(exp,res);
            }
        };

        // get-class methods
        virtual voltage& voltage();
        virtual current& current();
        // functional methods
        virtual double voltageQ();
        virtual double currentQ();
        // Aliases
        typedef voltage volt;
        typedef current curr;
        inline volt& volt(){return voltage();}
        inline curr& curr(){return current();}
        inline double voltQ(){return voltageQ();}
        inline double currQ(){return currQ();}
    };

    class source{
        public:
        // Organizer classes
        class voltage{
            public:
            virtual void offset(double val);
            virtual void high(double val);
            virtual void low(double val);
            // Aliases
            inline void off(double val){offset(val);};
        };
        class frequency{
            public:
            virtual void start(double val);
            virtual void stop(double val);
            virtual void center(double val);
            virtual void span(double val);
            // Aliases
            inline void cent(double val){center(val);}
        };
```

```
    // get-class methods
    virtual voltage& voltage();
    virtual frequency& frequency();
    // functional methods
    virtual void voltage(double val);
    virtual void frequency(double val);
    // Aliases
    typedef voltage volt;
    typedef frequency freq;
    inline volt& volt(){return voltage();}
    inline freq& freq(){return frequency();}
    inline void volt(double val){voltage(val);}
    inline void freq(double val){frequency(val);}
};

class system{
    public:
    // Organizer classes
    class beeper{
        public:
        void frequency(double val);
        void time(double val);
        void volume(double val);
        // Aliases
        inline void freq(double val){
            frequency(val);
        }
        inline void vol(double val){volume(val);}
    };

    // get-class methods
    virtual beeper& beeper();
    // functional methods
    virtual void beeper(double freq=0,
                        double time=0,
                        double vol=0);
    virtual int error();
    // Aliases
    typedef beeper beep;
    inline beep& beep(){return beeper();}
    inline void beep(double freq=0,
                     double time=0,
                     double vol=0){
            return beeper(freq,time,vol);
    }
    inline int err(){return error();}
};
```

```
        // get-class methods
        virtual measure& measure();
        virtual source& source();
        virtual system& system();
        // Aliases
        typedef measure meas;
        typedef source sour;
        typedef system syst;
        inline meas& meas(){return measure();}
        inline sour& sour(){return source();}
        inline syst& syst(){return system();}
    };
```

SCPI Implementation

What would the implementation of each of these methods do? Probably something simple like throw an exception. This is because a real implementation of this class would derive functionality from the base class. By having the base class implementation throw an error, non-derived (and, therefore, non-implemented methods in the derived driver) would generate errors, as we would expect. Here is a sample implementation of one of the methods:

```
    SCPI:source:voltage:offset(double val){
        throw Error(...);
    };
```

Using the Declaration

How do we make use of such a class declaration? Here is an example of how it might be used:

```
    SCPI *inst=...;

    val=inst->meas().voltQ(2.0,.001);
    val=inst->meas().volt().dcQ();
    val=inst->meas().volt().acQ();
    val=inst->meas().curr().dcQ();
    inst->sour().volt().offs(1.5);
    inst->sour().freq(2000.0);
    inst->syst().beep(3.0,2.0,2.0);
    val=inst->syst().errQ();
```

This example specifically avoids showing how the SCPI object is instantiated, since you typically would not instantiate a SCPI class, you would instantiate a derived class. We will discuss this next.

Sample Instrument Driver Implementation

Now that we have the basic infrastructure of a SCPI instrument, how do we apply this to a specific driver implementation? In order to implement a driver, we must create a class, derived from SCPI, that is specific to that instrument. Let us use, as an example, a simple DMM instrument implementation. We base our implementation on the HPE1410 VXI embedded voltmeter. This voltmeter has more functionality than is presented in this example. We are simply using a subset of the instrument for demonstrative purposes.

First, we need to create the hpe1410 class:

```
class hpe1410:public SCPI{
   public:
   class measure:public SCPI::measure{
      ...
   };
   class system:public SCPI::system{
      ...
   };
   virtual measure& measure();
   virtual system& system();
   private:
      // Instance variables
      measure meas;
      system syst;
};
```

Here, we create a class named hpe1410 that derives from the SCPI class. This class declaration shows us several things.

1. A declaration for each embedded class corresponding to each supported *base-node* in our instrument. In this simple class, we support the `MEASURE` and `SYSTEM` *base-nodes*.

2. Override the virtual *get class methods* for each of the supported *base-nodes*.

3. An instance of each supported *base-nodes*. These are marked as private, and are only accessible through the *get class methods*.

4. When we derive an embedded class from a class embedded within `SCPI`, we use the same name as the `SCPI` embedded class. In order to derive from the `SCPI` class, we need to fully qualify the base class name by specifying, for example, `SCPI::measure` instead of simply `measure`. The latter is the `hpe1410`'s version of `measure`, the former is the base class `SCPI`'s version of `measure`.

There are several things that are *not* needed in this class declaration:

1. A declaration for *base-nodes* that our instrument does not support. For example, in this case, we do not have to create a derived class for the `SOURCE` *base-node*. If, when using this class, a user tries to access the `SOURCE` *base-node*, the base class `SCPI` version of this method is used. This version, as we discussed in the last section, simply throws an error.

2. The inline alias methods for accessing the abbreviated SCPI names. The base-class version of these methods will work just fine and do not have to be re-implemented at this layer.

Now, we need to implement the measure and system embedded classes. We do this hierarchically until we have all the classes necessary to support the SCPI subset we desire declared appropriately. For each class, we must perform the following:

1. Override the *functional methods* we desire for each *terminal node.*

2. Create derived classes for each *organizer class* and *non-organizer class* we need for all supported *non-terminal nodes.*

3. Override the *get class methods* we need for all supported *non-terminal nodes.*

4. Create a private instance variable for each *non-terminal nodes.*

Once this is done, we will have a class declaration that looks something like this:

```
class hpe1410:public SCPI{
   public:
   class measure:public SCPI::measure{
      public:
      class voltage:public SCPI::measure::voltage{
         public:
         virtual double dcQ();
         virtual double acQ();
         virtual double frequencyQ();
      };
      class current:public SCPI::measure::current{
         public:
         virtual double dcQ();
         virtual double acQ();
         virtual double frequencyQ();
      };
      virtual voltage& voltage();
      virtual current& current();
      virtual double voltageQ();
      virtual double currentQ();
      private:
      // Instance variables
         voltage volt;
         current curr;
   };
   class system:public SCPI::system{
      public:
         virtual int error();
   };
   virtual measure& measure();
   virtual system& system();
   private:
      // Instance variables
      measure meas;
      system syst;
};
```

Now that we have the class declaration, we need to implement the derived methods. First, the *get class methods*. These are the methods that simply return a reference to the embedded class instances. Here are a couple examples:

```
SCPI::measure& hpe1410::measure(){
   return meas;
};

SCPI::measure::voltage& hpe1410::measure::voltage(){
   return volt;
};
```

We must write equivalent versions for each *get class method* in our entire derived hierarchy.

Next, we must implement the *functionality* methods. These are the methods that actually implement the real functionality of the class:

```
double hpe1410::measure::voltage::dcQ(){
    // Implement MEASURE:VOLTAGE:DC? Functionality
    // for the HP E1410 DMM
    ...
}
```

Notice how the name of the fully qualified method matches closely the ASCII SCPI fully qualified name.

Finally, we need to specify a constructor for our hpe1410 class along with any private data the hpe1410 class may need. We add the following to our hpe1410 class:

```
class hpe1410:public SCPI{
    ... rest from above ...
    private:
        IOIntf dev; // Used to talk to the instrument2
        ... // Any other private data
    public:
        hpe1410(char *visaName);
        // Any other constructors desired
};
```

The implementation of the constructor looks like this:

```
hpe1410::hpe1410(char *visaName)
    : dev(visaName)  // IOIntf constructor needs VISA
name
{
    // Initialize any other private data here
    ...
}
```

Now, how do we use this class? We can instantiate objects of type hpe1410 and use them directly:

```
hpe1410 inst("VXI0::24::INSTR");

val = inst.meas().voltQ(2.0,.001);
val = inst.meas().volt().dcQ();
val = inst.measure().volt().dcQ();
val = inst.meas().voltage().dcQ();

// This should fail (throw an error)
inst.sour.volt.offs(1.5);
```

---

[2] This is the same I/O interface class that was discussed in Chapter 9.

Summary

This appendix discussed a proposed object oriented instrument interface standard. In order to become a real standard, more work is needed to flesh out some of the details and create a set of workable rules and recommendations for the standard. This is a good starting point for the standard, but more work is needed.

In the mean time, users interested in this mechanism can create their own instrument drivers that follow these guidelines. At the same time, users can encourage their instrument vendors to develop object oriented drivers such as these. Only when enough user interest has been shown will the instrument vendors get together and work on a standard such as this.

The VXI*plug&play* Systems Alliance is the one standardization body that may be able create a standard such as this. The alliance, along with the help of the SCPI Consortium, may be the right set of people to work on this standard. If you feel this is a worthy standard that should be pursued by the alliance, please contact them directly and inform them of your views. The VXI*plug&play* Systems Alliance can be reached at:

VXI*plug&play* Systems Alliance
6504 Bridge Point Parkway
Austin, TX 78730

The SCPI Consortium can be reached at:

SCPI Consortium
Fred Bode, Executive Director
8380 Hercules Drive, Suite P3
La Mesa, CA 91942

B. Contents of Disk

Enclosed with this book is a floppy disk that contains source code for many of the sample code segments and applications discussed in this book. The code was initially developed using Microsoft Visual C++ 2.1 running on Microsoft Windows '95.

Installing the Floppy

You must copy the code to your hard disk before you can attempt to compile and use it. To copy it to your hard disk c: drive, insert the floppy into your a: drive, and execute the following commands from a DOS window:

```
mkdir c:\Ootm
xcopy /S a:\ c:\Ootm
```

The "S" in "/S" refers to a capital "S". Through the rest of this appendix, we will assume that the code has been installed into the `c:\Ootm` directory.

Makefiles

There are two makefiles of significance on the disk:

- `c:\Ootm\NonOO\Chapter4.mak`: This file builds the complete non-object oriented test application described in Chapter 4 of the book. The source code for this C-based example is contained completely within the `c:\Ootm\NonOO` directory. The executable that is created will be called: `c:\Ootm\NonOO\WinDebug\Chapter4.exe`.

- `c:\Ootm\TestSys.mak`: This file builds the complete object oriented test application described in Chapters 9-13. The source code for this C++-based example is contained completely within various subdirectories within the `c:\Ootm` directory. The executable that is created will be called `c:\Ootm\WinDebug\TestSys.exe`.

Directory Structure

The `c:\Ootm` directory is made up of several directories and subdirectories. Each directory contains either a portion of the object oriented test system `TestSys`, or the non-object oriented test system Chapter4, or other supporting files. The following is the content of each directory:

`c:\Ootm`

Base directory that contains the project file, `TestSys.mak`. Everything else is in a subdirectory of this directory.

`c:\Ootm\NonOO`

Directory that contains the makefile `Chapter4.mak`. Contains all files necessary to build the non-object oriented version of the test system.

`c:\Ootm\Error`

Contains the code that implements the Error class described in Chapter 14. This code is a complete implementation of this class and can be used in any application as is, but is also compiled into the `TestSys` application.

`c:\Ootm\Instrument`

A directory that contains a subdirectory for each instrument used in the `TestSys` application. It contains the code for the base class `Instrument`, discussed in Chapter 11. This code is also compiled into the `TestSys` application.

```
c:\Ootm\Instrument\Dmm
c:\Ootm\Instrument\Source
c:\Ootm\Instrument\Switch
```

Directories that contain the instrument classes for each of the specific test instruments used in the `TestSys` application. These classes are discussed in Chapter 11. This code is compiled into the `TestSys` application.

`c:\Ootm\IOIntf`

A directory that contains the `IOIntf` class discussed in Chapter 10. This code is complete as is and can be used in any application, but is also compiled into the `TestSys` application.

`c:\Ootm\Measurement`

A directory that contains a subdirectory for each measurement used in the `TestSys` application. It contains the code for the base class Measurement, as discussed in Chapter 12. This code is also compiled into the `TestSys` application.

```
c:\Ootm\Measurement\Frequency
c:\Ootm\Measurement\MaxVal
c:\Ootm\Measurement\ReadAtFreq
```

Directories that contain the measurement classes for each of the specific measurements used in the `TestSys` application. These classes are discussed in Chapter 12. This code is compiled into the `TestSys` application.

```
c:\Ootm\Misc
c:\Ootm\Misc\Dut
c:\Ootm\Misc\TestStation
```

This directory contains the implementations for the DUT and `TestStation` classes described in Chapter 13. This code is compiled into the `TestSys` application.

`c:\Ootm\Test`

A directory that contains a subdirectory for each test used in the `TestSys` application. It contains the code for the base class `Test`, as discussed in Chapter 12. This code is also compiled into the `TestSys` application.

```
c:\Ootm\Test\FrequencyResponseTest
c:\Ootm\Test\OutputAtFrequency
```

Directories that contain the test classes for each of the specific tests used in the `TestSys` application. These classes are discussed in Chapter 12. This code is compiled into the `TestSys` application.

```
c:\Ootm\Types
c:\Ootm\Types\Boolean
c:\Ootm\Types\Complex
c:\Ootm\Types\Data
c:\Ootm\Types\Signal
```

This directory contains the classes necessary to implement the new user-defined types `Complex`, `Data`, and `Signal` as discussed in Chapter 13. These classes are standalone and can be used as-is in any application. These classes are not used in the `TestSys` application or any other sample application on the disk. The `Boolean` directory contains a very simple Boolean type definition that is used in the `TestSys` application.

Extending the Directory Structure

As you develop your own applications, you may want to use this directory structure and extended it as necessary to satisfy your needs.

- As you add Instrument derived classes for the specific test instrumentation you are interested in, put them in a subdirectory of the Instrument directory, rather than an application specific directory, so they can be shared among many applications.

- The same process can be used for the Measurement and Test directories. As you create new Measurement and Test classes, if they could potentially be used in other applications, put them in the appropriate directories in this hierarchy, rather than application specific directories.

- As you find you need extensions to the `IOIntf` class, make them in the `IOIntf` directory rather than copying the class to an application specific directory.

- As you find you need extensions to the Error class, make them to the Error class defined in the Error directory, rather than copying the code and making changes in a given application directory. However, since the error codes you will be using will vary from application to application, you may want to put a header file with the appropriate error defines in your application specific directory. In addition, your implementation of the `Error::descript` method may be put in an application specific source file so that the error strings returned can be application specific.

- As you create new types, put them in subdirectories in the Types directory. Then, use these new types directly from these subdirectories.

These suggested rules can help make development of your test applications easier and allow you to leverage your code as easily and effectively as possible.

C. Solutions to Exercises

Part 1: Programming Test Systems

Chapter 1: Test Systems

Exercise 1-1

Here are two:

1. Collect weather information.
2. Collect noise data from an airport.

Exercise 1-2.

1. Temperature, pressure, humidity.
2. Sound levels (volume, frequency, etc.).

Exercise 1-3.

1. Temperature variations over time. High and low temperatures, etc. Trends can be used to predict future weather patterns.
2. Analysis comparing sound levels versus frequency, and sound levels versus neighborhood norms. Compliance with EPA guidelines, etc.

Exercise 1-6.

An example of a system that monitors a process using a process control test system is a home thermostat. It monitors the ambient room temperature and, based on the current temperature (along with trends of temperatures in the past), determines whether to turn on the furnace or not.

Exercise 1-8.

We will assume the following:

1. We want the average room temperature to be 72°F.
2. If the temperature drops below 71°F, the furnace should be instantly turned on.

3. If the furnace has not been on for at least 15 minutes, and the temperature is less than 71.5°F, then turn the furnace on.
4. If the furnace has not been on for at least 1 hour, and the temperature is less than 71.8°F, then turn the furnace on.
5. If the furnace is on, and the temperature reached 72.5°F, then turn the furnace off instantly.
6. If the furnace is on, and the temperature is at least as much above 72°F as it was below when the furnace was turned on, then turn the furnace off. For example, if we turned the furnace on at 71.8°F, then turn it off at 72.2°F. If we turned it on at 71.6°F, then turn it off at 72.4°F.

Given the above assumptions, our algorithm will look like this:

```
turn off furnace
offTime=currTime
loop forever:
    get the current temperature
    if furnace is currently off {
        if (temp < 71°F){
            turn on furnace
            onTemp=temp
        }else if ((temp<71.5°F) &&
                  ((currTime-offTime)>15min)){
            turn on furnace
            onTemp=temp
        }else if ((temp<71.8°F) &&
                  ((currTime-offTime)>60min)){
            turn on furnace
            onTemp=temp
        }
    }else{ // Furnace is apparently on
        if (temp>72.5°F) {
            turn off furnace
            offTime=currTime
        }else if (temp>(72+(72-onTemp))){
            turn off funace
            offTime=currTime
        }
    }
end loop
```

Chapter 2: Components of a Test System

Exercise 2-3.

Let us assume you want to build a 4x6 matrix switch, using 2x3 switch matrixes. In order to build this 6x9 matrix switch, you will need four(4) 2x3 switch matrixes:

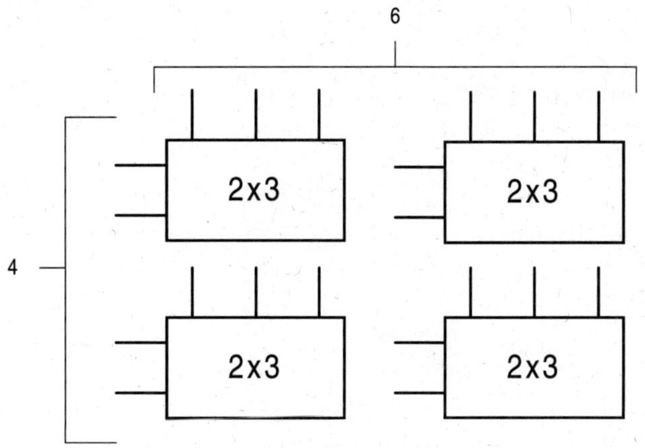

Chapter 3: Software for Test Systems

Exercise 3-1.

```
main(){
    INST src,dmm;
    double volt;

    ionerror(I_ERROR_EXIT);

    src=iopen("...");
    dmm=iopen("...");

    iprintf(src,"SOUR:FREQ 10e+3\n");
    iprintf(src,"SOUR:ENABLE\n");
    iprintf(dmm,"MEAS:VOLT:AC?\n");
    iscanf(dmm,"%g",&volt);

    printf("Voltage is %g\n",volt);

    iclose(src);
    iclose(dmm);
}
```

Exercise 3-2.

```
void CheckError(ViStatus err,char *str){
    if(err==VI_SUCCESS)
        return;
    printf("Error = 0x%lx: %s\n",err,str);
    exit(1);
}

main(){
    ViSession dRM,src,dmm;
    double volt;

    viOpenDefaultRM(&dRM);
    viOpen(dRM,"...",0,0,&src);
    viOpen(dRM,"...",0,0,&dmm);

    viPrintf(src,"SOUR:FREQ 10e+3\n");
    viPrintf(src,"SOUR:ENABLE\n");
    viPrintf(dmm,"MEAS:VOLT:AC?\n");
    viScanf(dmm,"%g",&volt);

    printf("Voltage is %g\n",volt);

    viClose(src);
    viClose(dmm);
    viClose(dRM);
}
```

Chapter 4: Programming a Test System

Exercise 4-1.

We could have tested several other miscellaneous values, other than the ones we called V_L and V_H. We could have, for example, tested all frequencies from 10Hz to 5000Hz with a step of 10Hz. This would have taken significantly more test time, but would have achieved a more complete test coverage.

Exercise 4-3.

Exercise 4-4.

Exercise 4-5.

Exercise 4-6.

The solution to these exercises is included on the enclosed disk.

Part 2: Object Oriented Systems

Chapter 5: Object Oriented Programming

Exercise 5-1.

Advantages of object oriented programming:

- By combining data and the procedures that access the data, it is easier to modularize an application, making it easier to document, understand, and support.
- Inheritance allows easy re-use of existing code and reducing the overall size and complexity of an application.
- Dynamic binding allows run-time determining what procedure should be executed. This allows procedures of the same name and general function to be implemented in wildly different ways for different uses.

Exercise 5-3.

Yes. Many object oriented programming concepts can be used in traditional programming languages. For example, C structures, along with creating naming of functions can replace classes and the methods on those classes.

Dynamic binding can be implemented in C by using pointer to functions and storing a pointer to one of many different functions into the pointer. Then, by calling the function pointed to by the function pointer variable, you are performing a form of dynamic function call.

Inheritance is an object oriented programming principle that would be very difficult to implement in a traditional programming language.

Exercise 5-5.

Since `vehicle` can also be considered an `asset`, the `vehicle` class can derive from `asset`. Then, when `plane` derived from `vehicle`, it indirectly derives from `asset`.

Another option is to have the `plane` class derive from `vehicle`, as in the original problem, then have a variable of type `asset` contained within the `plane` class. The `plane` class could provide methods for accessing the contained `asset` class. Sometimes inheritance relationships are called *is-a* relationships. In this case, however, the `plane` class would have a *has-a* relationship with asset instead of an *is-a* relationship. This may sound confusing now, but it will be explained more completely in Chapter 7, which discussed object oriented design techniques.

Chapter 6: Object Oriented Programming in C++

Exercise 6-1.

Sometimes a variable can only be initialized and not assigned. A simple example is a *constant* variable. Imagine the following class declaration:

```
class sample{
   private:
      const int a;
   public:
      sample();
};
```

In this case, the variable a cannot be assigned, since it is a constant. Instead, it must be initialized, which can be performed to constant variables. Therefore, the following constructor is legal:

```
sample::sample()
   : a(3)
{}
```

While the following constructor is illegal:

```
sample::sample(){
   a=3; // Illegal - a is a constant
}
```

Exercise 6-3.

```
class Vehicle{
   private:
      int speed;
   public:
      void operator +=(int change);
      void operator -=(int change);
};
Vehicle::operator +=(int change){
   speed+=change;
}
Vehicle::operator -=(int chnage){
   speed-=change;
}
```

Exercise 6-5.

A simple meaning can be to compare speeds. When applied to `vehicles` on both the left-hand and right-hand side, the >, <, >=, and <= operators can be used to decide which vehicle is going faster. When applied to a `vehicle` on the left-hand side and a integer on the right-hand side, then the speed of the `vehicle` can be compared to the constant speed specified.

Exercise 6-7.

By making all of the constructors *protected*, then the class cannot be instantiated and will generate a compile-time error. However, derived classes will still have access to the constructors. If the derived class has at least one *public* constructor, then the derived class will be instantiatable without the base class being instantiatable.

Part 3: Object Oriented Test & Measurement Components

Chapter 8: High Level OO Design of a T&M System

Exercise 8-1.

Other potential classes:

- ω_0, ω_1, ω_2
- bandwidth, β
- passband

Exercise 8-3.

The `DUT` class is a good spot to store test results, since a `DUT` instance is associated with each real `DUT` in the system. The `DUT` class can also be used to track the real `DUT` through the entire manufacturing process, and store information such as custom options installed, etc.

However, the `DUT` class itself serves no functional purpose to the testing process itself (we do not perform a measurement on the `DUT` class), so it is a periphery class to this test process.

Exercise 8-5.

By making `Object` a class, we can have that class perform actions that are common to all classes, such as logging results, etc. By implementing common actions in this class, they are available to all other classes transparently.

Exercise 8-8.

The first would correspond to a class design with X and Y Measurement both being classes, and X would have a pointer, or reference to the Y-Measurement class. In order to perform a Y Measurement, the X class would execute some method in the Y Measurement class.

The second implies, X is a class and Measures-Y is a method within the X class. Measures-Y is not a class at all.

Exercise 8-9.

Both `MaxValMeasurement` and `FrequencyMeasurement` would presumably have a separate instance of a `ReadAtFrequencyMeasurement`, both referring to the same DUT. Since `MaxValMeasurement` also uses a `FrequencyMeasurement`, that means the `MaxValMeasurement` instance would presumably have two instances of the `ReadAtFrequencyMeasurement` object.

This is a problem if, for example, the measurement object only performs the measurement once and caches the result. By having two instances of the `ReadAtFrequencyMeasurement` object associated with `MaxValMeasurement`, that means the `ReadAtFrequencyMeasurement` measurement could be executed more than once for each `MaxValMeasurement` requested. This is unnecessary redundancy.

A simple solution to the problem is to have the `MaxValMeasurement` and `FrequencyMeasurement` objects not have a copy of the `ReadAtFrequencyMeasurement`, but have a pointer to it. Both of these measurements could then share a pointer to the same instance of `ReadAtFrequencyMeasurement`.

The question then is, how is the `ReadAtFrequencyMeasurement` class instantiated, and how are the pointers filled in? An easy solution is that the `TestStation` can perform this function, much how it performs this action for the `Instrument` classes.

Exercise 8-13.

When we instantiate the Instruments, Tests, and Measurement classes and derived classes, we need to pass a pointer to the `TestStation` that created these objects. In a single `TestStation` approach, the pointer to the `TestStation` can be stored in some global variable. However, in a multiple `TestStation` approach, this is not desirable.

We can make this change now, even with a single `TestStation` implementation, so that if we later decide we want multiple `TestStations`, we can add them with no significant changes.

Chapter 9: Building an Instrument I/O Class

Exercise 9-2.

Exercise 9-3.

Exercise 9-4.

The solution to these exercises is included on the enclosed disk.

Exercise 9-5.

Assume the following class hierarchy:

class A derives from base class B which derives from base class C.

When you delete an instance of class A, if the destructor is not virtual, then only the destructor `A::~A` is executed. However, if you make the destructor virtual, then all three destructors `A::~A`, `B::~B`, and `C::~C` are executed. Usually, the latter is the desired behavior.

Chapter 10: Instrument Classes

Exercise 10-1.

Only one simple change is needed. We add an inheritance line to the class declaration. The code:

```
class Instrument {
    ...
};
```

will become:

```
class Instrument:public Device {
    ...
};
```

Exercise 10-5.

The `doIdleWork` method can be used for:

1. Sleep until an interrupt arrives saying the ready state of the instrument has changed.

2. Perform background actions required by the instrument before it becomes ready again.

Chapter 11: Measurement and Test Classes

Exercise 11-2.

Exercise 11-4.

Exercise 11-5.

Exercise 11-6.

Exercise 11-7.

Exercise 11-8.

Exercise 11-9.

Exercise 11-10.

Exercise 11-11.

The solution to these exercises is included on the enclosed disk.

Chapter 12: Building an Object Oriented T&M System

Exercise 12-1.

Here are two:

1. Have the `DUT` class return information about potential options installed in it, to help the `TestStation` determine which tests should be executed on the given DUT.

2. Have the `DUT` class store information as to how completely it was tested. In a real test system, the `TestStation` class may decide (randomly or using

some other algorithm) to only test a certain percentage of each DUT completely, partially, or at all. The DUT should store how completely it was tested so that post-testing analysis and correlation can be performed.

Exercise 12-2.

We choose to use the DUT serial numbers to determine what tests will be executed. We will execute the FrequencyResponseTest only on DUTs with even serial numbers. We will execute the OutputAtFrequencyTest only all DUTs with serial numbers that are not multiples of four. This algorithm, of course, assumes that the serial numbers are assigned sequentially. If this is not the case, a different algorithm is necessary.

The only method that needs to change is TestStation::connectDUT:

```
void TestStation::connectDUT(DUT *d){
    // Store away the DUT
    dut = d;

    // Calculate which tests to execute
    switch(d->getSerialNumber() % 4){
        case 0:
            numTests = 1;
            tests = new Test*[1];
            tests[0] = new FrequencyResponseTest();
            break;
        case 1:
            numTests = 1;
            tests = new Test*[1];
            tests[0] = new OutputAtFrequencyTest();
            break;
        case 2:
            numTests = 2;
            tests = new Test*[2];
            tests[0] = new FrequencyResponseTest();
            tests[1] = new OutputAtFrequencyTest();
            break;
        case 3:
            numTests = 1;
            tests=new Test*[1];
            tests[0] = new OutputAtFrequencyTest();
            break;
    }
}
```

The TestStation::testDUTmethod does not change, since it uses the numTests variable to determine how many tests to run. It also does not care which tests are run, since all it knows about is Test objects. The TestStation::disconnectDUT method also does not change, since it uses the numTests variable to determine how many tests to delete.

Exercise 12-3.

Only `TestStation::connectDUT` has to change:

```
void TestStation::connectDUT(DUT *d){
    int i;

    // Store away the DUT
    dut = d;

    // Calculate which tests to execute
    if( (d->getSerialNumber()%4) == 0 ){
        // Every fourth, run all tests five times
        numTests = 2*5;
        tests = new Test*[2*5];
        for(i=0;i<5;++i){
            tests[i*2] = new FrequencyResponseTest();
            tests[i*2+1] =
                            new OutputAtFrequencyTest();
        }
    }else{
        // All other duts, run all tests once
        numTests = 2;
        tests = new Test*[2];
        tests[0] = new FrequencyResponseTest();
        tests[1] = new OutputAtFrequencyTest();
    }
```

Exercise 12-4.

We add the following method to the `DUT` class:

```
class DUT:public Device{
    public:
        int getTestLevel();
};
```

This method will return a number indicating the level of testing desired. 0 means no testing, 1 means minimal testing, 2 means complete testing, and 3 means repetitive testing. The implementation of this method can use a variety of mechanisms to determine this value, anywhere from setting it in the constructor of the `DUT`, to calculating it based on the serial number.

The `TestStation::connectDUT` method needs to be modified in a straightforward manner, similar to the way shown in the solution for Exercise 12-2 and Exercise 12-3.

Part 4: Advanced Topics

Chapter 13: Creating OO Data Types

Exercise 13-1.

How about:

1. Perform base *e* logarithms with complex numbers.

2. Perform higher math operations, such as integration, differentiation, etc. with complex numbers.

3. Convert to and from time and frequency domain representations of numbers using base *e* logarithms and trigonometric functions.

4. Combine the `Complex` and `UnitData` class to provide a units for complex numbers.

Exercise 13-3.

The solution to exercise is included on the enclosed disk.

Exercise 13-4.

Adding overlapped units would require variations of the `normalize` function that convert the units of one instance to the same units contained in another instance, making the proper value changes as necessary. This is fairly easy for converting things like volts/amps to watts, but how about changing amps into units involving "seconds" and possible "electrical charge"? This could get considerably more complicated, for a general purpose class. But it is certainly possible and potentially quite useful.

Exercise 13-6.

In order to prevent the assignment of "`a=a`," you simply must check that the signals refer to different memory locations before proceeding:

```
Signal& Signal::operator=(const Signal& copySignal){
   //
   // Make sure we aren't doing a=a
   //
   if(this == &copySignal)
      return *this; // They are the same - do nothing

   //
   // Do the assignment
   //

   ...
   return *this;
}
```

The rest of the implementation is contained on the disk.

Chapter 14: Error Handling

Exercise 14-1.

The following `try/catch` handler will catch any `throw` of any type:

```
try {
   code that does a throw
}
catch(...){
   // The "..." means catch anything
}
```

The disadvantage of this approach is that the value thrown to us cannot be used, since we do not know what type it is.

Exercise 14-3.

In your procedure that calls the commercial C++ library, enclose calls to the library with the following `try/catch/throw` mechanism:

```
try {
    ... calls to commercial C++ library ...
}catch(const char *err){
    // This catch handler will convert the error from
    // a const char * to an Error instance
    throw Error(1, err, _MARK_);
}
```

Exercise 14-6.

The biggest problem with inheriting from Error comes in when we use the copy constructor to copy an instance of the variable. If we catch an Error instance using the following catch handler:

```
catch(Error err){
    ... process the error here ...
}
```

and we throw an error of a type that inherits from the Error class, then when we process the error in this handler, we have lost all detailed information we had in the inherited class. This, of course, can be fixed by providing a more specific catch handler:

```
catch(IOError err){
    ... process IOErrors here ...
}
catch(Error err){
    ... process all other Errors here ...
}
```

Another disadvantage has to do with saving and loading inherited error instances. This is discussed in Exercise 14-8.

Exercise 14-8.

The biggest problem is we need to know what type of error we are loading from the file before we can create the appropriate instance. In order to do this, we need some form of ID label at the beginning of the error that specifies which inherited error class this error instance refers to. This requires a change to the base error class as well, because it must save and load an ID label specifying that the base error class was used.

Exercise 14-12.

You could add run-time parameters to the `dumperror` application that simply takes errors from one file and stores some of them (the ones that make it through the filter) to a new file. The application can filter for things such as:

1. The time/date stamp being between a certain range.

2. Specific severity levels.

3. Specific error numbers.

4. Errors with or without cure strings.

D. Other Books of Interest

Other Books of Interest

The following books may be of interest in learning more about object oriented programming, design, and C++:

Lippman, Stanley B., *C++ Primer*, 2nd ed., Reading, MA: Addison-Wesley Publishing Co., 1993.

Ellis, Margaret A. and Bjarne Stroustrup, *The Annotated C++ Reference Manual*, Reading, MA: Addison-Wesley Publishing Co., 1990.

Standard Commands for Programmable Instruments, Version 1995, La Mesa, CA: SCPI Consortium, 1995.

IEEE Standard Codes, Formats, Protocols, and Common Commands, IEEE Standard 488.2-1992.

Standard Instrument Control Library - Reference Manual, Hewlett-Packard, E2094-90000, 1993.

HP VISA Transition Library - User's Guide, Hewlett-Packard, E2094-90002, 1995.

Booch, Grady, *Object Oriented Analysis and Design*, 2nd ed., Redwood City, CA: The Benjamin/Cummings Publishing Company, Inc., 1994.

Kernighan, Brian W. and Dennis M. Ritchie, *The C Programming Language*, Englewood Cliffs, NJ: Prentice Hall, Inc., 1988.

Glossary of Terms

abstract base class

A *base class* that cannot be instantiated by itself, but requires that a *derived class* implement additional functionality before it can be instantiated. In C++, an *abstract base class* either has *pure virtual methods*, or has its constructors marked as protected members.

base class

A *class* from which at least one other *class* derives from. A *base class* is a parent in an inheritance hierarchy.

C++

An *object oriented programming* language that consists of extensions to C.

class

A description of a collection of *member variables* and *methods* that act on the *member variables*. A *class* is generally not usable until it is instantiated into an *object*.

critical section

A section of code that is surrounded by operating system specific thread locking mechanisms that will allow only a single thread of control to enter the section at a time. This is accomplished by temporarily suspending threads trying to enter the section until any other thread executing within the section has left it.

derived class

A *class* that has inherited functionality from another (base) *class*.

DUT

Device Under Test. A physical, mechanical, or electrical device that is being tested by a test system.

inherited
inheritance

The process of one *class* deriving functionality from another *class*. Functionality can be both *member variables* and *member functions*.

inline

A procedure implemented within the header file along with the declaration of a

C++ class. Calls to this procedure produce a compile-time substitution of the code contained within the procedure, preventing a run-time need for a procedure call. Inline procedures are used to increase performance.

instance

A term used to refer to an *object*. An *object* is sometimes called an *instance* of a *class*.

instantiated
instantiation

The act of creating an *object* from a *class*.

instrument

A device that measures the physical, mechanical, or electrical state of a device.

member function

A function that belongs to a *class*. Typically, *member functions* are called on behalf of an *object* of the given *class* and perform operations on that *object*.

member variable

A variable that belongs to a *class*. A *member variable* is typically associated with an *object* and is used to contain the state of the *object*.

method

Another term for a *member function*. A function that belongs to a *class*.

multiple inheritance

The act of deriving functionality from more than one immediate *base class*. In a *multiple-inheritance* system, a *class* has more than one parent (this is opposed to having one parent, one grandparent, etc.).

object

An *instance* of a *class*. When an *object* is instantiated from a class, data space is allocated for the *object*. Multiple *objects* instantiated from the same *class* can exist simultaneously, each with its own set of independent data.

object oriented design

The process of creating the design of an application using *object oriented* principles.

object oriented programming

The process of writing an *object oriented* program.

OOD

Abbreviation for *object oriented design.*

OOP

Abbreviation for *object oriented programming.*

OO

Abbreviation for *object oriented.*

object oriented

A philosophy for creating programs based on principles of *classes*, *objects*, and *inheritance*.

protected

A *member function* or *member variable* that is only accessible from within the *class* and its derived *classes*.

private

A *member function* or *member variable* that is only accessible from within the *class*.

public

A *member function* or *member variable* that is accessible from within the *class*, its *derived classes*, and all other code not part of the *class*.

pass band

The portion of the frequency response of a mid-pass filter. The pass band is the frequencies that are allowed to pass through the filter.

polymorphism

Multiple *methods* of the same name that perform similar actions in different ways, depending on how they are used. In *object oriented programming*, this typically happens when a *method* of a *class* is implemented in different ways in different *derived classes*.

pure virtual

A *method* that is declared in an *abstract base class*, but has no implementation. In order to use this *method*, a *derived class* must provide an implementation.

thread-safe

Code that can be executed by more than one process thread of control at the same time. Usually, *thread-safe* code will not modify data structures or, if it does, will protect the data structure modifications with a *critical section.*

reentrant

Code that is *thread-safe* is also said to be *reentrant.*

virtual

A *method* that is bound to a particular routine at run-time instead of compile time. It refers to *methods* that are declared in a *base class* and implemented in multiple *derived classes.* The use of the *base class method* causes one of the *derived methods* to execute, depending on the actual *class* from which the *object* is *instantiated.*

LICENSE AGREEMENT AND LIMITED WARRANTY

READ THE FOLLOWING TERMS AND CONDITIONS CAREFULLY BEFORE OPENING THIS SOFTWARE MEDIA PACKAGE. THIS LEGAL DOCUMENT IS AN AGREEMENT BETWEEN YOU AND PRENTICE-HALL, INC. (THE "COMPANY"). BY OPENING THIS SEALED SOFTWARE MEDIA PACKAGE, YOU ARE AGREEING TO BE BOUND BY THESE TERMS AND CONDITIONS. IF YOU DO NOT AGREE WITH THESE TERMS AND CONDITIONS, DO NOT OPEN THE SOFTWARE MEDIA PACKAGE. PROMPTLY RETURN THE UNOPENED SOFTWARE MEDIA PACKAGE AND ALL ACCOMPANYING ITEMS TO THE PLACE YOU OBTAINED THEM FOR A FULL REFUND OF ANY SUMS YOU HAVE PAID.

1. **GRANT OF LICENSE:** In consideration of your payment of the license fee, which is part of the price you paid for this product, and your agreement to abide by the terms and conditions of this Agreement, the Company grants to you a nonexclusive right to use and display the copy of the enclosed software program (hereinafter the "SOFTWARE") on a single computer (i.e., with a single CPU) at a single location so long as you comply with the terms of this Agreement. The Company reserves all rights not expressly granted to you under this Agreement.

2. **OWNERSHIP OF SOFTWARE:** You own only the magnetic or physical media (the enclosed disks) on which the SOFTWARE is recorded or fixed, but the Company retains all the rights, title, and ownership to the SOFTWARE recorded on the original disk copy(ies) and all subsequent copies of the SOFTWARE, regardless of the form or media on which the original or other copies may exist. This license is not a sale of the original SOFTWARE or any copy to you.

3. **COPY RESTRICTIONS:** This SOFTWARE and the accompanying printed materials and user manual (the "Documentation") are the subject of copyright. You may not copy the Documentation or the SOFTWARE, except that you may make a single copy of the SOFTWARE for backup or archival purposes only. You may be held legally responsible for any copying or copyright infringement which is caused or encouraged by your failure to abide by the terms of this restriction.

4. **USE RESTRICTIONS:** You may not network the SOFTWARE or otherwise use it on more than one computer or computer terminal at the same time. You may physically transfer the SOFTWARE from one computer to another provided that the SOFTWARE is used on only one computer at a time. You may not distribute copies of the SOFTWARE or Documentation to others. You may not reverse engineer, disassemble, decompile, modify, adapt, translate, or create derivative works based on the SOFTWARE or the Documentation without the prior written consent of the Company.

5. **TRANSFER RESTRICTIONS:** The enclosed SOFTWARE is licensed only to you and may not be transferred to any one else without the prior written consent of the Company. Any unauthorized transfer of the SOFTWARE shall result in the immediate termination of this Agreement.

6. **TERMINATION:** This license is effective until terminated. This license will terminate automatically without notice from the Company and become null and void if you fail to comply with any provisions or limitations of this license. Upon termination, you shall destroy the Documentation and all copies of the SOFTWARE. All provisions of this Agreement as to warranties, limitation of liability, remedies or damages, and our ownership rights shall survive termination.

7. **MISCELLANEOUS:** This Agreement shall be construed in accordance with the laws of the United States of America and the State of New York and shall benefit the Company, its affiliates, and assignees.

8. **LIMITED WARRANTY AND DISCLAIMER OF WARRANTY:** The Company warrants that the SOFTWARE, when properly used in accordance with the Documentation, will operate in substantial conformity with the description of the SOFTWARE set forth in the Documentation. The Company does not warrant that the SOFTWARE will meet your requirements or that the operation of the SOFTWARE will be uninterrupted or error-free. The Company warrants that the

media on which the SOFTWARE is delivered shall be free from defects in materials and workmanship under normal use for a period of thirty (30) days from the date of your purchase. Your only remedy and the Company's only obligation under these limited warranties is, at the Company's option, return of the warranted item for a refund of any amounts paid by you or replacement of the item. Any replacement of SOFTWARE or media under the warranties shall not extend the original warranty period. The limited warranty set forth above shall not apply to any SOFTWARE which the Company determines in good faith has been subject to misuse, neglect, improper installation, repair, alteration, or damage by you. EXCEPT FOR THE EXPRESSED WARRANTIES SET FORTH ABOVE, THE COMPANY DISCLAIMS ALL WARRANTIES, EXPRESS OR IMPLIED, INCLUDING WITHOUT LIMITATION, THE IMPLIED WARRANTIES OF MERCHANTABILITY AND FITNESS FOR A PARTICULAR PURPOSE. EXCEPT FOR THE EXPRESS WARRANTY SET FORTH ABOVE, THE COMPANY DOES NOT WARRANT, GUARANTEE, OR MAKE ANY REPRESENTATION REGARDING THE USE OR THE RESULTS OF THE USE OF THE SOFTWARE IN TERMS OF ITS CORRECTNESS, ACCURACY, RELIABILITY, CURRENTNESS, OR OTHERWISE.

IN NO EVENT, SHALL THE COMPANY OR ITS EMPLOYEES, AGENTS, SUPPLIERS, OR CONTRACTORS BE LIABLE FOR ANY INCIDENTAL, INDIRECT, SPECIAL, OR CONSEQUENTIAL DAMAGES ARISING OUT OF OR IN CONNECTION WITH THE LICENSE GRANTED UNDER THIS AGREEMENT, OR FOR LOSS OF USE, LOSS OF DATA, LOSS OF INCOME OR PROFIT, OR OTHER LOSSES, SUSTAINED AS A RESULT OF INJURY TO ANY PERSON, OR LOSS OF OR DAMAGE TO PROPERTY, OR CLAIMS OF THIRD PARTIES, EVEN IF THE COMPANY OR AN AUTHORIZED REPRESENTATIVE OF THE COMPANY HAS BEEN ADVISED OF THE POSSIBILITY OF SUCH DAMAGES. IN NO EVENT SHALL LIABILITY OF THE COMPANY FOR DAMAGES WITH RESPECT TO THE SOFTWARE EXCEED THE AMOUNTS ACTUALLY PAID BY YOU, IF ANY, FOR THE SOFTWARE.

SOME JURISDICTIONS DO NOT ALLOW THE LIMITATION OF IMPLIED WARRANTIES OR LIABILITY FOR INCIDENTAL, INDIRECT, SPECIAL, OR CONSEQUENTIAL DAMAGES, SO THE ABOVE LIMITATIONS MAY NOT ALWAYS APPLY. THE WARRANTIES IN THIS AGREEMENT GIVE YOU SPECIFIC LEGAL RIGHTS AND YOU MAY ALSO HAVE OTHER RIGHTS WHICH VARY IN ACCORDANCE WITH LOCAL LAW.

ACKNOWLEDGMENT

YOU ACKNOWLEDGE THAT YOU HAVE READ THIS AGREEMENT, UNDERSTAND IT, AND AGREE TO BE BOUND BY ITS TERMS AND CONDITIONS. YOU ALSO AGREE THAT THIS AGREEMENT IS THE COMPLETE AND EXCLUSIVE STATEMENT OF THE AGREEMENT BETWEEN YOU AND THE COMPANY AND SUPERSEDES ALL PROPOSALS OR PRIOR AGREEMENTS, ORAL, OR WRITTEN, AND ANY OTHER COMMUNICATIONS BETWEEN YOU AND THE COMPANY OR ANY REPRESENTATIVE OF THE COMPANY RELATING TO THE SUBJECT MATTER OF THIS AGREEMENT.

Should you have any questions concerning this Agreement or if you wish to contact the Company for any reason, please contact in writing at the address below.

Robin Short
Prentice Hall PTR
One Lake Street
Upper Saddle River, New Jersey 07458